THE COURAGE TO SURVIVE

THE COURAGE TO SURVIVE

BY DENNIS J. KUCINICH

ISBN: 1-59777-568-1
Library of Congress Cataloging-In-Publication Data Available

Book Design by: Sonia Fiore

Printed in the United States of America

Phoenix Books
9465 Wilshire Boulevard, Suite 315
Beverly Hills, CA 90212

10 9 8 7 6 5 4 3 2 1

To the Good Sisters,
who taught me the power of prayer.

To Coach Peter Pucher,
who taught me the courage to survive;

To Dr. Javier Lopez,
who made sure I did!

Acknowledgments

I live each day in gratitude to my mother, Virginia and to my father, Frank for the great sacrifices they made to create from hope a family of seven children and to hold the family together against seemingly insurmountable odds. My heart's endless love is with my brothers, Frank Jr., Gary, Perry, Larry, my sisters Theresa and Beth Ann. We all shared the same wild ride and we have a common bond which is unbreakable. The Kucinich family stayed together through thick and thin and we are still together, in love and in spirit. Thanks, too, to my grandparents and to my uncles and aunts, especially Aunt Betty who would go to the race track to win money to buy me clothes.

I tried to write this book many years ago with the encouragement of my dearest friend, Shirley MacLaine, the irrepressible Bob Scheer, who told me to not to talk about the story, but write it; his wife Narda Zacchino, one of the world's great editors, and my daughter's mother, Sandra Horn. Despite their solicitude, I couldn't complete the story because it was just too painful to write. In 2007 I met Michael Viner in the green room of the Bill Maher Show and he offered to publish a book. This time I was ready.

Gore Vidal was one of the first people to read my reworked manuscript. His eagerness and enthusiastic response gave me great confidence in proceeding to share my story. I am once again grateful to Shirley MacLaine and Narda Zacchino for taking time away from writing their own books to help edit mine because they believe so much in the power of this, my story.

Finally, the extraordinary support of my dearest Elizabeth, my "Wifey," has enabled me to face all things, to be "as supple as the wind and take everything that comes with great courage." She has taught me to know love.

Chapter One

NEARLY EVERY NIGHT of my first two years, Mom rocked me to sleep while singing in her beautiful soprano the same lullaby:

Over in Killarney,
Many years ago,
Me mither sang a song to me
In tones so sweet and low.
Just a simple little ditty,
In her good ould Irish way,
And I'd give the world if she could sing
That song to me this day.
Too-ra-loo-ra-loo-ral,
Too-ra-loo-ra-li,
Too-ra-loo-ra—loo-ral
Hush, now don't you cry!
Too-ra-loo-ra-loo-ral
Too-ra-loo-ra-li
Too-ra-loo-ra-loo-ral,
That's an Irish lullaby.

My aunts brought books for me instead of toys. Mom taught me to sound out the letters as she read them aloud. Soon books stacked up alongside the walls of my bedroom. The works of Lewis Carroll, Mark Twain and Robert Louis Stevenson excited my imagination, and I was on my way to reading on my own. With Mom's prompting, I memorized Celtic poems and songs:

Oh ye'll tak the high road and I'll tak the low road,
And I'll be in Scotland afore ye.
But me and my true love will never meet again.
On the bonnie, bonnie banks o' Loch Lomond.

Powerful images of such intensity marched through my childhood dreams that for a time I could not wait to go to sleep to dream with my eyes closed and then awake early to dream with my eyes open.

Even the wallpaper came to life. The red-shirted cowboy sat on a fence. He wore brown chaps over faded blue pants. His spurred and starred boots were hiked up on the fence rails. Other cowpunchers were riding their horses. Oval lariats encircled little doggies that had strayed too far from the ranch. Some cowboys sat around the campfire after roundup, talking about home on the range. I swear I could hear the harmonica music. I stared at the cowboys in their neat groups. The great western panorama was on my bedroom wallpaper. Oh, to be a wallpaper cowboy and escape the confines of this crib, and get a good look at my first brother, Frank, born September 19, 1948.

The new baby took up much of Mom's time, but she still spent many hours reading nursery rhymes to me. I sat in her lap, her arms wound warmly around me. She held a book of rhymes. We recited together:

"This is the key to the kingdom. In that kingdom there is a city. In that city there is a town. In that town there is a street. In that street there is a lane. In that lane there is a yard. In that yard there is a house. In that house there is a room..."

It was great fun. My three-year-old repertoire was soon filled with songs of sixpence and mice running up clocks, silver bells and cockle shells. The fantasy of reading time gave way to the reality of our apartment: snapping mousetraps, silverfish and cockroaches. This was not the house that Jack built. This was the Cleveland apartment that Mr. Landlord owned.

When Mom was busy with my brother Frank, I looked at the pictures and read the words in newspapers. There were always plenty of newspapers in the apartment, because they served as our curtains. In the winter we stuffed papers between the windows and screens and under the door to keep out the freezing wind. We moved to an upstairs apartment in the same building where Mom kept the milk cold in the winter by putting it outside on the sill and fresh in the summer by placing it in an ice-filled galvanized tub. The apartment stairs were steep and dangerous. One of Aunt Betty's boyfriends took a tumble down the stairs once after Dad punched him. Dad also liked watching fights on a postage-stamp sized television we had for a few months.

Things were happening outside the apartment, too. Early in the morning, I watched as the sun lit up St. Clair Avenue. Trucks like my father's moved baked goods, soda pop, beer, fruit and vegetables to Diamond's supermarket across the street. My eyes followed the traffic. I spotted some red, white and blue mail trucks. Huge city buses were packed with people. Cars of all colors and a glistening red and silver stream of metal and firemen went back and forth all day.

A man wearing winter clothes sat on a buckboard atop a horse-drawn cart. Bundles of paper and rags were his cargo. The cart moved slowly. Its wheels clicked and clacked; his loud song, "Pay-poor r'eggs, pay-poor r'eggs."

Dogs played in traffic. In the evenings, wailing fire trucks with spinning and flashing lights zipped up and down St. Clair Avenue. Street shadows flickered underneath the soft green and orange neon glow of the nearest tavern. I jammed my nose against the top corner of the window. I looked down the street. I couldn't see the Epicure Café. Mom worked there late into the evening. She was a barmaid.

Dad did not like Mom working at the bar. They argued often about her job at the Epicure.

"Ginny, I want you to quit that goddamned job. I'll call your boss tonight and tell him you're not coming in," he would shout at her.

"Oh, no you won't!" She was angry. He held her tight so she couldn't move.

"Now let me go, you, you...." she tried but failed to free herself.

"You aren't going anywhere, Gin."

"Stop it! Frank! We need the money. If I don't work, we'll never get out of here."

"I'll make the goddamned money around here," Dad said as he forced Mom to sit down. "I don't want my wife working. I'll do the working around here. You stay home and take care of the kids."

"Oh, I get it," Mom cried, "You're just worried about some guy in the bar grabbing at me."

"I'd kill the son of a bitch," Dad vowed.

They continued yelling and pushing each other. Then Mom went to work.

I didn't like it when they fought. It made my stomach hurt. I didn't take sides; I was for both of them. I missed Mom when she was at work. Those were long nights. Dad went to pick her up at 2:30 in the morning.

Every time he left, I was afraid neither of them would ever come back. Frank and I were supposed to be sleeping, but we weren't. I waited anxiously at the window, searching the street for my parents. When Dad came back with Mom, as he always did, I climbed back into my crib. I shut my eyes and smiled. They were both home safely, so I could sleep peacefully. I could never understand why Mom and Dad fought. I know now there were two good reasons: money and sex. Mom eventually quit her job. She was pregnant.

Mom decided it was time for me to discover the world beyond the apartment. She led me to my new friend, Dwight. I met him inside the fenced-in driveway. He lived in the same apartment house. He was four, just like me. Once he threw a silver metal airplane into the sun. I caught it with my eye—seven stitches. Other than that, we never had a problem.

Holding hands, we went to Mauer's Drug Store together to buy licorice and strips of paper candy with the nickel I was told to share. We returned to play in the dirt alongside the ten-suite yellow brick apartment house.

A man crossed the street, looked down at Dwight and me digging a hole and then filling it back up again and asked me:

"What are you doing, playing with that n*****?"

I did not know the word or what he meant. I went inside to ask Mom.

"What's 'n*****' mean?"

"Don't use that word. It's a bad word," she said.

Whenever I repeated bad words I got my mouth washed out with Fels Naptha soap, fresh off the washboard.

"Mom, what does it mean?" I insisted. "A man said it to Dwight and me."

"Whoever told you that should have his mouth washed out. He was trying to hurt Dwight by calling him names."

I thought of a rhyme: "Sticks and stones may break my bones, but names will never hurt me."

"Dennis, names can cause people lots of hurt. Just remember, a person's color doesn't make him good or bad. People who happen to be white are no better than people who happen to be black," she said.

"But Mom, why did the man call Dwight a name?"

"Because he thinks he is better than Dwight. Because Dwight has dark skin."

"He called Dwight a name just because Dwight has dark skin?" I couldn't figure it out. So what if his skin is a different color? I didn't know that his being black and my being white made a difference. We often held hands. We went to the store together. We shared each other's candy. We played together in the dirt. There were lots of different colors. No one told me to stay away from any of them.

"Why bother Dwight? He's just a kid, like me."

"There is good and bad in everyone," Mom continued. "Don't pay any attention to people when they tell you not to play with Dwight. I'm not going to teach my children to hate. Now go on. Get back outside and go and play together."

Blacks and whites lived side by side in our apartment house. A black mother lost a baby at birth, just like my mother had before I was born. Blacks and whites wore the same kinds of clothes. We had the same kind of furniture—worn, sometimes with broken arms and legs. We both had leaky faucets and gurgling toilets. Our places had cracked walls with plaster falling onto the kitchen and dining room tables. Our apartments had garbage cans overflowing. Hungry rats scratched at our doors during the night. Bill collectors were at our doors during the day. We shared window-ledge refrigerators. White and black children bathed in the same curb puddles after a light rain. We raced together around vacant lots littered with flattened tin cans and shards of whiskey and beer bottles. We lived like blacks and blacks lived like us. If they were 'n******' we were 'n******' too.

Since I had been made more conscious of skin color, I began to consider other questions. Dwight had a dog. The dog was brown, too. I wondered if anyone would scold me if I played with his dog.

Dad backed up the orange wooden-slat trailer rented from Finn's. He moved out the kitchen table, the couch, two beds, and a small red picnic cooler in which Mom kept the meat. He placed his tiny television in a box. It worked off and on during championship fights. The refrigerator stayed. It didn't work.

Friends helped move cardboard boxes of clothes and paper bags filled with canned foods, cereals and bread out the door. I heard Dad and Mom talking about something called an "eviction." I didn't ask any questions. I said goodbye to the wallpaper range. I didn't have time to say goodbye to Dwight. The last I saw him, he was in the dirt, playing alone, probably waiting for me to join him.

We headed back to Grandma and Grandpa Kucinich's on Carnegie Avenue. It was the house we first lived in when I was born on October 8, 1946.

Chapter Two

THE FADED BROWN BOARD house at 2519 Carnegie Avenue lay on the outskirts of downtown Cleveland. It was set well back from the street. Its neighbor was an elegant Cadillac automobile showroom. The little house's black tarpaper roof had been beaten thin by years of rain, wind and heavy snow rolling in from Lake Erie. Blisters of paint tattered the side door entrance. A large "Bull Durham" sign, painted on the side of the house, was fading. The back yard barbed-wire fence was laced with a dried and weedy grapevine.

Five years before I was born, my father, Frank; my uncles, John, Pete, Paul, Steve, Joseph and George; and my aunts, Betty and Barbara, had all lived here with Grandpa and Grandma. When World War II began, Pete and Steve went off to war. Then, to bring an extra paycheck to his parents, Frank quit school in the eighth grade. He followed Steve into the Marines. Betty and Barb finished high school and went to work in factories to help win the war. George was a serious student, even in grade school; he wanted to be a teacher someday.

After the war, the boys came back to Carnegie Avenue. Frank was missing a kneecap but brought back jungle rot, malaria, and a Purple Heart. Pete's bronze and silver stars melted into a bottle of firewater. Steve contemplated the cosmos, and handicapping horses.

John didn't go to war. He went to jail for theft. When he got out of jail, he married a secretary and went respectable, selling used cars. Paul went behind bars for theft and took Pete with him. When they got out of jail, they set up an iron and steel scrap business.

All this was a bit much for my grandfather. He found peace on the noisy streets of the city on his ice delivery truck. Grandpa John "Eachega" Kucinich often took me with him on his ice run. His blue denim overalls crisscrossed broad, tough back muscles and strong shoulders, covered only by a thin white t-shirt. He coughed a lot as he spun the wheel.

The brakes squealed. I slid forward on the seat. My shoes touched the glove compartment. Grandpa stopped the yellow truck with the red letters "WHITE HOUSE ICE." He went to the passenger's side. He pushed down the chrome handle. He scooped me up under his left arm. He grabbed his huge steel tongs and walked to the rear of the truck. He flipped up the black canvas flap. He opened wide the scissor-like jaws and crunched the tongs into the steamy cake of ice. He slung the cold mass over his shoulder. Then he triumphantly carried ice and grandson through the swinging screen doors and into the half-light of a local tavern. Locked in his tight grasp, I spun past the polished black tabletops and the red-covered stools.

He hefted the ice into a tub behind the counter. He plopped me on the wooden bar and announced to the balding bartender wearing the white smock: "Here is my little Eachega. Give him pivo!"

Grandpa and I saluted our host's health: "Nas drovia." He finished feeding me the root beer, coughing as he walked me back to the truck.

"Little Eachega," he said, adjusting the visor of his old-country woolen button cap, "You stay with Grandpa. He show you beeg city." Riding in the truck with him was fun. I loved my Grandpa.

I couldn't even see over the dashboard, but with Grandpa as my guide I found out the city was much bigger than Carnegie Avenue. It was a city of taverns and churches on almost every corner. Grandpa seemed to know a lot of the people in the city.

His cough grew worse. He stopped driving his truck. He went into the hospital. I heard Mom and Dad talk about some breathing problem he had from smoking or from when he worked in the coal mines. I saw him in bed. A tent covered his chest and his head. He was having trouble breathing. He opened his eyes when Mom called him "Pa." He turned his head and looked at me. He raised his right hand, moving his index finger up and down, as if he was trying to say something or trying to catch his breath. I hoped he would feel better real soon so we could travel the big city together. I smiled at him. He nodded his head, stiffly. I think he was trying to tell me: "Eachega, I get off bet, I get trook. Vee go ride see citee. Trink pivo."

Mom and Dad led me out of the room. They were crying. Later on in the day, the phone rang at the house. Dad answered it. He said something to Mom, and they both cried for a long time.

As time passed, whenever I asked for Grandpa, Mom and Dad told me he was in Heaven. Okay, but I wanted to know when he was going to take me for a ride in his truck again.

Dad began to take me with him on his Star Elevator flour truck. He delivered to bakeries out in the country. High grass, tall corn: everything looked yellow and green for miles and miles.

A baker gave me a cloth hat with rings attached to it. It wasn't like Dad's dark green hat with the turned-up brim, but it was close enough. Once home I swallowed one of the rings from the hat and almost choked to death. Dad noticed I was turning blue.

"JESUS CHRIST," he shouted.

He grabbed my heels and turned me upside down with one hand while banging me between the shoulder blades with the other. No ring. Dad became very excited. I couldn't say much. He set me upright. He stuck two fingers way down my throat.

"Wait a minute. Ah, here it is. I got it!" I was through eating rings.

Carnegie Avenue had its hazards, particularly the pigs' feet jelly and knuckles that Dad insisted I had to eat to be a "good Cro." Uncle Steve terrorized me with hot yellow peppers.

"You're my first nephew," he told me. "I am going to show you what the world is all about." Then he passed me a cigar. It smelled bad. I turned that down. "Here, try this," he said. He then fed me green, rubbery Polski Wyrob dill pickles. They smelled okay and slid down fast into my tummy.

I was a good sport about it. That's why Uncle Steve took me with him to the racetrack. Uncle Steve had his own mathematics system. He said he used it to feed the horses at Thistledown and Cranwood Park. He said all horse races were fixed, but the horses had to be fed. He said his system helped him figure out which races were likely to be rigged. He also knew a lot of jockeys and trainers at the track and introduced me as a future jockey.

Back at Carnegie Avenue, Grandma Kucinich kept getting her hand caught in the wringer of the washing machine. Giant ants crawled in and out of the laundry pile. Ants were not much of a problem compared to other creatures.

Late one night there was a ruckus in the living room.

Uncle Steve had a gun in his hand. I had never seen a real gun before. Aunt Betty was calling out frantically, "Steve, don't shoot."

Dad, very agitated, whispered hoarsely, "There's the rat. There it is, there it is, behind the dresser."

Uncle Steve and Dad slammed the dresser against the wall.

I could hear an awful, high-pitched, blood-curdling sound. Then the room was quiet. Dad and Uncle Steve moved the dresser forward, cautiously.

"Got the goddamned thing!" Dad said matter-of-factly.

Steve brought a shovel and scraped up the big rat. It had a brown coat. Its face was smashed in. Its guts were splashed against the baseboard.

"Would have been less of a mess if I had shot it," said Uncle Steve, putting his German Luger back into its holster.

I was told to go to bed before I could see any more. Dad said the rat had been chewing in my baby brother Gary's crib. Uncle Steve had heard Gary cry and come running.

My new brother, Gary, had just arrived home. I was with Mom and Dad when they brought him from the hospital. Mom moved the blanket from his face. I could tell by looking at him that he had a lot to learn. No wonder he cried so loud when the rat jumped into his crib to welcome him home.

Dad was upset. "Where the hell was the dog?" he demanded. Aunt Betty took a pail of hot water and scrubbed the red-smeared wall near the dresser.

"The dog," explained a now wild-eyed Uncle Steve, "is afraid of rats."

Uncle Steve folded up a newspaper. He dropped the rat into a paper bag and took it outside. "The other rats will eat it," he said with a smile when he came back inside.

Every so often Uncle Steve would talk about that night and how he saved Gary's life. The story got better and better with each re-telling. "Yep, that rat could have chewed off Gary's nose. It could have taken one bite and the nose would have come off, just like that! Rats like to eat little children." He grabbed the tip of my nose. He pulled on it. He then displayed half of his thumb protruding between his index finger and his middle finger. It looked just like a nose!

If Uncle Steve was telling me all of this to get me to be afraid of rats, it worked. Every night as I was falling asleep, I listened carefully for faint sounds of scratching at the door. I waited. I was ready to scream bloody murder. I'd tell that rat to go away or I'd call Uncle Steve.

We came home late one night and as we pulled in the car's headlights beamed toward the back of the house. I saw a whole rat family meeting where the garbage was kept. Rudely interrupted, they turned around and quickly retreated into the night. I worried they would soon be back inside the house.

Chapter Three

THE FAMILY WAS GATHERED in the living room late one evening. I was supposed to be in bed, but I quietly stood in the hallway watching the animated adult discussion. Grandma Kucinich reached underneath the couch she was sitting on. She pulled out a small bag tucked underneath and took a donut out of the bag.

Aunt Betty called to her. "Ma, you know you aren't supposed to eat those!" She had a serious case of diabetes and was under strict orders to stay away from foods loaded with sugar, or die. Grandma Kucinich smiled, sat back and enjoyed her donut as Betty and others chided her. I was surprised to see her pitch forward moments later and fall to the floor.

"Ma!" cried Aunt Betty. "Ma!" I stood motionless, staring at Grandma on the floor, not really understanding why she wasn't getting up.

"Take her to the hospital!" someone shouted. "I think she had a heart attack."

Someone screamed: "She's dead! She's dead! Ma's dead!"

Uncle Steve spotted me in the shadows and snapped: "Hey, Dennis! Get back upstairs, now. This is no place for children."

I stood there, unable to move, transfixed at the sight of Grandma motionless on the floor. Mom came over and took me upstairs. She talked to me, but I didn't hear her. I was wondering why Grandma didn't get up. The next time I climbed a step and saw Grandma again, flowers surrounded her as she was sleeping.

"Grandma?" I called, waiting for her to wake up. Then Mom began crying and took me off the step. I stayed in the car as Mom and Dad stepped out into a pouring rain in Calvary Cemetery where the family buried Grandma.

The Kucinich family, which was drawn to the Carnegie Avenue as a homestead, splintered for a time after Grandma died. My uncles fought over who got what that had been owned by Grandma and Grandpa. It wasn't as if there was that much; people were arguing over a few pieces of furniture. We moved from Carnegie Avenue to a house off St. Clair Avenue, on East 72nd Place. We stayed there a few months, then moved to East 72nd Street, next to a dairy. The rooms were small, neat, and there was a side entrance. We lived down the street from one of Mom's favorite meat markets. We then moved to an apartment across from St. Vitus Catholic School. Mom took me there to enroll me in the first grade. They told her I was too young to begin the first grade.

"You don't know anything about him. He can read all the books. He's ready for the first grade." They looked at me. I was a little shorter than most my age, so they didn't think I was old enough. "Let's go, Dennis. Don't worry, we'll find you a place to go to school."

Aunt Betty and Aunt Barbara visited us frequently. They brought sweaters, shirts and books for Frank, Gary and me. Aunt Barbara was very beautiful. She had dark hair and dark eyes and was always high-spirited and very affectionate. She was widely travelled. She was a dancer who wore few clothes when she performed. She gave me my favorite sweater, one with cowboy Hopalong Cassidy on it.

Aunt Betty had red hair. She smiled more than anyone in the whole family. At Christmastime, Aunt Betty, Frank, Gary and I took the bus downtown to see the biggest Christmas tree in the world. It was at least 75 feet tall. How they got it inside Sterling Linder Davis department store was a secret. The tree was reflected in the eyes of every child. It had huge blue, red and green ornaments. It was dressed in rings of silver tinsel and colored lights.

It was the biggest, brightest and best Christmas tree God ever made. And it was in Cleveland, Ohio.

After marveling at the tree, we went with Aunt Betty to see Santa Claus. Frank was shy. Only Gary and I took a picture with the Man. Aunt Betty was so nice, except she bought us clothes for Christmas, not toys.

My uncles did not come to visit us. Dad told Mom they were still fighting over who should get the sofas, kitchen table and chairs from Grandma's house. Dad said as far as he was concerned they could have it all.

Aunt Barbara, Uncle George and Uncle Steve moved from Carnegie Avenue to the upstairs of a two-family home at 1377 East 30th Street, near the corner of St. Clair. Uncle Paul and his wife, Aunt Ann lived downstairs. One night, after Uncle George, Uncle Steve and Aunt Barbara painted the four rooms, Uncle Steve went to his job as an aircraft parts inspector at Tapco, Inc.

The night was chilly. A gas heater was turned on. Uncle George and Aunt Barbara went to sleep. Uncle Steve returned home in the morning and found Aunt Barbara dead and Uncle George in a deep coma. The gas heater had malfunctioned and spread carbon monoxide through the apartment. It was explained to me that Aunt Barbara went to Heaven, but I did not get this Heaven stuff. It seemed like a bad deal. One minute my Aunt Barbara was playing with us in the apartment, and the next minute my uncles said I would never see her again.

The Sisters of St. John Cantius High School, where Uncle George was an honor student, started a prayer vigil to the Infant of Prague asking for George's life to be spared. The hopes of an entire family were flickering with the votive candles lit in the parish church. Aunt Betty placed Infant of Prague statues throughout the house.

Uncle George had been the star of the family. All my aunts and uncles said he was headed for big things. He was very smart. He planned to be the first Kucinich ever to go to college. And Aunt Barbara was going to be famous in show business. After she died,

Mom and Dad were talking about a newspaper story describing Aunt Barbara as an "exotic" dancer.

"Mom, when can I see Aunt Barbara again?" I asked

Mom explained to me "When a person you love dies, only your love and your memory can bring them back."

After she was buried, Aunt Betty, who was Aunt Barbara's best friend, turned out the lights as she prepared to go to sleep in the room she had shared with Barbara, and heard Aunt Barbara softly say, "Good night."

"Barbara's spirit is still in the house," Aunt Ann said. "We should pray so that it will be released. She needs help to find peace." Aunt Barbara was only twenty-three years old when she died.

A puppy Dad brought home became my best friend. He said it reminded him of Brownie, a dog he had while he was in the Marines. I named my dog Puppy.

Mom said Puppy would never be paper-trained. I kept Puppy in the empty bathtub when I wasn't playing with it. During the day, Frank and I took Puppy outside to romp with us in the snow, and we shared samples of milk that a man from the dairy gave us.

When Dad said we had to move, I didn't mind. Moving was part of life. We moved from Carnegie to St. Clair to Carnegie to E. 72nd Street, to E. 72 Place, so why shouldn't we move again?

"We aren't going to be able to take the puppy with us," Dad said.

"Then I don't want to move. I want to stay here with Puppy," I began to cry.

'We can't rent a place if we have a pet," he said.

My tears wouldn't stop. I hated moving. What did people have against pets? That little dog wouldn't have bothered a flea. He was my friend. You just don't leave a friend behind. Who would care for him? Would they spoon-feed him dog food from the can like I did? Would they clean up after him when he messes in the tub? You just can't give a little dog a boy one day and then tell him

"That's it, find yourself another one." Dad said he would give Puppy to Uncle Pete to take care of. Uncle Pete had a front yard Puppy could play in, and I could see Puppy again real soon. Not good enough. This was my dog.

As we set out to find another place, Dad found out that Uncle Steve refused to return to E. 30th Street. He just could not bring himself to go back to the upstairs apartment where Aunt Barbara died. The gas heater that had caused Barbara's death had been repaired, and the upstairs was vacant. Steve had already paid the rent. We moved in.

The first thing I did was to run to Uncle Pete's to see Puppy. I looked in the yard. My dog wasn't in the yard. I went to Uncle Pete's house. I knocked on the door. Puppy didn't come to the door. Uncle Pete answered. He had on a t-shirt and overalls with suspenders. His black hair was greased back. He had a very scrubby beard. He smelled of beer. I think I woke him.

"Yeah, yeah. What do you want? What are you coming over here for? Do you know what time it is? Where's your father?" He gave me too many questions to answer.

"I came to see Puppy," I said.

"What?! Go home, will you?"

"I want to see my dog. Dad gave him to you to take care of for me. I thought he would be in the yard."

"You mean that little dog? That was a goddamned dumb dog. It got loose and ran away."

"Oh!? Ran away? Where?" I was seized by fear. My heart began to crash. "I'll go look. I'll find him. I'll call him, he'll come right away!" I turned around and called him:

"Puppy, here Puppy," I whistled, just like Uncle Steve taught me.

"Did you hear your father call you?" Uncle Pete asked.

"No. My Dad didn't call me. I want to see my dog. Where did he go?"

"Oh, all right. Your dog ran down there," he pointed between the houses, "and went out into the street, right under the wheels of a bus. It's dead. I told you it was a goddamned dumb dog." He pointed to a small mound of dirt near a side fence.

"That's where the dog is. Now get out of here." Please God, don't let it be true.   Please don't let Puppy be dead. He was my best friend. I never wanted to be separated from him. I wanted him to be there always at my side. I was so sorry we moved. I was so sorry we sent him over to Uncle Pete's. Uncle Pete didn't take care of Puppy. Uncle Pete didn't care at all. He said the dog was dumb, but Puppy was smart. He barked twice every morning when he wanted me to take him out of the empty tub/doghouse. He did that every morning. That dog was not dumb.

Was my little Puppy really dead? I would never see him again?! My head hurt from thinking. My face hurt from crying. I stood at the side of the fence, where Uncle Pete pointed. A small patch of ground had been broken. Was Puppy really in the ground? I sat down and smoothed the loose dirt with my hand. I just couldn't understand why Puppy was in the ground and not in my lap, licking my hand. My heart was buried with Puppy, by that side fence. I could not stop crying. I walked upstairs. I told my mom. She gave me a big, long hug. I kept trying to catch my breath in between sobs.

My world had become darker even though inside the apartment everything looked much brighter. I could smell the freshly painted walls. This was a nice place, but I sure missed Puppy. We had one more room than the last place. We needed it, because Mom said God sent another baby to her and Dad, a little girl named Theresa.

Theresa was born with a red mark on her forehead. Mom said it was nothing. The doctor told her it would go away. Other people had ideas how Theresa got that strawberry skin.

"Ginny, I'm telling you that mark has something to do with Barb. It's a sign from God," said Aunt Ann. "Theresa is taking Barbara's place in the family. Terrie will grow up and become a mother someday, to have the family Barb never had a chance to have," she continued.

"Ann, sometimes a birth mark is just a birth mark," Mom said as she changed Theresa's diaper.

"Ginny, you have to pay more attention to these things. There's always more to life than meets the eye," Aunt Ann responded.

Uncle George was in a coma for months as a result of the accident that took Aunt Barbara's life. Everyone in the family took turns visiting Uncle George in the hospital except me. No children were allowed in his room.

After many prayers and bedside vigils, Aunt Betty one day ran excitedly into the house. She was crying. But she was joyous.

"Frank! Ginny! He's awake! He's out of the coma! He's awake. George is awake! He's going to be all right."

Newspaper stories about George's recovery called it a miracle. He had been in a coma for five months.

"It was the prayers to the Infant of Prague," said Aunt Betty.

She placed a statue of the Infant on a stand in Uncle George's hospital room. She helped organize the prayers at the church and at George's school.

"We believed all along that God would spare his life," Aunt Betty said. "We prayed and prayed and prayed. The Bible says 'All things are possible to those who believe.' We believed, and now he's awake!"

Dad, Mom, Aunt Betty and I went to St. John Cantius Church to see Uncle George graduate with his class. When the Principal called his name, everyone stood up applauding, tears streaming down their faces.

Chapter Four

I LEARNED TO DRIVE a car in the summer of 1951. Lenny Gannon was Aunt Betty's boyfriend. He wore bright suits. He wasn't much taller than me. He laughed a lot. Magic tricks and practical jokes like hand buzzers and fake vomit spilled out of his pockets.

Uncle Lenny let me stand up in the front seat of his red Cadillac convertible as the car hurried along country roads. Uncle Lenny was using some of his magic. I thought I was the only one holding the wheel. The car slowed. He kissed Aunt Betty.

"Now watch where you are taking us," he said. I promised him I would be careful.

Lenny was a professional piano player. He taught me to play the piano. It was easy. Music was going on inside my head all the time. Beautiful music. Long-playing music where the notes climbed the scale right up to the stars. When I sat down at the piano the music just flowed. I went with Uncle Lenny to Ral-Cha's Cafe on Miles Avenue where he played regularly. His friends would gather around the piano and watch me play.

Dad wasn't at all happy about me playing the piano. Uncle Lenny told him about my piano-playing, and Dad was not impressed.

"Hey, look, this kid of mine is going to be a Marine like me."

Dad's colored pencil Marine portrait hung on the living room wall next to a picture of Grandma Norris. There was another picture of Mom and Dad getting married, with Dad in his service uniform. I wasn't sure what Dad meant about being a Marine, like him. Dad did imitations of Donald Duck, which made everyone laugh. Was Donald Duck a marine? Sometimes Dad did a pretty good impersonation of actor James Cagney: "All right you dirty rats" he'd bark in gangland-style greeting to the Kucinich kids as he came home from work. Maybe being a Marine had something to do with fighting for our country. Dad got into fights all the time. A marine had to be a good fighter, I gathered, but maybe not a piano player.

"He ain't going to be no goddamned piano player," he told Mom after Uncle Lenny left. I asked him if I could take piano lessons.

"This has got to stop now. What the hell kind of noise is this? Piano player my ass. That's for sissies. You'll be a marine. C 'mere kid, stand up straight. Be a marine. Piano player? Don't bullshit the troops."

That ended my piano-playing career.

Mom enrolled me in a pre-school program at Goodrich neighborhood house on the next block. There I discovered the joys of crayons, paper and scissors, finger painting, and Connie Austin. Connie rammed my scooter. She then gave me a kiss to make up for the collision. I was learning about boy-girl relationships. A *Cleveland Press* photographer took a picture of the event. Everyone in the house was excited that I had made the newspaper at age five. People kept talking about it for quite a while, as if it was some kind of accomplishment.

My brother Frank had accomplished something himself a few months earlier. The *Cleveland News* reported that Frank went downtown with another four-year-old to see President Truman, who was visiting the city. When the police brought Frank home, Mom was furious. She had no idea that Frank had left the yard. She didn't punish Frank, maybe because she liked Truman, or maybe because if Dad had found out, he would have given Frank a beating.

What they didn't know was that I was even more of a wanderer than my brother. I would slip out of the house and walk to Petri playground alone. Sometimes I went downtown alone. I walked a mile to Cleveland Municipal Stadium and followed closely a large person as he moved through the turnstile to watch the Cleveland Indians play. Baseball was such a frequent topic of discussion around the house that I decided to see a game for myself, from the bleachers. I couldn't see much from there, so I walked back home, my absence undetected.

Lenny and Betty got married. When they returned from their honeymoon, they bought me a small set of drums. They took me to Ral-Cha's Cafe to practice on the big drums. When I got to the bar I looked at the empty piano bench. My fingers again began to move quickly over invisible keys. I could hear the music, but my piano-playing days were over. My career as a drummer was about to begin.

Uncle Lenny gave me a toothy grin as people in the bar watched me practice drum rolls.

"He's got the beat. The kid's got the beat," Lenny proclaimed. "He's going to be a drummer, another Gene Krupa."

I didn't know about Gene Krupa, but if he was okay with Uncle Lenny, then he was OK with me. On the way home I asked Uncle Lenny about Gene Krupa.

"One of the greatest drummers alive. If you practice, you'll be as good as he is. People will come from all over just to hear you play the drums."

Good. Then I was going to be a drummer. I began practicing every night, upstairs at 1377 E. 30th Street.

I must have played too late one night. Dad came from his bedroom shouting, "Jesus Christ! What is this, World War Two? Jesus Christ, I fight the War and I come home to this noise!?"

"But Dad, I'm going to be another Gene Krupa. Uncle Lenny said so."

"Hey, piss on Gene Krupa. Piss on Uncle Lenny," he said. He took the drumsticks from me.

"When the hell am I going to get some sleep? I have to go to work in the morning. Gene Krupa? My ass."

Later that week, Mom gave the drums back to Uncle Lenny. For the longest time, whenever I heard a drummer or a piano player on the radio, I imagined that I was playing. I kept time with the music. I could always hear that music and I could hear Uncle Lenny encouraging me on the drums, "He's got the beat, he's got the beat; another Gene Krupa, believe it."

Summer was closing fast. I was on the threshold of new experiences. I was about to go out into that great world of hopes and fears. I was ready to find what Uncle Steve called my place in the cosmos. I was about to begin the first grade.

Chapter Five

I SLOWLY OPENED THE last compartment of the oak bureau. My dark blue school pants, white shirt and skinny black tie came into view. I was careful not to disturb my five-month-old sister, Theresa. She was blissfully slumbering about three feet off the ground in the half-open second drawer of the dresser. Socks, underwear and t-shirts were in other drawers. My cousin Mary Ann was waiting outside to walk me to school the first day. Mary Ann was much older than me. She was 7.

"Remember which way we are taking because you will probably be walking it alone."

Mary Ann lived right behind us with her dad, Uncle Pete, Aunt Marge and baby brother, Junior.

The morning air was fresh. The sun was shining upon my first day of school. I was worried. Would I see my friends? Would I meet new friends? Would I get chocolate or white milk at lunch? Did chocolate cost more than white or was it free, too? Older boys were sing-songing:

"First grade babies, Second grade tots, Third grade angels, Fourth grade snots."

"Hello, and what is your name?" a smiling Sister of Notre Dame greeted me. She had a long white cord belt draped around her black dress. She wore a silver Christ. Jesus hung fast to a black cross attached to her rosary.

"My name is Dennis," I said.

"You are in the first grade," she correctly assessed my condition.

I was ushered into Room One. The first grade. I made it! I never thought I would. I was sure something would go wrong. Maybe I wouldn't wake up one morning and then no first grade. It's not that I was a pessimist. Watching Grandma die suddenly in the living room, Aunt Barbara's death, the constant moving and Puppy getting run over, showed me life was so uncertain. I thought any moment could be my last. Possessed of this sense of fatality, I entered grade one.

Here I had a chance to show how much I had learned. Mom and Dad were going to be proud. The last few years, whenever Dad had friends over he asked me to read aloud stories from the newspaper, or he'd tell me to spell big words, like "Philadelphia." When I did he'd pat me on the head and say things like, "You are going to be a Marine, just like your old man."

Room One. The teacher was at the blackboard printing her name: Sister Mary Alice. She turned around. She was beautiful. I could hear sighs from half the room. She told pupils standing at the door to come in.

"Take any seat."

About six of us broke for the same seat, up front near her desk.

"Children, there are plenty of seats in this room," she laughed at the sight.

I sat a few rows back. I looked around the room. The blackboard had Jesus, Mary and Joseph lettered across the top. In the right-hand corner of the board there was a big chart with blue lettering inquiring: "Have you brushed your teeth today?" The answer was no. The top of the blackboard had letters A to Z stretching across the room.

"Good morning, boys and girls." She had a nice voice.

I could listen to her all day long, I thought.

"Good morning, Sister," the class responded.

"Now, when I call your name, you will stand up and say, 'Hello.'"

As the alphabetical listing advanced, a strange fear began to work its way up from my knees. I felt queasy. My chest tightened.

"Tom Bender."

My face got warm.

"Theresa Hiller…Anita Jelinek…"

I was about to die.

"Dennis, Coo, Ku-si, Cuh—How do you say your name?"

I stood up. I was flustered. I stammered. I just couldn't get it out.

"That's OK Dennis, you may sit down. Alan Petri… Carole Pianka…Tom Pluto…Tom Tomsick…"

One after another they stood up and said hello. I could not get that far. I was too flustered.

"Does anyone know what color this is?" Sister asked.

This was going to be easy, I thought; after all, I knew all my colors.

"Raise your hand if you know."

I raised my hand instantly for the chance to make up for the fumbled introduction.

Thirty-six pair of eyes focused on me as I stood.

"What color is this, Dennis?"

"Gr, Gr, Gruh, Gruh," what was this coming out of my mouth? I sounded like a growling dog. I could hear giggling.

"Try again, go ahead," Sister Mary Alice was being helpful.

"Grr, Gruh, Gruh,"

"Green," she offered.

I stood sweating in a room heated by my classmates' laughter.

"Green," it finally came out.

We took a recess break, and Sister walked up and down the aisles distributing chocolate milk. Children went for a walk, double file, into the asphalt-covered school yard. The ground was hard. You had to be careful not to fall down or you would be banged up. The church next door had wide grates covering up the basement windows. Sometimes people would lose money in the well. Kids would take a long stick, put some gum on the end and try to spear the coins with the gum.

The classroom had a carnival atmosphere. Crayons, paste, colored paper, scissors and colored chalk were plentiful.

"Now put away everything. Okay, boys and girls," she held up a book. I knew what a book was just after I was born. "What do you call this?" I raised my hand first.

"Dennis?"

"A bbb, bb, bubba," it wouldn't come out. What was wrong? Had my brain blown a fuse? I never had any problem with speaking or with getting my words out. When I recited for Mom, the words came out flawlessly. I read the paper aloud for many people. Why couldn't I get the words out of my mouth? I didn't know what was wrong. I was scared.

The laughter again. I knew they were laughing at me. I started crying.

"Now children, that is not nice." Sister admonished them.

After school, she asked me to come to her desk.

"Dennis, will you please give this note to your mother and father?" My eyes sought to hide in floor cracks. I nodded my head. I was afraid to speak. I kept the broken words to myself. Sister placed the note in my jacket.

On the way home, Mary Ann and I inspected elevators in the manufacturing and warehouse districts along Superior Avenue. I sat on a railing and took the envelope from my pocket. I read the note:

Dear Mr. and Mrs. Kucinich,

Dennis has a speech problem. I would like to discuss it with you. I think it would be to his benefit to attend special classes at St. John's College for speech therapy. Please call me at the school after 3:30 pm. Thank you.

Sincerely, Sister Mary Alice

"Mary Ann, what's this t-h-e-r-a-p-y?"

"I'm not sure, but it says here you got a speech problem. What kind of a speech problem? You saying dirty words?"

I wasn't dirtying words. I was breaking words. I was chewing them up and spitting them out in little pieces.

I had so looked forward to school. I didn't know why I had trouble speaking. At home Uncle Pete said I talked too much. "Children should be seen and not heard," Pete said. I knew the answers to all the questions. I just couldn't get the words out.

That evening Mom read the note to Dad.

"There's nothing wrong with him," he frowned. "Look at him. Hey, say something to me. Come on, kid, talk." I was silent. "See, there's nothing wrong with him. He's all right, ain'cha kid?"

The next day Mom used a neighbor's phone and called Sister. In a few days Mom and I were at St. John's College, a few blocks away from St. Peter's. A lady asked Mom some questions. I found out that I was about to begin t-h-e-r-a-p-y for stuttering.

The first session started with a list of words, all beginning with the letter 'b.'

"I will say the word, then you say the word," she said.

She was kind, like Sister. She did not wear anything to cover her head, which was probably smart, because it was warm in the small room.

"Take your time, Dennis. We have plenty of time. Now try again: BOOK."

"Buh-buh-"

I was trying, really. I think I first saw this word when I was about two years old. 'Book' must be one of the easiest words in the world for a first grader. Big deal, 'book.'

"Buh-buh-buh-bb." Oh! I started to cry.

"Just relax. Take a deep breath. Inhale."

Except when I was asked to recite at home, I was quiet. I had many things I wanted to say, but I was afraid to say them. I think that fear worked its way into my tongue. I was afraid of a lot of things. Afraid of the dark. Afraid Mom and Dad wouldn't come home. I was afraid when they fought. I was afraid one would hurt the other. Because when they fought I was afraid they didn't love each other. But when they weren't fighting, they were often kissing and hugging, so they didn't hate each other. I inhaled the chaos and the confusion and held my breath until the trouble passed.

My teacher was there at the right time and place. Had she believed that stuttering was a symptom of mental impairment, instead of emotional difficulty, I would have been sent to another type of school. Sister was the first person who saved my life.

"Exhale."

I knew I could do that right.

"Now say, 'buh.'"

"Buh."

"Try it again."

"Buh."

"Now try this, Buh, buh."

"Buh, buh."

"Buh, buh, buh, buh, buh, buh," she almost sang it.

I repeated the series.

"Now say buh, buh."

"Buh, buh."

"Now say 'book'."

"Book." No hesitation. I did it.

We went through a whole list of words that began with 'b.' I stumbled and stuttered all the way. At the end of the session she said, "You did very well today."

What a liar! I loved her.

"Next time we will try some more words."

Sometimes the lady would give me a list to take home and I practiced whenever things were quiet, which wasn't often. I was careful not to say words I didn't practice, so I kept much of what I knew secret, I bit my nails instead of talking, and when I ran out of nails to bite I wet the bed.

I went to St. John's College twice a week. It wasn't long before I learned how to say words beginning with the letters, *b*, *d*, *p* and *t*. Next we said another series of words which began with *f* and *v* and then another with *m* and *n*. This was hard work, getting my tongue and mouth in gear. It was like learning to talk again. I took many deep breaths. I relaxed and slowed down the words. The sessions were long.

I was in St. Peter's only a few months when I was offered a promotion.

Sister Mary Alice was anxious to get me to practice talking.

"Dennis, how would you like to be one of Santa's helpers?"

It seemed like quite an offer. I always wondered how people got jobs like that.

"The high school drama club has a Christmas Show, 'Santa's Helper.' We need two elves for two nights. You'll have to wear a brown costume, a green hat and green shoes."

"I don't have clothes like that."

"We'll make your costume. You'll just need your parents' permission."

When Dad came home, I asked.

"Ask your mother."

"Ask your father."

I asked my father again.

"Mom says it's OK with her if it's OK with you."

"No."

"No? Why not?" I wasn't supposed to ask Dad questions like that.

"No kid of mine is going to be no goddamned elf. You need a green hat? Here, try this!"

He placed on my head his green work cap with the multi-colored buttons and turned up the brim the way he wore it, except that it covered my eyes and ears. Maybe it was the brown costume that bothered Dad, because he wore green pants and a green shirt to go with his green cap.

"Now that's a truck driver's hat! You aren't going to be no goddamn elf."

I ran crying to the bedroom. That didn't work, so I came back to the kitchen.

"Please, Mom? Please?"

"Frank, I think we ought to let him do it."

"I said no. I mean no."

"Frank...." She took him into their room. It was quiet for a while. They came out. He stared at me, squinted his brown eyes and started to smile.

"OK, kid, you can do it. But don't thank me, thank your crazy Irish mother. She must think elves are Irish," he said. I don't know how she did it, but sometimes Mom could be very strong-willed. She blamed that on being Irish. And she had a real temper. That, too, she said, was because she was Irish. Dad was now laughing and why he changed his mind didn't really matter. I hugged them both.

At the announced moment I was nudged onto the stage at St. Peter's Auditorium. I looked out and couldn't see anyone in the bright lights, but I could hear a loud buzz as I stepped into view.

"Jinglebells, Jinglebells, come here, come here," Santa was up on his workbench, calling.

I had a long cloth strip with bells sewn onto it and I shook them as I walked to Santa.

"Here are the bells, Santa," I piped.

"Thank you, Jinglebells. Thank you."

Santa took the bells and put them around the neck of Rudolph the Red-Nosed Reindeer and, as the story goes, Rudolph could fly again and Christmas was saved. Before exiting Stage Right I turned around and bowed deeply to the audience, and it roared.

Chapter Six

MARY ANN AND I went back and forth to school together almost every day. Mary Ann was a big help, except when she was beaten up by her father, Uncle Pete. Then she wasn't much of a help to anyone. I don't know if she did anything bad, but she got beat a lot. I watched in horror as Uncle Pete would take out a big leather strap and chase Mary Ann around the house, the yard, and even down the street. When he'd catch her, and he always would, he would take her back home and then hit her until big red welts striped her legs. Sometimes the welts would open up, she would start bleeding, and she would plead, "Daddy, Daddy, don't hit me no more, please don't hit me, pleeease!"

Uncle Pete would hit her all the harder and tell her to shut up. It was just awful. Once I yelled at him for hitting Mary Ann and he made a move towards me, but then stopped. Maybe he was afraid of what my Dad would do to him if he hit me.

The tears would roll out of Mary Ann's big brown eyes and down her cheeks after she took a beating. She pulled out a hanky and wiped her eyes and blew her nose, and told me,

"I, I didn't do anything wrong. He just keeps hitting me." She looked up and both her eyes were black. "Mom says stay away from him or some day he's going to kill me."

Mary Ann's parents, Uncle Pete and Aunt Marge, met just after the war. Uncle Pete was a hero in World War II. He left the war with a strong taste for hard whiskey and his grade school education intact, but the war never left him. On the home front, he worked in the scrap metal business. I saw him out in the neighbor-hood in his red Dodge truck with the wooden slats sticking up from the flatbed, stopping here and there, picking up auto parts, stoves, sinks, ice boxes, old washers, any kind of metal junk.

Mary Ann said he spent a lot of time around the railroad tracks picking up scrap. Mary Ann used to joke, "Pa and Ma's in the iron and steel business. Ma irons while Pa steals."

Aunt Marge was a very frail Appalachian woman with deep-set green eyes and long brown-black hair, tied back in a ponytail. She stuck by her man no matter what. So when Uncle Pete was pitched over the counter at Kekic's Bar, his brain floating in the Sea of Calvert whiskey, Marge was there drinking right along with him—not enjoying it quite as much, but there just the same, with six-month-old Junior. Loosely wrapped in a cotton blanket, he kicked away at the ashtrays, spigots, glasses, bottles and everything else crowding him. His clean glass Even-Flo baby bottle stood nipple erect, like a prisoner of war among the helter-skelter Carlings and P.O.C. soldiers dotting the Formica terrain.

I often went with Mary Ann when she went into the bar to ask her father for money for food. "Get the hell out of here!" Pete would roar, "Don't bother me or you'll get it." Mary Ann would sob, and in a paroxysm of hunger run out of the bar, but before she got more than a few feet, an old lady who worked at Kekic's rushed out the back door with a small roast beef or goose liver sandwich. The old lady knew Uncle Pete, Aunt Marge and Mary Ann very well. She knew our whole family.

"I'm going to run away from home," Mary Ann would promise. "Sister Donna said don't do it, that I'll get in trouble, that they'll end up sending me to a girl's reform school, but I don't care."

I slept at her house one night and her father came in and took a cigarette lighter and started after her with it. Mary Ann ran past him, through the living room, past the four-foot-high brown-enameled gas heater and out into the kitchen, where she picked up a bread knife with an eight-inch blade. She brandished it, nervously, jerking close to her chest the wood handle with the three metal dots.

"Come on, you son of a bitch, I'll kill you," she yelled to Uncle Pete. The banshee-like cry flew through her tightly clenched teeth. Pete was snarling as he dove for her. She jabbed the knife out. He stopped.

"All right, give me the goddamned knife," he demanded.

"I'll give you the knife. Just come closer and I'll give it to you." Hysterically, she backed towards the door, while Pete stood at bay. She opened the door and fled.

I followed her. I ran towards the back stairs, but they were missing. There was a three-foot gap between the ground and the back door that led to the upstairs. With the terror of the image of Pete close behind, I levered a big board to the door's entrance and created a plank and ran upstairs. My heart was racing faster than my feet could carry me up to the top of the stairs. I pounded on the door, screaming for my Mom or Dad. No answer. The door was locked. The utility room that separated the back stairs from the kitchen blocked out any sound.

I ran back down the stairs. I saw Pete coming from the back of the house, carrying a belt he called a "Cat O'Nine Tails." I jumped to the ground, but a rusty nail hanging intercepted my left arm as I leapt. It ripped through my shirt, splitting my skin from the wrist to the elbow. I didn't notice I was bleeding until my mother fervently embraced me as I ran up the front hallway, yelling at the top of my lungs, "Uncle Pete's trying to kill us!"

When he wasn't drinking, he took my cousins and me to Tinker's Creek for picnics.

Chapter Seven

IN THE FIRST GRADE I learned that everyone has an angel who watches over them. At night I would pretend I was asleep, hoping to catch my guardian angel standing over me; but he was too smart and never let me see him. I knew he was there because nothing bad ever happened to me while I was sleeping.

Sitting at my first-grade desk, I could hear the second-graders showing off, singing, "Come to me, O little Jesus, come within my heart to rest," so loud that it was hard to crayon. I was sure I would never make it. I'd probably die first and go to Limbo because I missed out on communion.

On the way home from school, while walking up Superior Avenue, I'd pretend I was in line for my First Communion. Wearing pure white clothes, I saw myself kneeling before Father Schneider. I closed my eyes, stuck out my tongue on which he placed the white host with Jesus in it: "Ecce Agnus Dei." This worked out fine until I kept bumping into people coming out of the brick buildings on Superior Avenue.

Sister asked me to be in the First Communion procession.

"As an 'angel' you will walk in front of the second graders," she explained.

This was the biggest chance of my life. "Where will I get the wings?"

"You won't need wings," she continued.

"What?" I was confused and horrified at the thought of angels without wings, of dismembered Cherubims and Seraphims 'in unceasinging chorus praising' but waving wingless arms, stuck on earth.

"Dennis, we need eight first-graders to lead the second-graders into church. Walk when we tell you. Stop when we tell you. Sing one song and fold your hands like this," she said as she brought the flattened palms of her hands together and pointed her fingers up towards heaven.

I imitated.

"And that's all."

I told Mom and Dad about it. "You're no angel around here," Dad muttered, but he didn't say no. In fact, he didn't say anything else. He was reading a detective magazine, some kind of murder story. I started to read the magazine, but Dad took it away and said it wasn't for kids. At least he didn't object to the war movies we watched at school.

The first time we lined up for angel practice, the taller boys shoved me to fourth in line. Sister coaxed my friend Larry and me to the front. "You and Larry will lead the procession." Was I picked because I looked like an angel? Because I was the smartest? Because I was going to special classes to learn how to stop stuttering at school?

"You are the shortest," she smiled as she re-arranged the line. Sister gave us careful instructions on when to start, stop, what to do after communion. I didn't hear a word she said. Neither did Larry. Maybe the two angels behind us would know. They were taller.

It was still dark when I got up at six a.m. First Communion Sunday. I had a peanut butter sandwich for breakfast and I dressed.

At eight o'clock, I had to let Mom and Dad know I was leaving. I had to be at St. Peter's at eight-thirty, sharp. Dad was snoring like a Lake Erie tugboat, only louder. His face looked red. His big toe was sticking through one of his socks, out from under the covers. Mom was sleeping quietly next to him. "Dad, Dad," I called, softly.

"Dad, Dad." He still didn't respond. I shook him. He was snoring away. I couldn't leave without telling them. Suppose they thought I got kidnapped like that Beverly Potts girl from the West Side? I shook him again and spoke louder: "DAD!" He awoke, startled.

"Wh, wha, what?" His eyes, peeping through sleep-loaded lids, moved from one side of the room to the other as he cocked his head upwards. "Yeah."

"I have to leave now, Dad," I whispered. "I'm going to be an angel in the First Communion procession."

"You're not going anywhere. You are outside too much."

Maybe he didn't understand. "I've got to go now. I'm supposed to be at the church."

"Goddamn you, you're not going. Get those clothes off and go back to bed."

Mom was still sound asleep.

I was supposed to lead the procession.

"Dad, I have to go. I'm an angel." Sister was expecting me. The whole procession was depending on Larry and me.

"Angel bullshit," he said. He was angry now. He got up and took off my shirt and pants. He pulled off my black shoes without untying the laces and then removed my white socks. I was kicking and sobbing as he deposited me in bed. He went back to bed and I got right back up.

Theresa awoke from the commotion. The bureau rocked as she started crying from her drawer. I was afraid it would tip over, but it didn't. Frank and Gary woke up. They were closely crowded toward the wall at the other end of the black-striped mattress. I sat down and cried for about ten minutes straight. I could imagine Sister looking for me. Maybe she'll think I didn't wake up. Or maybe she'll think that I didn't want to be an angel. Or maybe I just forgot. I was sure going to be in a lot of trouble at school if I didn't show up. I could never tell her what really happened. I couldn't tell on my parents, it's something called squealing and I had heard from kids in at the playground that it's really a bad thing to do. I could do what Mary Ann did when she had trouble with her father—I could sneak out. I remember how she did it. She would get up. When all was quiet, she left. I also knew what happened to her when she got back.

I had to be in the procession. I got up. I walked scared stiff over creaking boards and accidentally kicked one of a dozen dark amber glass, blue and gold labeled bottles that were stacked on the floor, close to the living room table. They clinked like wind chimes and then went silent. I looked at the door of my parents' bedroom, and studied it purposefully. I jiggled the white doorknob. and moved the door open about an inch, then two inches. The door whined. I jumped and ran back toward my bed. I waited for the rapid pounding of footsteps. I heard only my heart booming in my ears. I walked back toward the bedroom. This time I moved the door open, slid inside and faced my sleeping parents. My clothes were in a pile on the floor, close to Dad. I held my breath and walked quiet as a cat.

"If You want me in that procession, Jesus, You keep my Dad asleep for a few more minutes, Amen."

I picked up the clothes that I had been wearing and left the room. I started crying as I put on my shirt, pants and shoes. I clenched my black tie in my hand; it trailed me down the stairs. I ran down the street as fast as I could. I was shaking. About two blocks from the house, I realized I forgot my socks.

On the steps of St. Peter's, a crowd milled comfortably in the unseasonably warm spring air. Tom Tomsick's mother. Adele, was there. She frequently invited me to their house to play with Tom. She treated me like I was Tom's brother. Dad and Mom didn't like that.

"If you like the Tomsicks so much, why don't you stay there?" they asked me more than a few times when I came home talking about the good time I had visiting with their family.

Mrs. Tomsick was motioning to me as I looked panic-stricken toward the church doors. They had already started, I was caught now; here I am running away from home to be in the procession and now I'm too late. I felt sick.

"Where's your mother and father?" Mrs. Tomsick asked.

I couldn't tell on my parents. I said nothing. She shook her head.

"Look at your hair, all messed up." She took out a comb and neatly combed my hair to one side, the way I liked it, that is, when I remembered to comb it. Dad usually tried to comb it straight back with some kind of heavy grease, like he said he did when he was my age. "And your tie." She took the tie and correctly looped it through.

Then, chuckling, she looked me straight in the eyes and while talking to me reached down and zipped my fly. "Now come on," she said, leading me through the adults, up the stone stairs of the church, into the marble-floor vestibule reverberating with organ music. I saw the girls in their brilliant white First Communion dresses with veils and boys in their equally shiny Panama white shoes, pants and tie. They had their hands folded like Sister showed us. They were holding 'Come O Jesus,' prayer books and rosaries, the first communion kit that came free, if you bought the blue pants and the blue coat. The second graders had not started marching. Mrs. Tomsick led me to Sister. I would be in the procession after all.

"My, my, Dennis where were you? We were worried about you," sister said as she set my hands and boosted me ahead. The organ music piped up even louder, the people in the church pews turned toward the center aisle, flash cameras clicked as wee angels led the holy battalion into church. During the sermon, I knew I was in trouble. I remember Sister saying in class that the Third Commandment was to Keep Holy the Lord's Day and the Fourth Commandment was to Honor Thy Father and Thy Mother. If you broke a commandment, God would punish you. I wasn't sure where I would be safe, because when I got home if God hadn't punished me by then, my Dad would.

When I came home, Dad was in the kitchen, sitting in his shorts, drinking a cup of coffee and reading the sports news. I said "hello" to him as if nothing had happened earlier in the morning; I pretended that he knew I had to be an angel and I had to go to church and I had to sneak out of the house, so no problem, Dennis, I understand.

"Where the hell were you?" he seethed.

I was silent. Dad stood up and reached to grab me. I backed up too late. I was in his grasp.

"What did I tell you, huh?" He shook me. "What did I tell you? What do you think you are pulling? I'll show you what happens when you don't listen to me." He picked up his leather strap, which had been draped on the doorknob of the bedroom.

"But Dad, I went to church." I began to whimper. I knew what was coming. He put me over his knee, and the belt began to sing against my body.

"No, no, Dad, please, I was, ouch, at church, yeow, at church, unh."

Dad wasn't impressed. It was no use. By the time Dad was finished, I believed I would have been better off if I had taken my chances with getting God mad instead of Dad. I had heard a lot of things about God, but He couldn't have been as handy with a belt as Dad was.

Don't get the idea that Dad had limited forms of entertainment. Dad observed his Sunday mornings by playing Croatian music on the radio. Tambura music, the music of beautiful Croatia, blasted through the upstairs as he ate his special breakfast of mustard sardines and pigs' feet in gelatin. Music of the old country was everywhere in the neighborhood: in bars, in clubs, in churches. Croatian was spoken on the street. There were many Croatian families living along lower St. Clair Avenue in small single-family homes with postage-stamp front yards.

They worked in steel mills, machine shops, auto and rubber factories. They drove beer, bakery, milk and general delivery trucks. They worked as mechanics and maintenance men. The more prosperous Croatians ran taverns, dry goods stores, insurance firms, funeral homes and other small businesses. No matter, Slovenians did not want their children marrying Croatians. Some Sunday mornings Dad brought me to an alley behind St. Clair

Avenue, where polka music wafted over mounds of old tires and piles of rusty auto parts next to Sterling Park.

We entered a kitchen where kids with serious faces, short haircuts, white shirts, ties and dark pants sat on folding chairs, holding white, yellow and red button-box accordions with black buttons popping through the mother-of-pearl facing. The accordions sighed and wheezed on command, tickled by short crawling fingers. Small shoes stomped up and down. Fathers winked and nodded at the children and at each other before downing the ritualistic boilermaker: a shot of whiskey and a glass of beer. "Nas Drovia." It seemed like every ethnic father wanted his kid to learn how to play the accordion, but Dad never asked me to play. I think he went there for a shot and beer and a chance to get out of the house to be with his friends. Some taught their children to speak Croatian. My Dad said he didn't think that was necessary.

"We are in America. Everyone should speak English." But he prided himself on being a Croatian. We went to dances, picnics and clubs where live Croatian music played and the men went around slapping each other on the back, poking chests, clapping cupped hands to the cheek, arm wrestling, trading stomach punches, all good friends. Most Croatians we knew had names that ended in "ic" or "ich." It took some people years to learn how to correctly pronounce the name Kucinich.

Koo-sin-itch, with the accent on the sin. The Sisters at St. Peter's were not sure how to say it. Some said "Q-sen-ik," "Ker–sen" "Goose–nitch," and worse. They really slaughtered the name so preferred to call me Dennis. This made me wonder if something was wrong with my last name. I thought it might be good to have a last name people could pronounce and a first name that was more like others.

That evening I asked Dad: "Can we change our name?"

"What kind of noise is this? What the hell is this kid learning in school?"

"Some parents are changing their names. Can we, Dad?"

"What, is this kid nuts or something?" he said to Mom.

"Listen kid," he stooped down for an eye-to-eye. "I gave you your name, my father gave me my name, his father gave him his name. The name belongs to our whole family. Be proud of your name. Kucinich is a good Croatian name. Make it better. Someday you'll know why it's good for you to be Kucinich and not Smith, Jones or Brown."

"But Dad..." I whined, "no one can pronounce it."

"That's their problem."

Mom joined in, in case I had ideas about my first name, "Your *grandmother* named you Dennis."

I couldn't argue with Mom and Dad. Other people could change their names, but I am Dennis Kucinich and that is that.

Chapter Eight

WE HAD LIVED AT East 30th Street for about a year and a half when the landlady asked us to leave. I took the No. 1 bus to St. Peter's and speech therapy during the summer from our new place at 589 East 101st Street, also off St. Clair Avenue. It was a two-family home. We moved into the downstairs. A family of four lived above us. Our house had two bedrooms, plenty of room. The kitchen had yellow window cabinets built into the wall. The kitchen table was a wooden square. Three vinyl-covered aluminum tubular steel chairs were neatly placed around the table. Mom was happy because the kitchen had a Magic Chef stove. In the living room there was a large bay window that proved to be a good place to hide when Mom and Dad had a loud discussion. Uncle Joe brought us a chair and a couch for the front room. It was a noisy street. The apartment house in back was busy at all hours with arguments between older men and young women and screams late into the night.

One hot summer day several police cars and two ambulances rushed to the back street apartment where a murder took place. I could see blood dripping through the white sheets covering the stretchers removed by the police. People milling on the other side of our fence said it was a gun and a knife fight over money. A neighbor said, "Doesn't matter. Those people are just killing each other all the time for one thing or another. What does it matter?"

A few days later Frank and I were playing on the roof of the garage when bricks that had fallen away from the decrepit apartment house behind us were being pitched in our direction, suddenly, in kind of a Philistine welcome wagon by our new neighbors. Up there on the roof when bricks, as opposed to stones, sail through the air, you have a little more time to step aside and avoid being hit, because bricks are red, easy to see and heavy for a kid to throw. It takes a while for a brick to get to its intended mark. You feel smart when you move out of a brick's path. But if you get hit with a brick, oh my God. "Look out!" I shouted at the top of my lungs to Frank, but it was too late.

The brick hit him in the side of the head. He just crumpled. He went down in a heap so fast he didn't have time to shriek. His grimacing face touched the hot tar roof of the garage. He lay motionless for what seemed like a long time. The blood trickled slowly from an indentation the brick left in his head, matting his hair. Then as I sat there praying, afraid my brother Frank had been killed, he jumped up. Tears streamed from his fierce glazed brown eyes. He cried out, he screamed vengeance. Frank wasn't very good at getting even. He was even smaller and skinnier than me. He was missing his front teeth from a previous fight, which made him appear charming when he smiled. Charming except when he was fighting. Then it made him appear tough. In any fight Frank was hard to keep down, but when he got up after getting hit with the brick, he was hard to keep up. I helped him climb down from the roof, down a fence, to the ground level and into the house, where Mom almost fainted when she looked at his head. She called a cab and took him to the hospital to have his head stitched. The doctors worked on him for a while. When Frank came home, his head was wrapped in a turban of bandages. Frank, Jr. started to cry the minute Dad came through the door.

"What the hell happened to him?" he demanded of Mom.

"He got hit with a brick. There was a fight on top of the garage."

"What was he doing there? What is going on with these kids?" he asked Mom.

"C'mere," he said, motioning to Frank, who could barely see from under the white swath.

"My head hurts," he moaned.

"Hey, cut that noise out," Dad said.

"But my head hurts," he winced.

"Hey, I got shot in the war!" Dad pointed to several scars on his leg and his side. "I saw guys who had their heads blown off. You still have yours on. Learn to fight back, kid." Frank, Jr. held his head and continued to cry. I think Frank was getting ready to be a Marine, he just didn't know it. Dad cared about Frank. He just wanted his sons to be tough. But Dad had something else to worry about—'layoffs' at his job.

"Ginny, they are laying off truckers. I don't know if I have enough seniority. The goddamned government is letting all kinds of people come into this country and now they are taking our jobs. Chrissakes, some of them immigrants can't even speak English. The Hungarians, they'll do the same work for less money. Next they'll be taking our jobs. We're getting screwed. Is this what I get for fighting for America? It's a lot of noise and bullshit."

Mom sat at the table listening to Dad's frustration as she put out a cigarette into an ashtray piled high with butts. She lit up again and drew in a deep breath of cigarette smoke, letting it out in a cloud.

"Jesus Christ, Ginny, I fought the Nips. I almost got killed. I don't want no goddamned handout. I just want a job. That's the least this friggin' country could do for me after I almost got my ass shot off."

Chapter Nine

WHEN THE LANDLORD came he said he had only rented to two kids, not four, and we had to move. Dad packed us into the dirty grey 1948 Dodge. It had an ignition that ground like a bad sinus. We drove for hours and hours. It was getting late. Dad drove down 30th Street, looking for rent signs, and then took the car under a railroad bridge, to the end of 30th Street, the edge of the industrial flats. It was just above the steel mill where a fiery fist shot out from the steel sleeve of a long smokestack and opened its flaming fingers thirty, forty, fifty feet until the night around it dissolved into its outstretched orange palm. The fingers of fire came together to form a torch. The light played upon the car, our shadows dancing in the interior. When I closed my eyes I could feel the light on my face. It was comforting. Even though I couldn't think of a single friend I had who moved around as much as we did, and even though I knew for sure most people just didn't live like this, I also knew our family was together, so what did it matter?

Dad went into the trunk and pulled out a couple of Army blankets. He threw one in the front seat and one into the back. He was tired. He had to go to work the next day. "Look, we are sleeping here tonight. We'll try again tomorrow."

Fortunately, the interior of the Dodge was carpeted. Mom and Dad slept in the front seat. Frank, Gary and Theresa shared the back seat. I slept in the footwell below the back seat. We weren't settled in too long when Gary decided he had to go to the bathroom.

"Jesus, what the hell now?" Dad got out of the car and opened the back door.

"C'mere," he took Gary to the back of the car, and Gary came back a minute later, wiping his hands against his pants.

"If anyone else has to go piss, you better do it now," Dad said, "or you'll have to wait until tomorrow. Then you can go to the gas station."

One by one we got out of the back seat and went to the rear of the car. By the time I got there, a puddle had already formed under the back bumper.

In the morning, Dad drove the car to another street off Perkins Avenue, parked it and then took a bus to work. During the day, Mom held Theresa while the three of us trailed her as she walked to a nearby store to buy some bread, bologna, peanut butter, jelly and cheese for lunch and dinner. She went to a drug store and bought some formula for the baby and stopped in a coffee shop where she mixed it and had it warmed. Frank, Gary and I played in the neighborhood where the car was parked while Mom sat in the car with Theresa until Dad came back to the car.

After work, Monday through Friday and on Saturdays, we drove through the East Side for days with our things packed in cardboard boxes and paper bags stashed in the trunk. Mom, Dad, Frank Jr., Gary, Theresa and me were living in a $95 four-door Dodge. Soon it was back to the edge of the mill for a place to sleep under the light of that glorious torch shining over the valley.

We started a new day. The car broke down in heavy traffic as we searched for our place. Dad commented that the person who sold him the car probably turned back the odometer. There was a commotion in the back seat of the car, we were fighting—until a man got out of the car behind us, pushed a handgun into Dad's face and said something about moving it, or else. That a gun could just come out of nowhere and be used against our father had us all very upset. Frank, Gary and I pretended that we helped Dad push the car to a nearby gas station. Dad gave the repairman some of the money we had saved for rent. He fixed the car and we were back on our way, scouring the neighborhoods into the night for a place to sleep.

Dad pulled into a side street parking lot, next to a hamburger shop with its hypnotic green and orange neon lights blinking against a white building, bidding us to come and eat. The smell of hamburgers coming out of the exhaust of the shop was just too much for all of us to handle, so we had a midnight snack.

"Eight hamburgers with onions, mustard, ketchup, the works," I said to the skeptical waitress. We ate. Then we headed for the edge of the hill to get some sleep. Once you have a full stomach, you can sleep almost anywhere.

Wherever we drove in the inner city darkness, my eyes would search for the emblazoned sky over the Cleveland flats for the torch which chased away the night. Every time I saw it, I was filled with wonder and awe, and I forgot that it was dark and we did not have a place to live.

Chapter Ten

AFTER LIVING IN THE car for a time, we moved into four rooms with Uncle Pete, Aunt Marge, Mary Ann and Junior, across from a soft drink bottling company on Perkins Avenue, about a mile south of 30th Street and St. Clair Avenue. We left a couple of weeks later, after Uncle Pete took a hammer and went after Aunt Marge for yelling at him when he flushed the family's aqua-blue parakeet down the toilet for escaping its cage.

That parakeet tried awfully hard to keep from going down the toilet. It beat its wet wings a few times and almost got away until Uncle Pete grabbed it and pushed his fist down the into the toilet bowl, all the time yelling at the parakeet, "I'll teach you a lesson, you son-of-a-bitch."

All of us who saw Uncle Pete kill the parakeet just cried and cried. Mom gathered us in another room while Aunt Marge looked white as a sheet, her mouth drawn tense, worried about what was going to happen next. Dad had some words with Pete, who stood there as if nothing had happened. "Let's go," he said. "We can't stay here anymore. Uncle Pete is just crazy."

Our family got back into the Dodge, the engine finally turned over and we were on our way to visit Dad's Croatian Godfather, Frank "Koom" Matkovich, who had just retired from the New York Central Railroad where he worked as an engineer for thirty-five years. It was only his second job in America. The first was in the coal mines where he worked with Pa Kucinich after they came over on the boat from Europe. Koom's small house was one of two on narrow Finney Avenue, between E. 82nd and E. 81st Streets, just above the NYCRR tracks, which passed under the Pennsylvania Railroad tracks at the rail crossroads near Broadway and Harvard Avenues. Many engineers, brakemen and freight men lived in the area. Both of the homes on the street, as well as the four homes whose back yards bordered to the west, were very well-kept. The yards were green. Violets, azaleas, and roses from his neighbors the Clearys, the Marshes and the Mickeys popped through the gaps in their fences, creating a natural wall of flowers. Corn, tomatoes and carrots sprouted from the Wolchkos.

The side door, with its eight clear glass panes, flashed open. Koom was tall at about 6'2", with jaundiced pale skin stretched tightly over his thin frame. He wore a blue-and-white striped railroad cap and bib overalls.

"Dobre dzienja," he greeted us.

"Dobre dzienja," my father replied.

Smiling, Koom reached out his hands and took Theresa from my mother and gave her a kiss, snuggling his whiskers over the baby's cheek, tickle, tickle. We trooped into the kitchen. My mother, father and Koom Frank sat down. Frank, Gary and Theresa went to the backyard. I stayed inside, listening.

"Koom, you need someone to take care of you, and we need a place to stay," Dad tried.

"Friends visit," Koom replied impassively.

"But they are not with you all the time," my mother added.

"Hi be hokay. No vant lot piple round."

"Koom, we will pay you. Sixty-five dollars a month." Dad started to get down to business. Koom Frank's lower lip unfurled, his head tilted back, revealing an angular jawline.

"You can keep your bedroom just like it is. Ginny will make your meals."

Koom gave this some thought. Sixty-five dollars a month, plus his railroad pension and his Social Security benefits and home-cooked meals. But he wasn't used to having so many people around, especially children. He opened an amber-colored bottle labelled

"Johnnie Walker," took two small glasses from a nearby cabinet and poured shots for himself and Dad.

"Nas drovia."

"Hvala," my Dad replied, tossing down a fourth drink, making a noise in his throat as his eyes watered a little.

"Hi tell you tomorrow. Sixty-five dole-ars, hmmmmm."

"Goodbye Koom. Laik a noch."

"Hi tell you tomorrow, Franic, Ginny."

So we moved to 8110 Finney Avenue in late summer of 1954. I was seven years old. We were cramped for space, but it was better than the car. My parents slept in a fold-out bed in the front room; Terry in a small bed in the corner of the dining room; Frank, Gary and I shared a bed in a street-light illuminated room overlooking Finney. Koom Frank stayed in the back bedroom with the door closed. We lived a short block from one of the liveliest corners in town.

Broadway and Harvard was a busy intersection. Within a radius of fifty yards a person could go bowling; get a haircut or a permanent; buy a new car or a new kitchen table; shop at Wahl's for groceries and fresh-cut meat; buy homemade bakery; get the latest news and racing forms and hundreds of magazines, dirty books and comic books at Dave's; buy a soda at Seymour's drugstore; get a watch fixed or a toaster repaired; buy a new tie, shirt, and pants; put money in the bank or take money out, to give to lawyers and doctors who had most of the second-floor business offices. You could buy saws, hammers, and nails on Broadway to fix up the house.

People crowded the sidewalks as they made their way in and out of the dozens of small businesses. Sundays, people jammed into the cathedral-like Holy Name Catholic Church. If you came a minute after mass started, you couldn't get a seat. Holy Name was the social and cultural hub of the community. Mom and Dad enrolled Frank and me in Holy Name Elementary School. Frank couldn't start school right away, because he had chicken pox.

Frank got over the chicken pox, began the second grade and was hit by a car at Broadway and Harvard. A trembling man in a dark suit and tie carried Frank in his arms as he knocked on the side door. Mom paled and told him to bring Frank into the kitchen. The man cradled Frank in his arms.

"I'm sorry, lady, he ran in front of my car. He was crossing in heavy traffic. I tried to stop. I think he's OK."

Frank was shaking and crying. Mom looked at the man in disbelief.

"Why are you bringing him here? Take him to the hospital."

"Lady, he fought me. He wouldn't let me take him to the hospital. He said he lived down the street and wanted to come home for lunch." Frank's arm was banged up. His face was scratched, but he was more upset about ruining his dark blue First Communion pants, which were his only good pair. His pants were torn at both knees.

"What do you want me to do?" the man asked Mom.

He gave her $50 and asked her not to call the police. Mom and Frank took a bus to the emergency room at St. Alexis Hospital, where he was X-rayed and sent home to bed.

Beyond our Finney Avenue backyard, past the rusting wire fence and scrub, a forty-five foot embankment led to tracks running northwest and southeast, bordered by two creeks with water spiders flitting around, chasing their shadows. On the other side of the tracks rock piles scattered willy-nilly resembling an undisturbed prehistoric site, the work of dynamite blasting years earlier to clear a path for the railroad.

The twenty acres of massive yellow-orange rock and grey slate had a hundred caves and crevices that were damp, cool and forbidding. It was neighborhood lore that some kids fell into cracks, rocks shifted and they were never heard from again. Initialed hearts pierced by arrows were etched with penknives into the rock J.T loves B. J., S. R. loves P. P., A. R. loves M. C.—and other immortal first-date pledges carved long ago. The perimeter of trees surrounding the rocks were places for owls to question strangers and crows to quarrel over wild cherries, while below lime-bellied garden snakes slithered in and out of their holes, seeking to avoid stray dogs and children who pretended to have encountered boa constrictors. Slender brown and green willow oaks proliferated around the rock piles and on the side of the steep decline. We'd cut down the stalks for use as bows to launch the whip-like arrow branches against outsiders. This panoramic sweep of tracks, creeks, rocks, wild grass, trees and wildlife was known as "The Gulley."

It was a magical kingdom of nature, tranquility, silence, danger and fear of railroad detectives catching you on the tracks as you hopped boxcar couplers to get to the rock pasture. The Gulley was a place to experiment, nestling atop a railroad trestle with your best friends to sneak a smoke. I tried to smoke during one nervous meeting before school and was a miserable failure, inhaling but not knowing how to exhale. I got sick on a few puffs and vowed never again. Besides, Aunt Betty said that "smoking stunts your growth" and I was already so short that I would have disappeared in smoke.

The Gulley was a place to have secrets. It was a friend to children. It was a haven for old men who rode the rails, the ones who lived in cardboard box motels with sterno stoves and red bandana knapsacks for pillows. The older kids told us, don't bother the hoboes and they won't bother you.

One afternoon I was chasing a butterfly through the Gulley. It had small ragged wings, tattered as though they had been sheared from a bolt of white cloth. It fluttered, rising quickly, dropping momentarily above the gaggle of purple and orange tiger lilies in supplication before the sun.

I watched quietly from behind a rust-brown chunk of rock. As the butterfly lit upon a sagging flower, I silently advanced. I wanted to catch it, just to look at it close and then to whoosh it back to the breeze. I reached. It escaped. Just as the butterfly vanished, an old man appeared in view.

I froze. I remembered lots of scary tall tales about the Gulley.

The man was sitting on a newspaper atop a flat rock. He wore a dark grey coat that had to be very warm. It hung on him the way it might hang on a coat rack, with plenty of room between the shoulders. His white shirt was soiled at the cuffs and torn at the pocket. He had the beginning of a beard on the sides of his face, perhaps to cover a reddish-blue mark on his cheek. He was staring intently at the squares of a checkerboard card with the reds and the blacks lined up to do battle. He did not see me. I turned to leave quietly. Do not disturb the strangers in the Gulley. He called after me, "Hey, sonny, you want to play me a game?"

"Nope," I turned, backing off. "I'm on my way home, goodbye." I waited to hear his footsteps, to see if he would run after me.

"Aw, come on, sonny, I won't hurt you. Just a game of checkers. I'll bet you don't know how to play."

"Bet I do."

"Why don't you come over and play a game?"

Uncle George and Uncle Steve showed me how to play, but I hadn't seen my uncles in a while. I wasn't sure, but I really didn't have to go home and the old man didn't look like he wanted to hurt little kids, so I went to the rock and sat across from him.

"Your move." He had two kings when the game ended.

"I'll play you another game," I said.

It was a faster game. He had three kings when the game ended on a fantastic triple jump.

"How did you do that?"

He put the pieces down and jumped them one-two-three. "Like that."

I still didn't know how he did it, but I wanted to learn because then I could challenge Uncle George and Uncle Steve, but he said he had to go. I scrambled up the hill, home in time to see the old man disappear into the green weeping willow trees far across the Gulley.

We played many times and I began to learn the game. I even beat him a few times, or thought I did, after he moved into the path of my kings.

His name was Mister. That's all I knew about him. He had one gold-capped tooth in his smile that gleamed whenever he made a good move on the board. I lived up the hill, but "Where do you live, Mister?"

He nodded over his right shoulder. "Over there." Over there was past the upper level tracks, beyond the waterfalls, the hobo camps, and through a thickness of trees. I was over there once.

"I live up there," I said, pointing to the top of the hill behind me.

After checkers one day I began to follow him. "I'm going to walk over there," I motioned to the steep climb ahead of Mister.

"It's too far for you to go, sonny, now goodbye."

I got the idea that he didn't want me to go with him, but I wanted to know where he lived. Maybe I could visit him at his house someday if he didn't want to come to the Gulley to play checkers. I turned away from him as if to head for home, circled the big rock pile and tracked him through the field, under the giant willows, up the steep path to over there. The streets looked much like up there, where I lived. Except for a green field and tall buildings, the area had houses that were not much larger than those on Finney Avenue. I watched Mister. He walked toward the buildings and past a sign that read "Ohio Department of Mental Health Turney-Warner Facility." He walked up two flights of stairs and entered a red apartment-type building, went through the door and did not come out.

We played checkers throughout that summer and then one day he stopped coming to the Gulley.

Chapter Eleven

KOOM FRANK WALKED through the Gulley every afternoon after his daily visit to the corner of E. 81st and Harvard, where he'd sit on the iron railing in front of an ivy-covered two-story brick garage and swap old-timers' stories with his long-time railroad buddies who used to work out of the Newburgh station at the trestle above Broadway-Harvard.

I never bothered Koom when he was there with his friends. They always seemed to be in such deep discussion, beating the air with their hands, nodding their heads up and down. Once in a while when I passed by, Koom would stop talking with his friends, pull me aside and give me a spare dime that I would use to buy sports comic books.

One day, when Koom was sitting alone on the rail, I asked if I could sit with him. He nodded 'yes.' I balanced on my wrists, watching traffic go by. My legs did not touch the ground. I was ready to talk with Koom just like the old men did. An old ice truck passed by, and it reminded me of my grandfather.

"Koom, you knew my grandfather, Pa Kucinich?"

"Hy new. Hy new. Hy cum frum olt cun tree. 'Eachega' you grandpa cum frum olt cun tree."

"Eachega," I said, "that's what Grandpa Kucinich called me. He called me 'little Eachega.' What's 'Eachega' mean?"

"'Eachega' nek nem, sum nek nem. Goot man Eachega, verk heart, verk like sumanagun. Too bet die yunk."

I wanted to know more. Traffic passed by; no one paid any attention to the old man and the little boy sitting on the railing.

"Koom, how did you and Pa Kucinich come to Cleveland?"

"Vee cum from Pennsylvanka. Vee vas hin New York. Ve cum on boads frum Olt Cun tree."

Koom Frank told me that his voyage started as he watched from the lowest deck of the full-bellied steamship as the huge lines were cast away from the pier. The buildings and shanties, then the firs and cedars dissolved into the twinkling blue Adriatic horizon. Zbogom Hrvatska! Goodbye Croatia! For 'Eachega' Kucinic it was farewell to the village of Batnoga. Zbogom Majka Kucinic stood at the door, sobbing deeply as her son left to seek his fortune.

"Eachega taut life be bedder here," Koom said to me. He hoped for a life better than the peasant lives of his parents, Josa and Mary, who were always hungry working someone else's farm, always broke, no rights. In America, Pa would not be a fugitive from his growling belly. Pa had a large appetite and small ambitions.

"He vant cum here buy shoose," Koom recalled with a smile. "Hi vant two tinks: Mek lots mooney, lif lung life." Koom spit lightly into his two hands, rubbing them together for emphasis. "Hi vant verk, mek mooney, no dik guttam ditches for sumbeetch diktatur.

"So, Daynee, hy get Hellis Highland, vait in lung line."

I imagined I was inside the Great Hall at Ellis Island. Multi-colored babushkas and dark woolen caps bobbed up and down in a sea of people as I paddled about.

"Daynee, Daynee!" Koom called me back from a day dream. "Ven Eachega see Eemegrayshun men. Eemegrayshun men say, 'vhut nem?' Eachega say, 'Nem Kucinic.' Men giff Eachega cart, spell guttam nem wrung," said Koom, shaking his head.

The immigration officer mispelled grandpa's name and then added an *h* to Kucinic, because that was how it sounded when Pa pronounced it. But that was the way everyone pronounced it in the old country and no one had trouble with it there, Koom told me.

"No verk New York. Baggars, teefs hall hover plays, vant mooney. Ve go Pennsylvanka, and ve dik ditches, verk coal mine." There were big mountains and hills everywhere, Koom said.

"Eachega no vant die, say 'No vant go Hell hin guttamn mine. Vee cum Hummerica to liff no die.'"

But it seemed as though the ground was intent on swallowing them up, one way or another. Back home a Croatian nationalist had tried to assassinate the Commissary, and then a Serbian nationalist shot and killed Archduke Ferdinand. Koom said that when Pa left the old country there was always talk of war. If he stayed at home he would have to fight for some foreign government which took over his homeland. What a crazy life, either way you chose you die: In the old country his name would be inscribed on a marker in the blood-soaked soil of Europe. In America he would cut his epitaph with his own fingernails into a massive soft black tombstone in Pennsylvania.

"Eachega say 'Koom, vee nut seff hin guttamn mine, nut seff hin Olt Cun tree.' But tek Hummerica henny day."

I asked Koom about my grandmother, who met Pa in Pennsylvania. "Goot voman. Verk heart. Vun day Eachega go peeg hroast. Hi use tell hem, hi no get merry, hi mek lots mooney, hi yeet, hi hrest, hi get troonk, vife no like get troonk, mek menny troobles, no merry."

But Pa wanted to get married. Maybe it was the tambura music at the roast, or the euphoria of a day away from the mines, or the smell of jagne roasting on a spit, but the fire danced in John's eyes when he met Mary. Somewhere between the coal mine and the church they fell in love. They were married at the Visitation of the Blessed Virgin Mary Church in Mt. Pleasant, Pennsylvania.

Koom said there were more coal mine disasters. Everywhere they looked they saw men whose strong bones had been shattered against shifting mountains of rock, whose spirit alone clung to crippled bodies which would soon be of no use to anyone.

"Eachega no vant die yunk. Me knee dir. Merry vant life. Vife vas from coal femly." Mary Kucinich understood. She knew coal mine country just as she knew many young women who gathered on dusty front porches, sitting in a semi-circle of rocking chairs to sew and weep. She did not want to spend her years this way, black gold, black clothes. She wanted a family.

Koom said he left Pennsylvania for a job with the railroad, in Cleveland, Ohio, to the northwest.

"I tell Eachega: Cum Clevelund, Hrvatski dom. Lots jobs, mek lots moony."

Pa and Ma arrived in Cleveland, in the summer of 1915.

Cleveland was America's sixth largest city, a brawny iron and steel capital, located on Lake Erie. Everywhere could be heard the industrial orchestra, the full-throated horns of large ships laden with iron ore and pig iron working their way down the Cuyahoga River with the help of tuba tugs; the freaky violin of railroad cars braking into the broad-shouldered industrial valley, loaded with coal and iron ore; the crashing cymbals as melted ore poured from the blast furnaces and pounded into mammoth cradles; the calliope of factory whistles; automobiles tuning their horns downtown and the electric street cars clanging triangles as they bustled around Public Square. Cleveland had the sound of excitement and the smell of money.

Cleveland was where John D. Rockefeller started out. He built Standard Oil and then moved to New York, returning to Cleveland during the summers. There were other millionaires in full-time residence in great mansions along flower-decked, tree-lined streets not far from downtown. Their names were easy to pronounce: Mather, White, Hanna, Wade, Johnson, Brush. They founded the shipping, sewing machine, electric and motor car companies and steel mills, but Cleveland's massive industrial sinew was built by the chugging human engine of Polish, Ukrainian, Croatian, Italian, Jewish, Irish, Hungarian, Slovenian, Slovak and German immigrant workers who peopled shanty towns on the steamy perimeter of the valley. Their dreams as boundless as the tempest-tossed Atlantic across which they made their voyage west, the ethnics offered themselves as humble oblations to idols of iron, steel and oil. Grateful to work long hours for low pay, they gave of themselves and their children to bring wealth and a new population to Cleveland, grateful to come to a place where they could build churches, schools, labor halls, and dance halls to celebrate the community of the old country and new fortune.

Like many new immigrants, Pa Kucinich started out on the streets of the city of Cleveland. "He buy veggen, pik hup screp. Hef lots kits, no mek mooch mooney. Hef John, Pete, Paul, too maynee kits. Lifhin two hrums. No mooney, no pay hrent, get kick out, cum me for mooney, say 'Koom, troobles, gut beek troobles. Haf new bebby Steef.' Hi gif mooney, he go pick hup more screp, hef more kits."

Pa collected enough scrap to buy an old ice wagon and a couple of sick horses who jerked and slobbered along the route. Pa became an independent iceman. He didn't have to worry about feeding his family, which was good news because he had another son, Frank, and two daughters, Betty and Barbara. Then came the Depression. Pa lost the ice cart and couldn't afford to feed the horses. The family was evicted from their home near the railroad tracks, in the shadow of Holy Name Church. They resettled in a Polish neighborhood a few blocks away.

"Dey liff down stritt," Koom pointed down Harvard Avenue. I suddenly became aware of the traffic again. I imagined how difficult it would be this day for a horse-drawn cart to manuever between the semis and the fast-moving autos.

"Eachega pik hup screpp, verk heart. Pete, Paul, Yahn no verk, sumbeetches steel." Koom said Uncle Pete and Uncle Paul got into trouble for stealing wire from railroad freight trains.

"Eachega, Mary, tell dem kits, 'Mek honest liffing. Verk heart, no steel, guttam no steel, starff first.'"

Ma and Pa Kucinich had pride. Koom, Pa and a half-million others translated their Croatian dreams into American dreams: Work hard, get ahead. Pa and Ma knew they had gone about as far as they could go and they weren't getting too far, but their children could go farther. They could get an education, work their way up, become big deals or something. And their children's children? Ah, in America anything is possible.

"Your fadder Franic, gut men. Verk heart, sumbeetch verk heart. Goot Cro. You be goot Cro, too, sumday I tink, Daynee, but verk heart. Verk heart."

Chapter Twelve

M Y NEXT-DOOR NEIGHBOR was a crew-cut, red-haired
Slovak teenager named Gene Wolchko. He played football with me
in the street when he wasn't practicing for the Southeast Lions
team. After school started I didn't see much of Gene. I saw his
mother in the backyard one afternoon and asked about Gene. She
took me around to the front of the house and pointed to an upstairs
bedroom that overlooked Finney, same as mine.

"He's up there, studying, doing homework."

Days and weeks passed. Indian summer faded into autumn
and still no Gene. Finally his mother let me visit him in his room.
Books were piled onto shelves which Gene's father Mike had made.
Mike was blind. What he couldn't see with his eyes, he could see
with his hands. The shelves were finely crafted.

"Hey sport, what do you say?" Gene looked up from a pile
of papers.

"Just wanted to say hello. When will you be able to come
outside again to play?"

"Not right now. I have to study."

"Why do you study so much? Don't you ever get a chance
to have fun?"

"I'm having fun. I'm learning. I want to do well. I just
started high school and some day I want to go to college. You'll
have to study some day too."

So I'd stand in the alley, alone at twilight, throwing the ball
up into the coming darkness, until it disappeared and then flashed

by the street light into sight, back down into my outstretched hands. I waited for him to come out. He seldom did. I wondered about all the time he spent reading books. He liked books. I did too, but every time we moved I had to leave my books behind. So I learned to like playing out in the street.

One rainy November evening Gene knocked on my door and asked me to take a walk with him through the fields and over the railroad tracks, to the Miles Park Library. The last time I'd seen a library was when we lived across from one on E. 30th Street, near St. Clair Avenue. It had been demolished to make way for a freeway.

This was the first time I'd ever been inside a library. It was as quiet as a church, except for people standing around saying "Shh, shh."

The aroma of thousands of books permeated the gigantic reception room.

"You have a library card?" Gene asked.

"Nope."

"Want one?"

"What's it cost?"

"It's free."

"OK."

I filled out a form with the help of a small gray-haired lady. She gave me a temporary card.

"We will mail you a permanent card," she said.

I followed Gene into a section marked 'History.'

He took four books. I saw a room marked 'Grades 1-6' and walked over to it. Even though I was in the fourth grade, I browsed through all the books in this section and none interested me. I moved to the sports section and picked up a volume entitled "Pride of the Yankees."

"How old are you?" the librarian inquired in a friendly way.

"Nine."

"Then this book is out of your age group, sorry," she said.

"I'll take it for him," Gene intervened.

That was the start. I mean, if Gene could stay up nights

studying, so could I, even if the books had nothing to do with schoolwork. It was easier to stay up late without worrying about waking up anyone because Mom had another baby, Perry, who cried late into the night, so I read in the kitchen while Mom rocked the baby to sleep. There were now eight of us living at Finney Avenue. The library gave me a chance to be away from home until late each weekday.

A note from the principal of Holy Name Elementary provided me with wider access to all the books at Miles Park. So night after night, when the house was quiet, I read in the bedroom by streetlight, at the top of the stairs by hall light, and in the kitchen over the heat register. I paged through volume after volume of sports, mysteries, ghost stories, lives of the Saints, science fiction, autobiographies and adventures. I journeyed to worlds far beyond Finney Avenue, Cleveland, America—for free. The thought of being able to borrow so many books boggled my mind. They became my most important possessions, even if they really belonged to the library. It didn't matter that the car didn't work or the TV set was broken. Books took me wherever I wanted to go. They took me to the Great Pyramids, to the battlefields of the Crusades, to the streets of France during the revolution, to the gridiron where Jim Thorpe romped, from earth to beyond the stars. I became a time traveler.

The more I read the more I learned that people do not live the same the world over. I learned that great civilizations had once existed then they crumbled, long before I came into this world. I learned that history was once everyday life and all kinds of people—kings, serfs, presidents and ordinary citizens—experienced a fading away of glory and hardship. If they didn't have much, they didn't lose much; no one can have everything, but everyone can *be* something. What a person can be is not necessarily determined by social rank or wealth, but by how much he or she knows and how hard he or she works. Through my reading I began to understand that our family didn't have much, except fights.

I didn't know what Mom and Dad were arguing about, but they were battling again in the kitchen. I stayed behind the living door listening, filled with the fear of being discovered.

"Now cut that shit out, Ginny."

"Listen, you Croatian son of a bitch."

Call it love at first fight. Butter knives, forks, spoons, pots, pans and steel griddles would fly, dishes would break, windows would smash, doors would crack, screens would be knocked out, holes would be put in every wall of our rented place. Monday, Tuesday, Wednesday, Thursday, Friday, Saturday, Sunday night at-the-fights, every one a knock down, drag-'em-out bout. Sometimes a split lip, sometimes a bruised arm, sometimes a chipped tooth, inflicted carelessly amidst screams and roars, taunts and threats, dangerous home-grown violence.

Not wanting to get drawn into the battle, I cowered underneath beds, in corners and in upstairs closets, staying out of the crossfire. Through it all, I worried that Mom or Dad would get hurt real bad. In nightmares I saw red images of soaked towels wrapped around heads, necks, arms; blood spattering on the floor. I saw black images of death. Though they almost killed each other, Dad called Mom at least a half-dozen times a day every day he was at work. She waited for his calls and watched the clock for when he would come home. When he walked through the door Mom and Dad would kiss for a long time and then tell each other: "I love you" before they started fighting. This kind of love was very confusing, very hard to understand and very upsetting. It definitely wasn't like the love television or movie families showed each other. After going to bed, Mom and Dad would hold each other as they fell asleep, and awaken in the morning ready for a new day of fights.

I coughed whenever they fought. When the police came to the door and said they should quiet down, I coughed. When I overheard Mom and Dad talk about moving again I coughed and could not stop. I was having trouble breathing. I was taken to a doctor, Homer J. Daus, on East 71st and Superior Avenue.

"Doctor, I need air." (Cough. Cough) God, help me get some air. (Cough) I. (Cough) Can't breathe. (Cough. Cough. Cough. Cough. Wheeze) Open, open the window. Please, Doctor. I'm hot. (Cough. Cough. Wheeze) My, my chest is. (Cough) heavy. My (Cough) chest is hot." (Cough Wheeze) I knew what it felt like to be dying as the fire spread from my chest to my throat, then to my eyes and my brain. Dear God, things are getting dark. The world is coming to an end; someone is turning off my air. I need air. I don't want to die.

"Dennis is going to need rest and quiet," the doctor said.

Mom nodded without speaking.

"He is to stay in bed for the next ten days. Then you call me."

Mom nodded again.

"I'm afraid he has bronchial asthma."

Mom frowned.

"I'm not sure how this got started, but we have to be careful. If it gets worse I'll have to put him in the hospital," said the doctor.

I continued coughing. I wanted to stop. I didn't want to go to a hospital. (Cough) (Cough) (Cough) "Doctor, erg, Doctor!"

"Yes? Dennis, what is it?"

"(Cough) I (Cough) (Cough) have to go (Cough) to SCHOOL," I managed to gasp the last word without a cough. I had so much to learn, so much to do. I was working on becoming the best speller and best reader in my class. Sister kept a chart on the wall to mark each student's progress. I was leading in a number of subjects. I would fall behind if I didn't go to school. I'll wait until Dad gets home. I'll tell him the doctor wants me to stay in bed because I have asthma. I know what he'll say. He'll say "Asthma, my ass! Asthma? What the hell is asthma? I had yellow fever in the Marines. Be a marine! Go to school, sure you can go to school. Nothing wrong with you, kid." I knew I could count on Dad.

"I know, Dennis, I know," the doctor said. "But school will have to wait until you are well. For now you are going to have to stay in bed." Boy, was I mad.

Friends brought books from school. When I wasn't coughing, I read. I wished I could find a book that could tell me how to get rid of asthma, how to breathe with the bricks on my chest, how to get well. Mom put Vicks Vap-O-Rub on my chest every night and smoke in my lungs during the day because she smoked three packs a day. But maybe that wasn't as bad as the chemicals that drifted into our home from the industrial flats, or the pollen from the roaches that were running relays in the kitchen. It was a pretty lonely time. The rest of the family stayed away from me because they didn't want to catch whatever it was that I had.

The coughing spells would come without warning and could last for hours. When one ended, momentarily, I was so weak I would fall asleep.

Chapter Thirteen

I SLOWLY MOVED FROM the cot in the living room to answer the front door. Uncle Bill Norris stood on the steps. He resembled Grandpa Norris, except that Uncle Bill was tall, thin and did not have a red face. His hands were behind his back. He was trying to conceal a package. He had a smile that lit up his face and mine.

"Stay away from the door," Mom called from the kitchen.

I stood still, wheezing heavily, as Mom opened the door for her oldest brother, my godfather. I hadn't planned to spend this day in bed. After all, a tenth birthday is a cause to celebrate the discarding forever of the one-digit existence and embrace the emerging possibilities of ages eleven, twelve, and the teens.

"Happy birthday, Dennis," Uncle Bill said as he handed me the package he had been hiding. "It's a shirt," I thought, disappointed because I was hoping to get a magic set, but I knew Mom and Dad couldn't afford it. Not that I would mind getting a shirt, but a shirt wasn't as good as a magic set. I had read a great book about Harry Houdini, so this week I wanted to be a magician. I couldn't remember ever reading a book about shirts.

I wheezed a "thank you" and started to cough. I had difficulty stopping the cough. I sat down on the edge of the thin mattress of Mom and Dad's foldaway, the veins of my neck popping up as the coughing became more labored. I strained to gain composure.

"He's got asthma," Mom said to Uncle Bill, whose smile suddenly changed to a look of pained concern.

"I can't stay, Ginny. I have to get back to work. Dennis, I hope you feel better and I hope you like the birthday gift."

I thanked Uncle Bill and waited until he left to see what kind of shirt he bought me. I shook the package. It rattled. Shirts do not rattle. I tore off the wrappings and, WOW, A MAGIC SET! I was so excited I worked myself into a coughing spell, but I didn't care, because I was on my way to becoming a magician and, if I got good enough, maybe I could make this asthma disappear.

Fat chance. I studied Houdini and Madame Blavatsky, and they didn't know anything about getting rid of asthma. During the next five months of recuperation at home I started a World Explorer's stamp collection and I began to read volumes about Marco Polo, Magellan, Vasco De Gama, Christopher Columbus, and Ponce De Leon. The more I read about world exploring, the more I understood that explorers were dreamers who dreamed with their eyes open. Dreams moved them towards a destination. Before the explorer set out to find a new world, he had to have been there already in his inner vision, using the compass of his heart. I knew that many people had told the explorers they could never make it, that their journey was too long and others had tried and died. But the heart of an explorer knows he must try, no matter what the risks. Sometimes, if you have only the courage to survive, you can change the outcome.

Dreams, courage and desire were the stuff of my recovery. That, Mom and Dr. Daus. When the black and white television worked, I watched an animated cartoon character named Jiminy Crickett sing the theme song of "The Walt Disney Hour." That song spoke to me personally.

"When you wish upon a star,
Makes no difference who you are.
Anything your heart desires
Will come to you.
Like a bolt out of the blue,
Fate steps in to see you through.
When you wish upon a star
Your dreams come true."

One night when I wasn't coughing, a mild autumn breeze rattled through the living room screen. Suddenly I could hear Jiminy Crickett singing his song. We didn't have a record player, and the television was off. No radio could be heard from the houses nearby, but I could hear that song just the same. I think all children have special radio crystal sets tucked away so they can hear music older people can't hear.

I got up from my cot and went to the front door to listen to the music. The street light and the tree behind it kept the sky from view. I put on my pants, shirt and shoes and went out the back door towards the back yard. I climbed the wooden fence post and vaulted the rusty wire fence. In seconds the music grew faint and I was standing in a silent field, the Gulley below invisible in the darkness, the sky above blanketed with stars. One shiny star was winking from a thousand miles away. I looked at that star for the longest time, until I was quite sure that it was the only star in the sky. Then I made a wish, and the star winked back.

After that night, whenever I got a chance, when the house was still except for the snoring of people and the chugging of the refrigerator, I returned to the field above the Gulley to wish. I wished all kinds of good things for Mom, Dad, Frank Jr., Gary, Theresa, and Perry and Koom Frank. There were so many stars to make wishes upon, I made wishes for everyone in the whole world.

I was away from school for most of the year. I finally got over my asthma. At first Dr. Daus said I would outgrow it. Then he decided to give me injections of aminophyllin, and the asthma began to go away. It was a cold, rainy day when I rejoined my fifth grade class at the century-old Holy Name Elementary school building, darkened by decades of steel mill soot. Inside hundreds of children were standing in the hallways and along winding staircases singing "It's a great day for the Irish." "They are practicing for St. Patrick's Day," Sister said. Mom had prepared me well.

At Holy Name if you didn't have an Irish name you could pass by singing Irish. Sister handed me a sheet of songs, and I was singing Irish. At Holy Name the sunrise was recorded only over

Dublin, and it set on Galway Bay. The wooden hallway floors were the Auld Sod and all good 'Namers kissed the crucifix on their rosaries and the blarney stone in their green-and-white-shamrocked dreams. I liked singing Irish songs so much that I joined the choir. To my dismay, the choir didn't sing Irish songs. They sang Gregorian chants, in Latin. I learned the Gregorian chants, but during the Sunday masses, if I didn't like the particular song the choirmaster picked, I sang Irish lyrics to the music. I decided I would take the name Patrick for my confirmation. My mother was Irish, so I was Irish. Dennis John Patrick Kucinich!

I was happy to be back at school. While things were going well for me there, Mom and Dad were having difficulties at home. They were having a time of it trying to make ends meet. It may have been that Dad's eighth-grade education and five young children never gave him a chance to hold onto the money he made. He drove his truck five days a week, except when he was in the hospital with a bad knee or kidney stones. But a lot of bills were not paid. Doctor bills, lawyer bills, car repair, TV repair, loans from Dad's friends, loans from the Teamsters—and Dad and Mom still had eight people to feed, including Koom Frank. After work one night Dad looked at the mail, shook his head, tossed the letters on the table and put his hands in his pockets.

"Son of a bitch, I don't know why I'm working so hard. I make it, they take it. We can't keep up, we can't keep up, Ginny. I better go to see the lawyer on Saturday. I think we are going to have to file for bankruptcy."

And soon there was one more mouth to feed. When Mom came home from the hospital with our new baby brother, Larry, she wasn't herself. She spent her days in the kitchen, making formula for Larry and crying. When Dad suggested that she go back to the hospital, she refused.

"I don't want to go back to the hospital. I can't take this anymore," the anguish in her voice found that place that only a mother's voice can reach. I felt deeply sorry for her, and a twinge of panic too. What was happening to Mom?

The tears would eventually turn to shouts. Life was so hard for both of them. Fighting was not their only recreation, but other than sex it seemed to be the one they indulged in the most. Frank, Gary and I took up the violence where Mom and Dad left off. We scuffled from room to room. When Dad came home Mom would give her report, and then Dad would beat the hell out of us with his leather strap. The strap wasn't bad, but the buckle left an impression.

Koom Frank stayed away from all of us. He stopped going to the corner. He kept himself locked in his room for days, emptying the foul-smelling contents of his brass spittoon onto the bathroom roof, where it slid down into the gutter just above the entrance to the kitchen. It was so bad we stopped using the side door entrance. The roof above was streaked with yellow and brown stains. Flies picnicked in the gutter. Above it, inside the upstairs window, Koom held private conversations in Croatian with himself and sometimes cried out for his sister who had died in the old country. Whenever I heard his long sad sobs come through the walls it would make me cry, too. The constant bombardment of noise inside the house could have caused anyone to put his hands to his ears and shout "Enough!" I knocked on his door, to let him know we loved him and try to get him to come out.

"Please Koom, please come out. Let's go downstairs. Let's go for a walk to the corner. Please come out of your room."

"Daynee, no bodder, no feel goot, no slip, no bodder, go vey."

He would not leave the room. Trapped among noisy people who did not speak his language, locked up in his room with his spittoon and his trunkful of fading memories, he could not be consoled. He had been so generous to us. If if wasn't for Koom Frank we would be out on the street. He gave us his home. Now, behind the doors of his upstairs room, he made plans to return to Croatia, booking his passage home with imaginary agents, arguing the price of the ticket at the top of his lungs, telling them he had to get back now to see his sister. He couldn't wait any longer to leave.

He had to return to the old country because things hadn't worked out for him in the new one.

Dad said Koom Frank needed to see the doctor. He went up to Koom's room and brought the old man out, then carefully escorted him down the stairs. Koom moved slowly. He entered the kitchen where not so long ago he had welcomed us to his home. His skin was a waxy yellow. His cheeks were sunken. His brown eyes had a wounded look to them. His grey beard had not seen a razor in many weeks. His stringy hair was uncombed and shaggy by his ears. His hand moved to his head. He pulled something off his scalp, looked at it carefully, made a face and then cracked the thing between long nails. He tried to smile briefly, nodding.

"Come on, Koom. Come on," Dad supported him by the elbow, guided him to the car and took him to the doctor.

Dad came back alone. The doctor told him Koom was losing his mind and should be put in Turney Road, the same place Mister Checkerplayer-in-the-Gulley lived. Koom Frank was okay before we moved into Finney Avenue. I am sure that once he had committed himself to stay in his bedroom, his only escape was to exchange one reality for another. I hoped our dear Koom would find his mind again. I was very worried that Mom was losing hers.

At least I could go to school and not have to think about it every moment. I was on my way to school, after stopping at Wahl's to get some chocolate cupcakes and fresh-cut bologna for lunch sandwiches. As I was crossing through Holy Name's churchyard, a strange taste came up from my stomach and caused my tongue to lurch back in my mouth, as if to block it out. It was a sour substance. My saliva began to run thin. My throat tightened as a yellow, sulphurous odor worked its way up from my belly. It wasn't bad food. I hadn't eaten breakfast. It wasn't the air. The mill wasn't blowing clouds of rotten eggs into the neighborhood today. No, this odor was working its way up from my belly. It tasted bad. It smelled awful. It hurt. I tried to throw it up. Nothing came out. My face got red as I gagged. My eyes popped a little. The veins at the side of my neck and at my temples began to bulge. I felt as if an invisible hand had grabbed my guts and twisted them into a big, wet, red and yellow knot, forcing up the hot juices that were now flowing out through my mouth.

I was glad no one could see me do a slow-motion jackknife to the pavement. I would have been embarrassed if anyone would have watched as I rolled around on the ground. I could have told them I was inspecting the undersides of the fire escapes along the high school next to the church, but they would not have believed me. They would have said, 'Just a dumb kid rolling around the asphalt for no reason.' No, when it happened the first time I was thankfully alone. These spells came over me many times, usually in the morning. They never lasted more than a few minutes. I was seldom late for school. I didn't say anything to anyone about the pains. I didn't want to get sent home sick. I didn't want to go to the doctor. If I went to the doctor it meant I was sick.

Just about the time I stopped stuttering, I was afflicted with asthma. Now I had asthma *and* something churning in my gut. Not that I couldn't handle it. I could handle anything. When that yellow smell began to flood my senses, I had about two minutes to get to the bathroom. Most of the time I didn't think about being sick, because I think you can get sick just thinking about being sick. I didn't ever want to miss a day of school. This desire helped me practice the power of mind over matter. Sometimes it worked; other times I vomited and coughed. I still went to school, but I knew I was really sick. Matter over mind. Maybe this wasn't going to go away. No amount of praying and wishing seemed to be working. There was a war going on inside me, or maybe I invited the war inside my body: the fighting and the arguing at the dinner table, the constant threat of moving again and many times staying up late at night to watch my four brothers and my sister when Mom and Dad were not at home.

Chapter Fourteen

SISTER BERNARD ANN handed me a stiff paper card written in English and Latin.

"Take this home. Memorize the responses and you can be an altar boy."

"An altar boy? Wow." You couldn't volunteer to be an altar boy, you had to be asked. I had good grades from the start, except in handwriting, which I flunked in the first year. I wanted to live up to Sister's expectations. I set aside ghost stories for a few nights of spiritus sanctus and memorized Latin.

The alarm went off at 4:00 a.m. I was up earlier than the paperboy. I had always wondered who got up so early. I quickly found out: No one else.

I arrived at the Holy Name sacristy at 5:00 a.m. I turned on the lights. The immense silence invoked a fearful reverence. I was the sole mortal occupant of the House of God.

Monsignor's green and gold vestment hung neatly in an open closet. I took up the black cassock. My name was printed on a white tag inside the collar. I buttoned the cassock. The top of my white shirt showed through. It looked like I was wearing a Roman collar. I stared into the mirror for a moment. Ten years old, and already I was Father Dennis John Patrick—Kucinich! I donned an oversized white surplice and reviewed the carefully choreographed lessons I learned in altar boy class:

Hold the cruets this way.

Don't touch the hosts.

Don't touch the chalice with the cruets when you pour the wine.

Don't spill the wine.

Don't pour too much wine.

The unspoken sacrilege: Don't sneak a swig of wine. The priest will know. You will go directly to Hell. I had all the rules down.

The other server arrived. Monsignor Clarence Elwood arrived, in a hurry. He took off his coat, looked at me and smiled.

"Good morning, my son." It was the first time a priest spoke directly to me when I wasn't in a confessional.

"Good morning, Monsignor."

"Is everything ready?"

"Yes, Monsignor."

Never before had I seen a priest change from his black suit into his mass vestments. I thought of Clark Kent, rushing into a phone booth and coming out in his blue-and-red Superman costume.

I turned on all the lights in the sanctuary. It lit up the space brilliantly, the white light bulbs soaring heavenward toward an enormous mural of the Holy Trinity. Monsignor nodded, I tugged gently at a chain of bells, and the six elderly women who regularly attended early mass rose from a kneeling position and blessed themselves as the service began.

I genuflected before the altar. Monsignor took the silver chalice to the tabernacle. He transferred the hosts from the white gold ciborium. He returned to the foot of the altar and blessed himself. He began, just like in the Mass card:

In nomine Patris,	"In the name of the Father,
et Filii et Spiritus Sancti. Amen.	and of the Son, and of the Holy Spirit. Amen.
Introibo ad altare Dei"	I will go to the altar of God."

He began Mass.

"Ad Deum qui laetificat juventutem meam,"	"To God, who gives joy to my youth"

My first response.

He looked up past the winged canopy hovering over the altar and implored:

"Emitte lucem taum, et	"Send forth your light and
Veritatem tuam…"	and your truth…"

The marble altare Dei, a vision of white and gold, was bathed in a rainbow arc of lights streaming from the stained glass.

Holy men and women soared above the sky-blue Persian carpet on which two small altar boys stood with Monsignor. He took up a large host. He bowed and then he held the Host up high.

"Hoc est enim corpus meam."   "This is my body."

It was a mystery that Jesus could fit into that wafer of bread. One of the benefits of being an altar boy was that I could get a little closer to figure out if it was some sort of trick.

The altar boy across the steps shot me a hard, sideways glance and whispered harshly. "The bells, Dennis, the bells," I heard him just in time to grab the handle of the small set of six silver bells. I shook them. The breasts of the faithful were beaten in expiation.

Monsignor's strong hands grasped the highly-polished chalice. I saw the compressed reflection of the small congregation rise with the cup as he lifted it up above his glasses. He closed his eyes for a moment, his thoughts on the wings of a prayer sent to heaven.

"Hic Est Enim Calix Sanguinis Mei,	"For this is the Chalice of
	My Blood.
Qui pro vobis et pro	Which shall be shed
Multis effundetur"	for you and for many others."

The Chalice, the Sangreal of the Last Supper, the vessel of Salvation was before my eyes, held closely by Monsignor and before him by Joseph of Arimathea as he caught in it a drop of blood from Christ crucified.

This triumph of life and death, of spirit over body was, I learned from reading, a preoccupation of the Knights of the Round Table as they consecrated their lives to a search for the lost Holy

Grail. I knelt before Monsignor, knighted by the imagination of loyalty to some mystical Arthurian Court, a squire under the protection and strength of God and good in the gold Grail. In the consciousness that collected during the early morning prayers and walks to the back of the church, running atop spinning cinders along silent rails reaching out toward infinity, somewhere between the library and the sanctuary, my own quest began. I followed it down the pages of Mallory and St. Matthew. I began to feel a sense of duty, an obligation to try to do good.

At Finney Avenue, I came to love learning and serving mass. I received communion every day. I was sure I was going to be a priest. It was a time when I contacted the spiritual dimension, a vast world inside that I explored through constant prayer and reading the lives of the saints. I came to believe in a higher purpose for my own life, one that transcended the turmoil at home, getting worse by the day. I wondered how many of us in the house of chaos were playing in the shadows that claimed Koom Frank's sanity. I wanted to help my family. I wanted to help all people. I was developing a powerful sense of mission, to be of service to God and humanity, to help people who didn't have a place to live, or food to eat, or the clothes they needed, or the love they needed. I knew these were among the most important days of my early life, and I spent many of them alone at all hours of the day, in the back pew of an the empty Holy Name church, calling upon the Saints to intercede in everything I saw and felt. Invoking powers on high, teetering between worlds of madness and hope, I began to think of the future.

I prayed very hard to try to create a better future for our family.

I prayed we would stay on Finney Avenue. Please God, don't move us again.

I prayed my mother and father would not fight anymore, that they would stop drinking and smoking.

I prayed the daily screaming at the dinner table would stop.

I prayed my asthma would go away.

I prayed my mother would get over her nervous condition that became serious just after my new brother Larry was born.

I prayed the terrible pains and that awful yellow smell from my stomach would stop.

I thanked God, in advance, for answering my prayers and for keeping me alive. I prayed and I coughed.

Chapter Fifteen

"FOR GOD'S SAKE, Ginny, why don't you go and get your tubes tied? How many more kids are you going to have? You can't keep having kids. It will kill you," Aunt Ann Kucinich said to Mom.

It was the first time we had seen Aunt Ann since her car went out of control and smashed into a tree at 100 mph. Aunt Ann travelled in the fast lane with Aunt Barbara on the showgirl circuit. Family rumor had it that at one time she was a girlfriend of someone who had been in the notorious Purple Gang of Detroit.

It took a team of plastic surgeons to reconstruct her fine features—they had been destroyed in the accident. She had been pronounced dead on arrival at the hospital. They put a sheet over her until an attendant noticed some movement of her crushed legs, legs which had once danced on stages across the country. If ever there was a survivor, it was Aunt Ann. She was one tough cookie.

"Does Frank think that all you are is a baby machine? When do you go out shopping? When was the last time you went to the beauty parlor? When's the last time you bought a dress? My God, woman, this just isn't fair. You aren't supposed to spend all your time having kids!" Ann blinked as she talked.

"Oh," Mom sighed, "Frank says everything will be OK. But I don't know." She was shaking, as she had been for several weeks. Her coffee lapped along the brim of the cup. She put it down to avoid a spill. "I'm losing it. I can't handle the kids. I just can't get out of this house. I'm here all day, cooking and cleaning. You wouldn't know it to look around. There's no money, I can't buy anything. Look at the kids, we can't get them anything. Koom Frank is out of the hospital. He stays in his room all day, moaning and groaning. This place is driving me crazy."

"You've got to stop having kids," Aunt Ann insisted. "Look, if you want Paul and me to take care of Perry and Theresa and the baby for a while, we'll be glad to take them to my brother's farm in Michigan."

"But we are such good Catholics," Mom's thoughts had been trailing, seeking to find an explanation for six children.

"Ginny, I'm going to tell Frank what I think of all this," Ann said.

"No, please, Ann, don't. I…I'll…everything will be OK, I'm just tired."

"No, Ginny. Everything will *not* be OK," Aunt Ann said emphatically, as she reached out to steady Mom's shaking hand.

Later, Dad gathered all of us into the car. We drove to Uncle Frank and Aunt Marion Norris' home on Kirton Avenue, on Cleveland's west side. It was the week before Thanksgiving.

The Norris house was crowded with four adults and nine children. I doubled with cousin Ray in his upstairs bedroom. Frank and Gary stayed with Richard and Wayne in the other room. The rest of our family took over the basement and another down-stairs bedroom.

It was a vacation from Finney Avenue and we were all together having fun: playing scratchy records on the old Victrola in the basement, walking the nearby railroad tracks, flying kites in the school yard of Annunciation Catholic Church.

On Thanksgiving morning, it was hard to sleep. The smell of mince, apple, and pumpkin pie drifted upstairs. Aunt Marion was preparing a feast. Frank, Gary and I weren't used to eating breakfast, but we sure weren't going to turn down any food from Aunt Marion. After breakfast, she asked us to go outside while she finished cooking dinner, but every twenty minutes or so we would come back to the dining room table to watch the growing spread of relishes, carrots, celery, olives, cranberries, mashed potatoes, jellies, applesauce and yams steaming, begging to be eaten.

"Sure, Aunt Marion, we'll wait."

"Why, for heaven's sake, you would think you children never eat," she laughed.

"Thank You, Lord, for this food," Uncle Frank, his head bowed, led the prayers before this beautiful Thanksgiving meal. Aunt Marion served as referee while Frank, Gary and I knocked the stuffing out of the twenty-pound turkey and fought with our cousins over who would get the drumsticks.

After dinner, Dad took me aside. "Your mother is going into the hospital."

I knew it wasn't to have a baby. She had been sitting quietly at the dinner table, silent as she had been the last few days. All of us had tried to talk to her, but she didn't have anything to say. The last thing I had heard from Mom was a few days earlier in the kitchen of our Finney Avenue home. She was smoking a cigarette and sipping a glass of beer as she stared out the window. She rested her chin in the palm of her hand and breathed deeply, whispering secrets to something or someone outside the window. Then the long breaths began and a high-pitched cry came from deep inside her, dropping slowly into silence. Mom's face would change. Her eyes told me she was far away, but her tears were all over the kitchen table, and her cries knifed into my heart. No, this time she wasn't going to the hospital to have a baby. Would the doctors help her to recover her strength? Would they be able to help her find the laughter that she had lost?

"I'm taking her to the hospital this afternoon," Dad's voice cracked. Life had become too much for Mom to handle. She had pressures on her that often drove people to drink. Six small children were pulling at her apron strings, one a brand-new baby. Our financial situation was always shaky. She went out with my Dad often, but she never had any freedom of her own. I saw that she had gotten old fast. Her spirit was withering. She had lost herself and tried to find relief in pools of golden liquid from dozens of bottles of beer every week.

"We can't stay with Uncle Frank any longer. This house is too small for thirteen people. Uncle Frank is going to take all of you to a place to stay until your mother gets well." Dad had tears in his eyes.

Uncle Frank and Aunt Marion were two of the nicest people, but how nice could they continue to be when faced with another, larger family with no other place to go? We really liked staying with our cousins, Ray, Richard and Wayne. I wished we could have moved in with the Norrises, but then Uncle Frank and Aunt Marion may have had a lot less for which to be thankful. This wasn't the first time we'd been in a place where there were way too many people. I had a feeling of what to expect, but as many times as we had moved, nothing in my life thus far could have prepared me for what would happen next.

Chapter Sixteen

DAD PUT COATS on Perry and baby Larry and left with Mom. Uncle Frank asked us if we were ready to leave.

"Where are we going?" I asked.

"You'll be fine, don't worry. Come on, Frank, Gary and Terry."

We slowly climbed into his car and travelled down an unfamiliar highway. Traffic was light on this cold Thanksgiving afternoon.

"Where…are you taking us, Uncle Frank?" I asked haltingly.

"There is a nice home nearby, where there are boys and girls whose mothers and fathers are having problems. Children stay there until the problems are solved."

"What kind of a place is it?" I was worried. I had an awful feeling I might never see Mom and Dad again. I didn't like the way we left Kirton Avenue. There were too many things that were left unsaid. What about this place where Uncle Frank was taking us?

"It's called Parmadale."

"Parmadale. Uncle Frank, isn't that some kind of orphanage?" Fear began its clammy clutch on my arms, my chest, in my gut. Was Uncle Frank taking us away to an orphanage? When Frank, Gary and I fought with each other, Dad would tell us, "Some day your mother and father won't be around anymore and then you'll be sorry!" Was this the day? Was this what he meant? Would we be given up for adoption? Didn't they want us? Were we going to be all right? Were Mom and Dad going to be all right?

My thoughts sped in circles. I had a feeling of being lost, abandoned inside an eternity of questions without any hope of an answer. Frank, Gary and Theresa weren't asking any questions. They had fed themselves so well at Uncle Frank's that they had fallen asleep.

Uncle Frank tried to reassure me. "The people here are very nice to children. Don't worry."

"Uncle Frank, can't we stay with you, pllllease? I promise we will be good." His eyes blinked as he looked through his thick glasses, straight ahead to the road.

We headed down a long drive toward a row of forbidding brick buildings nestled among a small forest of evergreen trees. Wisps of smoke rose above a range of chimneys. Uncle Frank ushered us through a door into a darkened reception room. A Sister entered the reception room and spoke briefly to Uncle Frank.

It wasn't until Uncle Frank kissed us goodbye that it sunk in we were being left in a strange place without our mother and father or aunt and uncle. Frank, Gary, Theresa and I stood huddled inside the entrance to the parlor of the building and looked at each other in shock. Gary started to cry. Theresa was already crying. I nudged Gary to stop. Frank was crying, "I don't want to stay here!" I didn't want to stay here either. I turned my face toward the door that Uncle Frank had just closed. I wanted to run, but I didn't know where to run to. The room melted in watercolors.

"Come," Sister said to Frank and me, taking us into her spreading arms and bringing us close to her. A second Sister arrived to help with Gary and Theresa.

"What about Gary and Theresa? What about my brother and sister?" I asked, choking back sobs.

"They will be fine," Sister said. "They will be in other cottages."

We did not want to leave each other. We had never been separated before. "Please keep us together," I begged Sister. I didn't know if I would ever see my brothers and my sister again.

Sister gently coaxed Frank and me down a long hallway and up a flight of stairs.

"We have rules here. If you obey them you will not have any problems at Parmadale," she said.

Rules?

She led me to a room full of beds with crisp white pillows atop green army-type blankets. "You will sleep here. Everyone must be asleep by 9 p.m. We get up at 6 a.m."

Frank was taken to another section of the cottage.

I soon learned that Parmadale wasn't an orphanage, a place for children from broken homes, or even a place for children whose parents were sick. It felt more like a jail. When I got up at six the next morning, I asked someone as we were being led to the washroom: "How often do you do this?"

"Every day," was the answer from another boy, who seemed surprisingly calm considering the circumstances.

"Every day, a shower?" I couldn't believe it. "And you have to brush your teeth every day too? Suppose I don't want to brush my teeth?" I mean, they can't *make* you brush your teeth. It had never occurred to me that teeth were something you planned on having a long time.

"You have to brush your teeth. That's the rules. There's a dentist here, he checks." The boy gave me a wide, "look-Sister-no-cavities" smile.

I didn't need a dentist. I'd never seen one. The jawbreaker gumballs from Wahl's grocery store machine were my dentists. They pulled out most of the teeth I didn't have any use for. This was pure torture, to be forced to wash up and to have to brush my teeth every morning. I had an out.

"I don't have a toothbrush!"

"They'll give you one."

"They'll *give* me a toothbrush?"

After a week or so I got into the daily routine. Up at 6 a.m., make the bed, wash, brush teeth, go to Mass at the chapel, pour milk in the cafeteria, eat breakfast, dry the dishes, go to class where I daydreamed about home. There was a music class, which was great. I wondered what Dad would say when he found out that I learned to play the clarinet. I could hear the music again, and no one cared how long or loud I played. I hadn't heard anything from Dad, and it really bothered me. I didn't know if Mom was any better. I saw Frank a few times in the cafeteria and was sorry I ever fought with him. I asked Sister about Gary and Theresa. "They are fine, just fine." That's all they ever told you at Parmadale.

"They are younger," one of the Sisters explained when I asked about my siblings. "That is why they are in other cottages, but we take good care of every child here. We'll take good care of your brother and sister, don't do any more worrying about that," Sister tried to convince me.

"Can I see them?"

"I'm afraid we can't arrange that just yet, but you'll see them soon."

If they were "fine" then why couldn't I see them? Had something happened? Had they been adopted and Sister didn't want to tell me? And what had happened to Perry and baby Larry? What had happened to our family? It had suddenly scattered to the winds. This was my worst fear, that Mom and Dad would be gone, that I would be separated from my brothers and sisters and not be able to see them ever again.

After school and on weekends, clusters of children played in the courtyard and hills behind the cottages: some sledding, some throwing balls, others rolling in the snow. One day, as I looked far across the field, I saw a short figure in a brown corduroy jacket and black cap kicking through the snow. It was Gary. He was far across the field. I wanted to talk with him. I had never been away from him for so long. I wanted so much to see my little brother. I ran to him as fast as I could run. I knew I would never fight with him again, Jesus, I just wanted to see my little brother. Why couldn't I see him like I did at home, every day? I ran to him, faster than I had ever run before. It was getting hard to breathe. I just about got up to him. I was so happy. I knew he was all right. My brother, how much I missed him, he'll be glad to see me. I'll go around him, I'll come up from behind him and surprise him. "Gary!" He turned.

It wasn't him. "I, I'm sorry, I thought you were my brother."

It was another boy about his size wearing a coat that looked like his. He gave me a funny look. "I don't have a brother," he said, turning away to continue trudging through the snow. I slowly walked back to my group. My stomach hurt, badly. When you spend time with people every day you take them for granted, especially when that person is a brother or a sister. Then a day comes when they are not around and nothing is right, things don't fit together. My mind kept skipping spaces. Time didn't move. My thoughts froze.

On Christmas Eve, I could not stop coughing. I was sent to bed. I met emptiness in the quiet white infirmary bathed in the still radiance of red bulbs floating against a silver Christmas tree. The tree sprung from a terrazzo floor. There were no presents under its artificial limbs. Music crept in faintly from another floor. I tried to shut out the Christmas music. The silver tree and the red bulbs began to bleed into liquid darkness. On this Holy Night I wept for evenings that were far from silent. What I wanted for Christmas was our family to be back together. I did not want anything else, except to get older fast, so I could take care of my mother, father, brothers and sister. I was not an orphan. I hated being like an orphan. I prayed, Sweet Jesus, who came into this world with Joseph and Mary, please don't make me an orphan on your birthday. My chest and neck hurt from coughing. I was having a lot of trouble breathing. I fell asleep, not knowing if tomorrow would come.

On Christmas Day, I had stopped coughing. I was let out of the infirmary to join all the children in the cottage, who were gathered in the main lobby to receive hardtack and to open gifts sent by friends and family. Frank and I stood together. We looked around, but there was nothing under the tree for us. Oh, who cares about Christmas? The other children later gathered in the gym for a movie and to sing songs, but I couldn't sing. The music had gone out of my life.

New Year's Eve was very quiet at Parmadale. It was almost midnight. On previous New Year's Eves I stayed up to wait for Mom and Dad to come home with their funny hats, paper streamers, horns and cranking winding noisemaker contraptions, smelling of perfume and beer, whiskey and smoke.

Tonight there was only the smell of the antiseptic floors, the freshly laundered sheets and pillowcases and ghostly apparitions of New Years' past, of people dancing, kissing, hugging, holding beer glasses high, as balloons and streamers flung towards the praying clock. Mom and Dad would not be celebrating this New Year. I would not be waiting up for them to come through the door, singing and laughing, taking turns shouting out "Happy New Year." I buried my face in the pillow and cried all I could possibly cry. In that flash flood of tears, that most intense moment of loneliness, a resolve began to build in my heart. I vowed to face the coming year, to withstand anything that came my way, to not cry anymore, to promise God that if He gave me a chance I would be somebody, someday, so I could help my parents, my brothers and my sister and other people like them who were poor, and lonely and without hope.

I knelt beside my bed. "Jesus, help me to have the strength. If You give me a chance, I'll make things different for our family. We will be together again. Someday, somehow, I'll try to help make this world better for Mom and Dad and my brothers and sister. Just get me out of here, Jesus, just get me out of here. Please bring us back together. Amen."

The Sisters took good care of all the children. We were never hungry. We had time to pray, time to learn and time to play, all very important things to children. But there was one thing they couldn't give us. I was luckier than most other children at Parmadale. Some came from broken homes; their parents were divorced or put the children in a home with no intention of coming back. Other children really were orphans, with no one to take care of them but the Sisters. I felt so bad for them. It made me want all the more for our family to be back together. My heart would not rest until we were all back together, somehow, somewhere. During those days at Parmadale, the four Kucinich kids received the best care we'd ever had. They were also the worst days of our lives. I could not imagine what it was like for my mother and my father, being away from the family they loved.

Chapter Seventeen

MY PRAYERS WERE answered. After we spent eight weeks in Parmadale, Dad came to get us. This was one happy day. I raced through the halls repeating "We're going home! We're going home!" I made my bed one last time, military-style, careful to tuck the corners. I gathered up the few things I was given at Parmadale—a comb, a toothbrush, pajamas, socks and a book—and put them in a paper bag. I ran downstairs, sprinted to the front door and jumped into Dad's arms. Mom was better, he said. Her nerves were settling down. The doctor wanted her to get more rest. Dad said we were going to go away from the city for a while, to a place where there was plenty of peace and quiet.

We stopped by another Parmadale cottage and picked up Gary and Terrie. My heart was bursting with happiness; our family was getting back together again. We were going to be with Mom soon. I was very excited. We stopped the car briefly at Finney Avenue and filled the trunk of the car with a few boxes of clothes. I wanted to take the big dictionary that Dad had bought for me a year ago. It was the best birthday gift I had ever received. He said there wasn't room. I also left behind a stack of books that I had taken out of the Miles Park library. The books were long overdue and I knew there were going to be fines accumulating for not returning them. There was one thing I did not want to leave at Finney Avenue. At the last minute I secretly stashed under the front seat of the car the magic set Uncle Bill Norris gave me for my birthday. Then we headed for the hospital to pick up Mom.

Mom looked very thin and frail. Her face was a pale ivory. She had lost a lot of weight. She had tears in her eyes as we approached. We children converged on her from all sides in a flurry of hugs, kisses and tears of happiness.

"I'm going to be all right. Just be good and help me," she said in a weak voice.

"Mom, we missed you so much," I said as I held her tightly.

"We thought we would never see you again," Frank said. We made a lot of promises right on the spot. We promised to help. We promised no more yelling and screaming. We promised to do everything we could to make sure we stayed together.

"Hey, where's Perry and Larry?" Gary asked

"We are going to see them very soon," Dad promised. "They have been well cared for."

As the car moved out onto the highway I asked, "Where are we going, Dad?" not that it mattered because wherever the place, we were all headed in the same direction.

"Millington, Michigan, to stay with Uncle Paul and Aunt Ann. They have been taking care of Perry and baby Larry the last few months."

Michigan! That seemed very far away, almost in another country. I had never been out of the Cleveland area. In fact, we had never left the east side, except for visiting Uncle Frank and Parmadale.

We drove through a snowstorm, west along the lakefront road through Toledo and into Detroit, Michigan. Late that evening, Paul and Ann met us in the small farming community of Millington. We ate chicken dinners together at Schumaker's Restaurant, and then they led us to an isolated farm.

The kerosene lamps of two small houses blinked through the windows like fiery cat eyes. We got out of the car and the only sound we heard was the opening and closing of a slight, rickety wooden shed braced by the sharp wind. Exhausted, we tramped into the kitchen of our new residence.

"Uncle Paul, where's the bathroom?" Frank asked.

"Put your coat back on," Uncle Paul said. "You too," he motioned to Gary and me.

"Why do we have to put on our coats to go to the bathroom?" I asked. He led us out into the freezing night. He pointed to the rear of the house to the shed, whose door had been keeping time with the wind.

"It's in there." He was kidding. "Go ahead, look for yourselves." He wasn't kidding. We looked inside the shed.

No light, no sink, no towels, no roaches. This wasn't a bathroom, just a bench with a hole in it. Uncle Paul pointed to it.

"You sit there and do your business." He held up a roll of toilet paper and put it on a nail inside the outhouse.

"It's all yours," Uncle Paul said, laughing as he saw the look of disbelief on our faces.

It was a great reunion when Aunt Ann and Uncle Paul brought Perry and Larry into the room and all eight of us were together for the first time in a long, long time. I cried when I realized that at one time I had been sure this was never going to happen. I was so happy that we were together again as a family. I never wanted to be apart from my mother and father and brothers and sisters again. We got along better than ever. It was a whole new adventure for all of us.

In the next few months, while the snow was still covering the farmland, we learned about outhouses, quilting, crossword puzzles and tracking rabbits quietly, step by step, through rows of mulberry bushes. When we were snowbound, Mrs. Geneva Frost, the neighbor who lived in the small house in front, read to us from the Farmer's Almanac while we sampled her fruit preserves and fresh bread. This wasn't the old peanut butter and jelly routine we had done for years, either. These were preserves and bread Mrs. Frost made right before our eyes. It was amazing. We had absolutely the best food we'd ever had: mashed potatoes, roast beef, chicken, yams, green beans, apple, cherry, and berry pies. Mrs. Frost and Aunt Ann helped Mom by cooking meals for our family. I couldn't wait to get home just to smell the food. It was like every day was Thanksgiving!

I took many long walks in the woods during those cold winter days. The air was clean and sharp and kind to my lungs. I hadn't had an asthma attack since I left Parmadale. I trudged often through the whiteness, alone with my thoughts about our new life. I felt a sense of oneness with the snow, the trees and the bright winter sky. When it grew too cold, I could follow my tracks back home and go into our warm home and talk to Mom, who was doing a lot better.

Frank, Gary and I enrolled in an elementary school in Millington. It was the first time I attended a public school. It seemed different, because there were no prayers, no masses, no time off for holy days, no pictures of Jesus in the classroom, no catechism tests. I missed serving mass. I felt somewhat empty. A school bus picked us up every weekday and carried us to a modern school with a new gym and great lunch food. I made new friends easily, but since none of the other children lived near our farm there was no chance to play together after school.

When Spring came, under Mrs. Frost's direction, we learned how to plant onions, carrots, watermelons, strawberries, and leaf lettuce. She had an encyclopedic knowledge of the Burpee catalogue planting schedules. The clear stream in front of her house was teeming with newly-spawned pollywogs constantly trying to evade youthful fingers dipping into the water.

Dad couldn't get a decent truck-driving job in Michigan, so after a while he travelled back and forth from Cleveland. It must have been very painful for him to leave his beloved wife and family, travel hundreds of miles away and spend the week alone. We missed him greatly during the week. He drove about seven hours back and forth every weekend to spend time with us. One week he decided to take a plane to Cleveland so he could stay with us longer. Just as he was leaving for the airport to fly to Cleveland, Mom became hysterical and insisted he stay. To pacify her, he missed his flight. The next morning a radio broadcast announced that the plane had crashed, killing all aboard.

On most Saturdays Mom and Dad were together. Sometimes they would go dancing at a pavilion overlooking a green lake. They danced for hours. We children sat and watched Mom and Dad as they swept across the floor. When they danced slow they held each other tight, just like lovers in those movies we watched on television during evenings at the farm. They were easily the best dancers in the place. Other people would stop dancing and watch Mom and Dad when they were doing the "jitterbug."

When it was time to leave the pavilion I sometimes thought Dad would drive off into the lake, because he and mom were so happy they had trouble seeing the road, but we always made it home. Each time we arrived safely I knew I had to make good on another promise I made to God, providing He got us home in one piece.

The school year ended early so that farmers' children could help with the planting. Our crop of fruits and vegetables didn't take long to plant, so I spent time exploring, following streams into the nearby woods, studying the budding green leaves slowly patching over the sky. I learned all about farming by visiting our neighbors. I rode a tractor, milked cows, cleaned out horse stalls and jumped from haylofts into mountains of straw—until I found out that the same straw had been used to line the floor of rabbit hutches. Gary and Frank were too little for this kind of wandering. Theresa and Perry played in the farm house. Larry was still in a crib that Paul and Ann bought from a neighboring farm family.

Frank and I built up a big mound of sand behind the outhouse, digging up the soil with our hands and contouring the ground below the mound. Then we rolled ourselves into balls inside big old tires and discarded washing bins and took turns riding down the "hill."

Dad played softball with us a few times. He could really hit the ball. He had trouble fielding because his knee would give out. But when he played ball with us, those were the best softball games in the world.

In the city there weren't many chances to watch pollywogs grow to be frogs, as I did at the stream in front of Mrs. Frost's house. I enjoyed the satisfaction of planting things and watching them grow, but we weren't on the farm long enough to harvest the crops we planted.

Dad came home one weekend and said we were going to move back to Cleveland. Mom was stronger. She was laughing again. I had come to love the farm, but Dad said he wanted us to move back to Cleveland because that was where his work was. Theresa and Gary did not want to leave the farm either. They threw a tantrum, but we jammed into the car again, ready to go. We promised Mrs. Frost, Aunt Ann, Uncle Paul and our other friends that we would come back to visit, and then we headed back to Cleveland.

Chapter Eighteen

IT WAS THE SUMMER of 1958. Cleveland didn't look much different.

"Ginny, we can stay with Koom Frank. I talked to him, he said we can come back anytime we want."

"There's too many bad memories there, Frank, I can't live there," Mom said, as Dad drove past the picnic benches, baseball diamonds and sailboats on Cleveland's lakefront.

We stopped the car and Dad bought a newspaper and asked me to read the ads for apartments for rent, east, while he drove up and down the streets of our old neighborhoods. I circled a few listings with a pencil and handed him the page.

Dad was on the pay phone for a few minutes. I heard him say "Three kids." If he said six kids we would be refused immediately, and the eight of us could end up sleeping in the car.

"Three children are too many?" Dad said incredulously.

Dad tried another number.

"Three kids, yes, I drive a truck." His smile beamed as he got into the car and we drove to Hough Avenue, near Crawford Road. We waited in the car, down the street from the apartment, while Dad paid a fifty-dollar deposit and a month's advance rent. A half-hour later, after the landlady had gone, we went up the stairs to inspect our new home in the city. Three small rooms. Dad said it would do until he could find something better. The apartment didn't have a stove or a bed, so we slept on the floor until Dad went out and bought three mattresses.

Mom cooked from an electric skillet Aunt Ann had given to us. We ate grilled cheese sandwiches, hot dogs and hamburgers on alternate nights.

The landlady showed up the first Saturday. Before Dad went downstairs to let her in, he told Gary, Frank and me to go down the backstairs so she wouldn't see us. A man and a woman who lived in a downstairs suite observed our exit.

"Hello," the woman said, "are you the children who live upstairs?"

"Nope, just visiting," I said, as I pushed Frank and Gary into the next yard. My brothers didn't understand. They began to make faces; they pushed back and hollered. We spilled out onto the sidewalk, bickering, rumbling down the street, then hiding behind a parked car until the landlady left the building.

Once the landlady arrived on a weekday and we did not have a chance to run down the backstairs, so Frank, Gary and I hid in the closet of the main room. Hiding in the closet was much more fun than running down the backstairs. Whenever anyone would show up at the front door we would pretend it was the landlady and do a "hiding" drill. Apparently our drill had some flaws. The landlady said we had to move. We moved to another apartment a few doors down, until the landlord came to collect the rent. He saw all the children. Mom looked at him and knew there was trouble coming.

"Lady, you've got too many kids in this place. We told you when you moved in, three children and you have, how many?" He did a head count. "Six! No, we can't do that," he said, shaking his head with finality.

"They're good children," Mom's voice quivered. "They aren't causing anyone any problems. Look, we're keeping this place clean and everything," she pleaded.

"Yeah, that's what you say now, lady, but in a few months they'll tear this place apart. We can't let that happen. I'm sorry, but you have to move."

"But…."

"I'm sorry," he said, his lips closed and his chin bunched.

"Please don't make us move," she said, but to no avail.

The man left and Mom looked at me with tears in her eyes. "What do people have against children? Don't children need a place somewhere to live? Weren't the people renting to us children at one time in their lives? Not everyone can afford to buy a house. What is a large family supposed to do?" she asked. "What am I going to tell your father?"

There was not a shortage of housing. But all you had to do was to read the newspaper ads and you would see the unwillingness to rent to children was so bad that people would come right out and say it in black and white. Discrimination based on the number of children in a family is almost as bad as discrimination based on color. Many of the children I met in school came from large Catholic families where the parents owned their home, lived in the same neighborhood and went to the same school for most of their lives. But as renters with a large family we were out of luck and sometimes out on the street. It seemed no one, not even other Catholics, were going to rent to a family with six children, even if the kids were saints—which we certainly were not. After a while we just plain expected to get evicted as soon as we moved into a place. That way we were never disappointed. But expecting it never stopped Mom from crying, nor Dad from sweating out where in the world the eight of us would move to next.

The summer wasn't a total loss. I learned what alleys to avoid so I wouldn't get mugged. Three black children stopped me in an alley near Hough and Crawford as I was returning from the store.

"What's you got in the bag, boy?"

"Nothin', just some cigarettes for my mother."

"He got some cigarettes for his mutha," said the tallest boy, as he looked at his friends who were laughing.

"Good," said the smallest boy. He was not smiling. "Tell your mutha I like to smoke, suckah." He grabbed the paper bag that contained cigarettes and a get well card.

"Got any money?" The third boy was not to be denied his chance.

I didn't have anything in my pockets except a few bottle caps I was saving for the R C Cola hockey ticket promotion, where you turned in a dozen bottle caps in exchange for a free ticket to a Cleveland Barons game. I didn't want anyone going through my pockets. And I sure didn't want anyone taking my bottle caps.

"No! Leave me alone." They shoved me to the ground, ripped out my pockets, looking with confusion and contempt at the bottle caps.

"Silly little mutha," one of the boys said as he threw the bottle caps down the alley.

"This is our alley, suckah, stay out." Fair enough, I thought, as I lay on the ground, fair enough. They left and I collected most of the bottle caps. I stayed out of their alley after that.

Chapter Nineteen

THE NEW SCHOOL YEAR was about to begin. We needed to find a place somewhere so we could go to school. We returned to St. Clair Avenue to check rentals near E. 105th Street. It was warm in the car, even though all the windows were rolled down and the vents were open. Frank, Gary and I used newspapers to fan each other and Mom and Dad in the front seat until Dad told us to stop it because he couldn't see out the rear window. The street smelled of tar and the tires were sticking to the surface. This was a good day to be swimming or exploring caves; it was an awful day to be looking for a place to live.

A cardboard sign above a delicatessen snapped me from a daydream: "FOR RENT." We were only a few doors away from the E. 107th Street apartment we'd lived in seven years ago. Dad copied down the telephone number on the sign, pulled into a Gulf gas station and made the call. The landlord didn't object to the number of children—"four" as Dad claimed during the phone conversation. Lucky for us, the building's custodian did not take a head count when he accepted the month's advance rent.

Our old neighborhood looked different. Some of the movie theatres had closed down. A number of businesses had changed names. Some had new steel gates folding in front of their windows. A discount department store had moved into a building next to a Masonic Temple, and a storefront Baptist church had been established. Still, this was familiar territory. I could recall places and friends who had lived here, and it gave me a feeling of security. Perhaps our family would finally take root in this neighborhood where Dwight and I had played and grow like the maple trees that lined East 107th Street. I hadn't even walked up the steps of our new apartment when I decided I liked it here. This would be like old times, as if we had never left. This was our neighborhood.

Forest Hills, a large city park up the street from the apartment, had baseball and soccer fields and plenty of green, open space surrounded by densely populated apartments and one and two-family homes. Gary, Frank and I spent our first summer days in the new/old neighborhood playing softball in the park, challenging all comers. During one pick-up game, players from the other side told us that bigger kids were going to "clean out" the park and Forest Hills pool, a few blocks away.

"I didn't know the park and pool was dirty," I said.

"No, they're going to get rid of the n******," said one boy.

"Yeah, n****** carry all kinds of disease," said another. "We're supposed to stay away from them."

He didn't seem too smart. If you are supposed to "stay away" from someone, why bother them?

I thought about the man who had told me to stay away from Dwight seven years earlier. I wondered what Dwight was doing now. I wondered if these kids had met the man who told me not to play with Dwight. I wondered why they were allowed to say the word "n*****," and what all this had to do with softball and Forest Hills park and pool. Maybe they lost a softball game to people with dark skin and were still mad about it.

"Come on, let's play softball," I said, as two of our opponents kept talking about "n******" and what was going to happen in the park. They seemed more interested in talking about a fight than in playing softball. It was a lousy game and they were lousy players. We beat them easily, and we weren't that good.

When white teenagers finally showed up one day at Forest Hills Park with chains, rocks, knives and baseball bats, small black children saw them and ran out of the park. But their older brothers soon arrived for revenge.

"Let's get out of here," I said to Gary and Frank. We ran from the softball field, turning briefly to watch the two groups moving slowly towards one another.

We heard what sounded like gunshots and bolted for home. Gary ran directly into the path of a panel truck. He was struck squarely. He sailed through the air in a seated position for about ten yards, landed on his feet, and kept on running. The terrified driver stopped to help Gary but couldn't catch him. Gary's black and blue legs frantically propelled him through St. Aloysius' school yard to his hiding place, behind an apartment building on East 109th Street. He rested, out of breath and afraid, but he refused to go to Forest City Hospital to be checked out.

"What's wrong with you, Gary? You could be hurt bad and not know it!" I tried to reason with him but he made a face that meant, "No," and I could see arguing was no use. Later on, after everyone had forgotten about Gary and the panel truck, he showed me his bruises. He didn't want to go to the hospital because he had messed his pants.

The park was no longer safe. I spent my time trying to find old friends. I discovered that they'd all moved. But it was easy to find new friends in the summer, and it seemed as though every kid on the block was out on the street, playing cowboys and Indians, cops and robbers, zooming their homemade orange crate roller-skate scooters up and down driveways on E. 107th Street or playing stickball between the two- and three-story buildings. My new companions lived in a dark three-story brick box wrapped in multi-colored laundry strung out on a criss-cross of ropes and plastic clothesline and hung over sun-bleached wooden railings. It was in that apartment house on a rainy August morning when I discovered a dusty coal cellar loaded with empty mason jars and massive feathery cobwebs. This was the perfect creepy location for my first try at being a professional magician in front of an audience.

When the weather was nice, my neighbors Spider, Ken, Al and I were off climbing roofs and jumping fences. We slammed our fists on the fenders of slow-moving cars, then lay down, playing dead in the street. One day, however, it was raining, and there was nothing for us to do. If we stayed inside our apartments long enough we would get only in trouble with our mothers, so I didn't have any problem getting Spider, Ken and Al into the basement where they shared orange-crate seats.

I turned on a light bulb that hung from the ceiling. Its tungsten filament cast a dim light, providing a properly dark room. I draped my t-shirt over a cardboard box—the book suggested a cloth be placed over the magic table for performances. My friends were impatient and restless.

"Aw, he's no magician," said Al.

"I'll show you," I said as I pulled a magic wand from a black top hat, bought for thirty cents from the Salvation Army. I placed the magic wand on the magic t-shirt. "Just watch."

"You don't know magic!" exclaimed Ken.

Little did they know I had worked with magic before—well, kind of. I'd done plenty of reading about Houdini and other great magicians. I had also began my studies learning what magic is not. Uncle Lenny once shook hands with me and I got a strong buzzing electric shock. That was not magic. He gave me a flowered glass for my ninth birthday. The glass leaked when filled to the petals. Not magic. Other times I took a fake black widow spider to school at Holy Name, but everyone knew it was a fake. I put phony rubber vomit on Mrs. Byrne's desk, who was so outraged that she took a swing at me. Not magic. Novelties, tricks, harmless practical jokes—there was no mystery to any of these. Real magic had mystery, the element of the unknown.

I stirred the magic hat and pulled out a number of colored handkerchiefs from the tip of the wand. Only Al was impressed by this opener, perhaps because he had a runny nose and a short-sleeve shirt.

I opened a small container to reveal a red ball, secure in the center.

I closed the container, tapped it twice with the wand and then shouted the magic words from the instructions that came with Uncle Bill's magic set:

"Abracadabra, hocus pocus," adding "ad Deum qui laetificat, juven tutem meam" for effect. The container was opened. The ball...gone!

"Hey, how did you do that?" The question every magician dreams of hearing. Only I didn't hear it. I got the idea I wasn't getting through to my audience; they were sitting there bored, grim-faced and fidgety.

"All right, I'll cut out the small stuff and get to the big one. Gimme anything you have in your pockets—yo-yos, bubble gum, baseball cards."

Rocks, a peach stone and two pennies were produced and placed inside the plastic doors of the yellow, green and red-terraced mini-Buddhist temple magic box. I shut the doors. My friends started. Since I had their valuables, they obeyed when I demanded that they remain seated so as not to disturb the Genie of the Magic Lantern. I said the magic words, tapped the box and opened the doors. The rocks, peach stones and two cents had vanished.

"Where's my money?" Ken asked belligerently.

"Wow," Spider exclaimed, but all he had in the box was a rock. Ken walked behind me to try to discover the secret. Never do that to a magician. "Get out!" I demanded.

"I want my two cents back," he insisted.

"OK, sit down and don't get excited." Magicians should always try to avoid injury to self while performing, the handbook of magic said.

"Presto chango, everyone gets his stuff back, here's your two cents." I packed up the magic and removed the mirrors from the box. I headed for home, satisfied that my practice had helped. For my next Cellar Magic show I charged admission, one penny per person. I made eight cents.

Chapter Twenty

DAD AND MOM WANTED us to go to St. Aloysius Catholic School, two blocks east of where we lived. I went to the convent and was told we would have to pay a book bill, but Dad had just paid the rent and bought a used television so he could watch war movies. We didn't have any money left. He kept us captive before the television whenever *"The Sands of Iwo Jima"* or *"Guadacanal Diary"* or other World War II films were on, so we could see how the Marines did it. I knew all about the halls of Montezuma and the shores of Tripoli, but not a week went by without Dad trying to recruit me. I was convinced I would be a Marine, just like Dad.

When I came home complaining after a street fight, he'd say, "Look, if you are going to be in the Marines, you gotta be tough." If I didn't like a chore Mom gave me to do, Dad would tell me later, "Hey, you're going to have to work hard, or you'll never be a Marine." When Dad and I would get into arguments, he'd take a belt to me, and if I so much as whimpered, he'd say, "Huh! You won't make a pimple on a Marine's ass." But sitting in front of the television set to watch the USMC in action was all I had to do to get Dad's approval. "You're a good gyrene, kid, a real credit to the Corps!"

Summer Sundays were a slog, with Dad watching the Marines trekking through the televised hell-hot jungle, and me observing the sunny skies lighting up the newspapers lining our windows, calling me to step out of the dark oven known as our apartment. The battles were not only on television. Most of the time they were financial struggles in the kitchen. Late one night, I watched Mom and Dad sitting in the kitchen beneath a dim yellow light, somberly counting pennies atop our chipped white metal-topped kitchen table. I knew every single penny was important to our family. Every single penny was needed for food and shelter and clothing. A utility bill was due. Click, click, click... the pennies dropped one by one as they were sorted and counted. Click, click, click. With painful efficiency columns of stacked pennies soon lined the table. They were put in wrappers and would be taken to the bank the next day to pay the bill.

I did everything I could to bring some money into the house. Martha Schaeffer owned the delicatessen below our apartment. I asked her for a job and for a time I earned a quarter here and a quarter there helping with chores at the store. Plus, when people wanted soda pop I opened the bottles for them and collected the R C Cola bottle caps to get more hockey tickets.

I was elated to start school again. Dad and Mom had a meeting at St. Aloysius to tell one of the Sisters that we couldn't afford to pay the book bill on time, because Mom had just had a miscarriage and we had more bills. Every penny was scraped together to try to pay them. The school had to be paid. Dad tried to remain optimistic. He told the Sister the school would not have to wait long for money because he was hoping to get an increase in his serviceman's pension. The Sister told them they would have to pay about seven dollars each for the book bills for myself, Frank and Gary. And if they didn't have the money the children would not be able to attend St. Aloysius. "You shouldn't have children if you can't afford them," the Sister said. Mom came home with the old Irish fire in her eyes, raising holy hell.

"That's all the priests tell you, have children. A woman is supposed to have children. That's why we got married. We've had a lot of children, six, and that doesn't include the two I lost. Because we're good Catholics and have a big family, we have nothing but trouble finding a place to live. Now the Catholic Church doesn't want to help our children get in Catholic schools?

'Shouldn't have children if you can't afford them.'" She mimicked the Sister's lecture. "Piss on them!" Mom seethed.

"Ginny, calm down," Dad said. "I'll be goddamned if I am going to beg them, but we'll find a way."

"How, Frank?" She looked at me and the other kids. "We don't have the money. You'll go to public schools, just like in Michigan. Oliver Wendell Holmes and Patrick Henry schools are not that far away."

They spent the rest of the evening smoking cigarettes, drinking beers and talking religion. Mom stopped going to church after that.

The next day I told a new friend from around the corner on East 107th that we had to go to public school because we couldn't pay the book bill at St. Aloysius.

"Other people don't have money, either," he said. "Last year, my Mom paid my book bill late. She went to see Sister Leona, and Sister Leona said it was all right to pay late."

"Where is this Sister Leona?" I asked.

"At the convent. She is the Principal."

Mom and Dad didn't have the money, so I decided to make one last-ditch effort to go to Catholic school. I wanted to continue serving mass. I walked to the St. Aloysius convent door and rang the doorbell a few times. A heavy-set Sister came to the door. She wore a black habit with a broad white bib.

"Sister Leona, please," I said plaintively.

"Who shall I say is calling?" the bemused Sister looked at me. She had a peaceful, round face and her eyes looked as if she knew a good joke and couldn't wait to tell it.

"My name is Dennis Kucinich, Sister."

"And what shall I say this is about?"

"Sister, it's about a book bill for me and my brothers."

"Well, you came to the right person, I'm Sister Leona." She invited me to come inside the convent. I sat down on a small couch.

"Sister, I want to go to school here," I said. "I have served Mass at St. Peter's and at Holy Name. I want to keep serving."

"That's wonderful. We can always use more altar boys. We have quite a few masses each week at St. Aloysius."

"But Sister, another Sister told my Mom and Dad that we couldn't come here." I wanted to go to Catholic school so badly that I began to get real emotional, barely choking back tears and mixing up the message. "Sister Leona, that Sister told my Mom and Dad if they couldn't afford kids, don't send them to Catholic school." I hit the word school hard, and I stretched it so long that water came out of it and spilled onto my shirt. I started sobbing.

Sister Leona was aghast. She quickly sat next to me and put her arm around my shoulder. "Now, there, there, my child, you shouldn't ever have to worry about things like this. Your parents were told if they couldn't pay the book bill, you couldn't go to school here?"

"Yes Sister, something like that," I sniffled.

"We'll we can take care of that right now. You wouldn't mind working to pay the book bill, would you? You could even earn extra money to pay for your lunches. I could use some help around the school with the floors and all. Would you like to help around the school?"

"Yes, Sister." Oh my God. My heart jumped up. I didn't even ask what it was she wanted me to do. I hadn't even thought about money for lunches, but it looked like that was going to be taken care of too. I was ready to scrub floors, do anything, just as long as we could all go to school at St. Aloysius.

"We have a janitor here who is very busy. It would be nice if he had a little helper."

"Sister, I'll work, I'll pay off all book bills and everything else."

"It won't take that long to pay them, Dennis, we wouldn't want you to ignore your studies here at St. Aloysius."

"Oh, yes Sister! Of course, Sister. Thank you, Sister. I can't wait to go home and tell my Mom and Dad." I got the job! I went inside church to say a prayer of thanks.

Mom and Dad wouldn't have to worry about the book bill, lunches or anything else. Frank, Gary and I would be able to go to St. Aloysius. I would get a chance to serve mass, scrub floors and play football, all because of Sister Leona.

A huddle of Catholic Youth Organization (CYO) football hopefuls was already scavenging through boxes of old equipment when I showed up at the narrow locker room underneath St. Aloysius' gym a few days before school started. I submarined my way through the crowd to "helmets" and came up with a mean-looking black and white leather Michigan State model. It was the first helmet of my life, and I didn't mind that it kept falling over my eyes. It would keep me from losing my ears when I was slammed to the ground during scrimmages. The football practice pants were outsized, like winter pajamas.

I ran flatfooted through my pass patterns at Forest Hills field. The torn old pair of cleats I had fished from the locker room dustbin were a few sizes too large, but a few extra pairs of socks and who would know the difference? Maybe my feet were just too small for my age.

If I ever got off the bench, God help the other team. As it was, I had time to think during the regular season games and plenty of time to study the cheerleaders jumping up and down on the cinder track behind the bench.

At the start of each game our St. Aloysius football team prayed to win. We joined hands in the center of a huddle and the parish priest very solemnly started *The Memorare*:

"Remember O most gracious Virgin Mary that never was it known that anyone who fled to thy protection, implored thy help or sought thy intercession was left unaided. Inspired by this confidence, I fly unto thee, O Virgin of Virgins, my mother. To thee I come, before thee I stand, sinful and sorrowful; O Mother of the Word Incarnate, despise not my petitions, but in thy mercy, hear and answer me. Amen."

The energy of spiritual inspiration charged from the center of the huddle, the captain of the team beseeched "Our Lady of Victory...."

The team in unison: "Pray for us!"

The captain again: "Our Lady of Victory…."

The team once again, with voices rising: "Pray for us!"

Then, so loud that everyone in the stadium could hear us: "Our Lady of Victory…."

"PRAY FOR US."

The team on the other side of the field couldn't hear a word we were saying. They were also loudly invoking the power of heaven.

We prayed hard. When we lost it provoked deep thoughts. Were the other team's prayers better than ours? Did they have a connection with God that we didn't have? I caught up with Sister Leona as she was leaving church after Monday morning mass and asked her how could we lose, when we prayed to win? If anyone would know anything about prayers, she would. I had to find out: Does it pay to pray when you play?

"It's wrong to pray to win," she said. I was very surprised at her answer. I didn't understand. She prayed all day. She had us pray many times a day. We prayed to win before every game. We were good Catholics. How were you supposed to win, anyway, if you didn't pray?

"Sister, we pray before every game and…"

She raised her right hand and waved her index finger, like she was going to teach me something.

"It's fine to pray before every game, but it is wrong to pray to win because God doesn't play favorites. Only one team can win; God can't let both teams win. When you pray, pray to do your best and maybe you will win, and maybe you will not win. God doesn't make any guarantees, not to Principals and not to young football players from St. Aloysius."

From then on, whenever I stretched my arm toward the center of the huddle of hands, I prayed to do my best. I prayed to get off the bench too.

I also joined the basketball team and the school guards. And I began to serve mass again, including at weddings, where altar boys were each given a few dollars by the best man. I liked to serve and to volunteer. It was a way to learn new things, to make new friends, to feel like I was doing something important and to stay away from the apartment.

At St. Aloysius, I developed the school yard skills essential for survival in life. I could hold a line during "Red Rover" and "Pom Pom Pullaway." Leonard Smith knew how to break a line. While I had my arms interlocked with those of my schoolmates, ready to stop anyone from passing through our line, Leonard ran straight at me, punched me in the face and broke my nose. As I sank in agony to the ground, Leonard easily passed through the gap. I went home.

"Dad, he just punched me in the face and I didn't do anything to him. What are you going to do about it, Dad?" I asked when he arrived home early in the evening.

"What? What do you mean, what am I going to do about it? What is this noise? Hey, kid, fight your own battles."

I was very upset. I wasn't sure what I wanted him to do, but I wanted him to do something because I would have a broken nose for the rest of my life.

"Kid, don't worry. Look at my nose. Croatians all have broad noses. Now nobody will think you are Irish," he said as he looked closely at the purple circles widening under both of my eyes. "You know, I think your nose *is* broken. Come on, we better go get it fixed," Dad said.

He took me to a doctor at Forest City Hospital.

"You vill fill pray-shure, no pain," the man in the white coat said as he fingered my nose with his burly hairy hands.

"Honly pray-shure," he said. Sure, easy for him to say. I was bleary-eyed and weak. I couldn't resist his hammy hands as they explored my nose like it was a piece of putty.

The Doctor lied. I felt both pressure and pain. Pain so intense my scream drowned out the sound of his reassuring voice while he cracked my nose back into place. I don't know what bothered me more, the pain or listening to the sound of my nose cracking. He put a face-mask bandage on me. I looked like something out of a horror movie, wild purple-rimmed eyes and white tape. After a while I got used to my new nose. I also learned when to duck when a punch was thrown.

I learned new prayers. At midday when the church bells tolled, all students stopped whatever they were doing. They set down the baseball trading cards being flipped against the building, held back the marbles from the chalked ring, laid down jump ropes, put down lunches, closed school books, stopped in their tracks and bowed their heads to say the "Angelus."

As hundreds of small lips muttered the prayer a siren began to wail.

St. Aloysius students were shepherded into the hallway of the school. Sister put us in single file and marched us down the basement stairs as the siren pitch became louder.

"Get down, like this," Sister said, crouching low alongside the pastel-colored cement block wall.

"Put your hand over your head, like this," she instructed, "one hand behind the head, the other bracing the forehead."

The cry of the sirens, the fear of the unknown; what would happen next?

"Get down, get down now, would you?" cried Sister as the sirens called. "Whatever you do, don't look up," she warned us.

"Keep your eyes shut, children, or you may be blinded by The Flash," Sister had urgency to her request. Some kids were getting scared and wanted to go to the lavatory. I shut my eyes real tight, so the flash wouldn't get them.

"Don't move until you hear the 'all-clear' signal," Sister was very serious, and we remained frozen into position. And then those words which came easily when you believed that you were going to die: "Oh my God, I am heartily sorry for having offended Thee."

Someone behind me called the drill stupid. Without turning, I answered:

"You won't think it was stupid if the Communists attacked." We had been taught that the Communists were so bad they didn't even believe in God. We had to be prepared if THEY attacked.

My God, we had to be prepared. Let's face it, everyone was talking about the Communists these days. There were stories about the Communists in every newspaper. I heard radio reports talking about the Communists. Someone said the Communists had even been on television in front of the United States Congress. It seemed they were everywhere. Sister often led us in prayer for the conversion and redemption of the godless, atheistic Communists. Maybe we could save the Communists from themselves.

What was a Communist? I didn't know, but when someone is trying to kill you how much do you need to know about them? You just have to be prepared. As I ducked down, I held onto my head, tightly. I wished everyone in the school's basement would be quiet, so I could listen for the buzzing of Communists airplanes and the whistling of Communist bombs. It was terrifying crouching there, like being afraid of the dark. The much-feared Communists never came, except in my dreams when they launched rocket attacks on St. Aloysius. I saw the long slow trajectory of the missile. It arched in the sky and then headed right for the school. I hid under a desk and escaped unscathed, thank you Jesus, we won. ST. ALOYSIUS 1, COMMIES, 0. Once you learn to survive the Communists, you can survive anything.

Chapter Twenty-One

I DID NOT KNOW if I could help to defend St. Aloysius against the Communists by being a school guard, but at least I could help other children cross the street safely. The spring-alarm Big Ben clock jangled at 6:30 a.m., but I was already awake and standing by the oven, trying to get my school guard's shoulder-and-waist white belt dry from last night's Ivory soap scrubbing. As a lieutenant in St. Aloysius' school guard brigade, I was responsible for meeting all the guards at the school yard at 7:15 a.m., to make sure all street positions were covered. Other than the belt, my uniform consisted of a badge, worn where the white cloth strip crossed the heart.

I liked being a school guard. The badge gave me a feeling of responsibility, almost like being a policeman, a Texas Ranger, or maybe a Marine in waiting. I wasn't particularly keen on the belt, because it reminded me of Sergeant Garcia's belt in Zorro and it led to school guards engaging in deadly sword stick fights with the crossing flags. My lieutenant's badge had a red crest, which I pretended meant courage. A Captain's badge was blue. New guards had plain but bright silver ones. All the badges had a bald eagle perched protectively over the top, which made school guards look official, especially to first-graders.

I scraped together two Skippy peanut butter and Welch's grape jelly sandwiches, fending off errant roaches who missed their light-switch cue to return to the cracks and recesses of the apartment's walls. I took a fork and retrieved the belt from the inside of the oven. It was hot and damp. I took the red badge, opened up the big pin at the back of it and threaded it through the belt, almost stabbing my left hand.

In the front room, I put on my only pair of school pants: turquoise blue with black piping, twenty-five-cent Salvation Army issue. I buttoned up the obligatory white shirt, clipped on a dark blue tie, scooped up a reader and a spelling book, neither of which I ever read at home, stuffed the peanut butter and jelly sandwiches into a brown lunch bag, grabbed my coat which was hanging on the bathroom doorknob, and met our family dog, a shaggy bundle of black and white patches named Spotty. Uncle Paul and Aunt Ann brought him for us from Michigan.

This was no ordinary dog. He was a water spaniel, so naturally he caught fish in park streams. But he had other talents, like capturing rats in the back yard and snagging steaks from picnic grills in the parks where we went to play. He was a great dog. Whenever we moved we never had to worry about him complicating the back seat. But he was not apartment-trained. "Hello, Spotty," I said, gingerly sidestepping his unique greeting, left in little rolls marinated in urine on the floor. He barked, waking up everybody in the apartment. I picked my guard belt off the oven top and exited, hustling down two flights of wooden stairs, pausing to check the "Apartment 5" mailbox, opening the green wooden framed glass door then making a right turn and heading for St. Al's.

Traffic was light on St. Clair Avenue. A fine spray of iced rain shimmered like a frozen morning dew. I was first to show up at the guards' rendezvous. I walked around the school yard, trying to keep warm. Minutes later, Tom, then Bob, then Robert and eventually Mike and Ray showed up for duty. The janitor opened a door where we kept the yellow safety flags with the centered green crosses, which symbolized, I was told, not Jesus but safety.

The captain reminded us:

"Look both ways before you step off the curb. Keep the flag out far enough so cars can see it. Wait until the person crosses the street then go back to the curb...and no horsing around."

The instructions were easy, but every once in a while a guard would forget, like the time a dozen angry pupils rousted me from a daydream by calling from across the street. "Hey, let us cross." I took the job seriously enough to arrive early every day. I made sure that everyone crossed safely. Around school, guards were always considered to be more alert than pupils who weren't, and I did my best to live up to the reputation. The half-hour of duty passed slowly on cold mornings when the damp guard belt clung to my jacket, advancing the chill of the wind. I ignored the cold. I kept concentrating on the hot chocolate that awaited all guards at the end of a winter morning's duty. When I rushed in from the cold the other guards were already at the table inside the school. They mixed the chocolate powder with hot water. I got the last packet. The cup warmed my hands. I stared into the rising steam, thinking how lucky I was to have hot chocolate on such a cold morning. How happy I was to be going to school. How glad I was to be going to St. Al's Catholic school.

Protecting others gave me a strong sense of responsibility. I developed it with the help of Sister Mary Alice, who wanted me to be an angel; Sister Bernard Ann, who wanted me to be an altar boy; and Mom and Dad, who wanted me to be a babysitter. When others depended on me, I thrived. I gradually became aware that in one way or another we all depend on each other.

After football practice I scrubbed floors at the school to pay the book bill for myself and my brothers and sister. If I finished cleaning the floors before seven o'clock, I would spend time in the gym alone practicing basketball. All the practice helped me make St. Al's team, which played in a Catholic Youth Organization league.

At practice, the gym was alive with the mechanical pounding of basketball dribbling drills. I quickly put on a pair of tennis shoes, eager to get my four-foot-one-inch frame into action.

"Why don't you play on the other side of the court?" Robert motioned with his head to the other side of the gym, which was empty, "with the midgets," he laughed.

"I'm better than you are," I said, knowing I wasn't as good, but with all my practice I could keep up with anyone. He took a shot and missed. I took a shot and missed. We were even.

"Hey, Robert, I hear they're moving onto your street," called Tom, flipping a basketball against the wall to practice his chest pass.

"They'll never last," replied Robert. "The ones on 115th Street were there just a couple weeks."

"Who you talking about?" I asked, but I knew.

"The 'n******.'"

"The WHO?"

"What are you, dumb? 'N******' are moving across the park to E. 116th Street. They shouldn't be here, my parents said, they don't belong here," said Robert.

Young whites got into trouble for stoning the house of a black family that moved into the parish. School yards, public parks, and sometimes the streets became racial battlefields where Italians, Slovenians, Irish and Blacks acted out the frustration and the hostilities of their parents.

Morris, by far the best player on our basketball team, came over from the far side of the gym for a drink of water. He caught the conversation.

"We ain't no 'n*******,' we are colored people, and you better remember that. Maybe we don't want to live near you, 'white cracker,'" Morris spat between his teeth, challenging Robert. He was also the best street fighter.

"We weren't talking about you," Tom looked at Morris and shrugged his shoulders.

"You talking about colored people that way, you talking about me, too," Morris replied. He was angry. I saw a fight coming. I nudged him back to the basketball drill. I remembered Dwight and me playing in the dirt as I watched Morris drive hard towards the basket.

Chapter Twenty-Two

WHEN I CAME HOME after basketball practice, Mom gave me the news. "Your father is in the hospital." Her green eyes were red-rimmed. She held a damp Kleenex to try to stem the congestion of tears.

A crate had slipped off the tailgate of his truck, Mom told me, reinjuring his right knee that had been shot out by machine gun fire on Bouganville in the Solomon Islands.

Mom was fearful. She and Dad were inseparable. The thought of facing any day alone without him was too much for her to bear. She didn't know if he would be home for Christmas. She would have to handle things alone: the six children, the bills, the landlord.

She wiped her eyes and walked over to the kitchen table. She sat on the torn red vinyl-covered chair and lit up a Camel cigarette.

"We'll wait until Dad gets home. Then we will put up a Christmas tree. He may not be able to walk for a while. Why are so many things going wrong?" And then she called all the children together and said: "You kids are going to have to be good."

Later, as she sat at the kitchen table nursing a beer and smoking one cigarette after another, she began to reminisce about her Frank. I was her audience.

It was a Christmas a dozen years earlier. Dad had just been released from Great Lakes Hospital in Chicago. "He was on crutches then," Mom recalled. "I'd hate to see him on crutches again. It was so hard on him. He suffered so much, and he never complained."

She told me of their first holiday together after the war.

They were riding the trolley car. It moved through the holiday traffic along bustling Euclid Avenue. Cleveland's main street glistened in holiday colors. Recently discharged from the Marines, Frank came home with a Purple Heart and a metal plate in his knee. This was his first Christmas home. He was away from the crowded troop carriers riding the waves. No "hit the beach" commands. No machine-gun fire rattling death. The crowded trolley passed a throng of people huddling in front of a brightly-lit Christmas display window. More and more people jammed onto the trolley. Suddenly it all came back to Frank. It wasn't a trolley. It was a troop carrier. He was on it. He was moving toward the beach with his buddies, again tempting sudden death.

"I gotta get out!" He shouted loudly from the back of the trolley. "I gotta get out. Let me out!!"

"I tried to quiet him down." Mom then described how he limped toward the rear door. It did not open. He gave it sharp rap with his crutch. The door relented. He hobbled down to the street, sweating from fear of violent death. She wiped his forehead and sheltered him in her arms as they rode in a taxi home.

"He needs me now," Mom said. "I wish I could be in the hospital in his place."

Mom went to a closet and took out a brown metallic picnic basket. Whenever we moved, that basket was the first thing she put in the car. I never asked about it. I figured it must have some very important stuff in it. Once, out of curiosity I had tried to pry it open, but it wouldn't give. Now Mom gave a strong tug at the lid; it opened with a pop. She took out a stack of letters bound with a piece of white string. "These were letters Dad and I wrote after we first met," she said, with a faint smile.

She untied the string and set the letters on the table. As she began reading, her forehead suddenly furrowed, her eyebrows lowered, she bit her lip and tears started to trickle down her face. I put my hand on her shoulder and smoothed her cheek. She sobbed, whispering, "Dad's hurt. We don't have any money for the rent. We can't buy you kids clothes. We don't have enough money for food. Dennis, this is not the way Dad and I planned our lives. We wanted things to be a lot better for you kids."

She retied the string around the bundle of letters and put them back into the basket. I kissed her on the forehead and then embraced her, holding her until she cried herself to sleep in my arms. I gently woke her and helped her from the chair into bed. I went back to the table. I wanted to learn more about Mom and Dad. I quietly opened the basket. I had a sense of reaching into deep family secrets. I hesitated, wondering what Mom would think if she knew I was reading her letters. I stared at the open basket for a moment. I had to know what was in those letters that made her cry. As I picked up the bundle of notes I could feel my heart beating faster. I loosened the string binding them. They spread out in my hands. I opened up the first envelope with a March, 1945 postmark. I began to read:

U.S. NAVAL HOSPITAL
NEW RIVER, NORTH CAROLINA
MARCH 1, 1945

Dear Virginia,
I can't get over meeting you and falling for you the way I did. I only hope things turn out all right for you back there, and keep yourself in good shape. Don't drink too much. We really did together. If you only knew how much I love you. Well there isn't much I can do about it. Last night on the radio they were singing "Oh How I Miss You Tonight." And I really miss you, Virginia. If you recall I went out with you at every opportunity that you gave me and I'm glad that we both kept our senses. Every time we were together it was like two fuses ready to blow out, and that's unusual as hell.
Love Always, Frankie

U.S. NAVAL HOSPITAL
NEW RIVER, NORTH CAROLINA
MARCH 7, 1945

Dear Virginia,

Have you been down to Gazelle's or Carney's or places? Are you having a good time? Honey, tell me some of the things you do and remember what I told you about everything. If Buddy comes around and you feel different, tell me, don't pull any strings on me, because I'll be looking forward to things. Fair Dinkum, honey?

Well honey, I'll write soon again. I was never much of a long letter writer but maybe you can write me some long letters and I'll be expecting them soon. Honey, don't mind the writing because I've been out of practice. Gung Ho. Give the family my regards.

Love always,
Frankie

MARCH 15, 1945

Dearest Virginia,

I haven't received a letter from you as of yet, but I'm looking forward to it. I hope there isn't anything wrong at home.

Well Honey, I hope my other two letters have reached you. By now you could have wrote me, unless things have changed since I left. Well maybe I can't blame you, and I won't. Ever since I've left you things haven't been the same with me. Look honey, if you don't want to write, well just drop me a card and I'll understand and won't bother you. I guess Buddy must have been back. Well I knew something like that might have happened. Well anyway, I'll admit we had some swell times together, even though I didn't turn out too good for you, well I tried and you can't blame me for trying. Well, I'll be signing off for now, but will send you my new address, Fair Dinkum?

I love you always, Frankie. Gung Ho.

PHILLY
APRIL 11, 1945
(Five days after they were married in Cleveland, Ohio at St. Thomas Acquinas Church.)

My Dearest Darling,
Honey you don't know how much you love someone until you are away from them, and I do love you terribly, for always and always...
I remain your loving husband,
Frankie

APRIL 17, 1945

My Dearest Wife,
Gee honey I miss you so. I just can't help it. I can't change anything, or draw my money till I reach my next station, so honey if it's not too hard to go to work and keep yourself going until I give you the word which shouldn't be too long at least some time next week I hope.
I'll always love you with all my heart forever because I think you'll turn out to be the best wife any man ever had. So I'm saying goodbye for a little while.
I love you always,
Your husband, Frankie

CLEVELAND, OHIO
APRIL 23, 1945

My dearest husband,
Gee honey, it was just like a dream talking to you tonight. Honey I miss you so much it isn't funny but I promise you that I will keep up, so don't worry. I have been worried about you. Talk about sleeping? I just can't. Every night I pray hard for you and Sunday I said a special prayer. Church seemed so funny to me this Sunday. I don't know why but

it was just like we were marching down the aisle to get married and it brought back pleasant memories. I will never forget them and I'm glad that I have them to look back on. Honey, I love you so much I would give a million bucks to be near to you but just talking to you seemed to console me somewhat. At night when I go to bed I hug my pillow and imagine you are near. Honestly honey, I can't wait to see you so I hope you can get that leave.... It's getting late now so I'll be saying good night. Remember I'm praying for you, so please keep your chin up. Just a little lonely tonight, that's all.

Good night honey.
Love, Ginny

U.S. NAVAL TRAINING CENTER
GREAT LAKES, ILL.
APRIL 23, 1045

Well Dearest One,
Honey I did some squaring away and had an allotment made out to you and after all this and that I'll only get $28.00 pay the 4th of May, that isn't much is it? ...Honey, please don't get drunk or anything like that, because I love you and will always till I die. Things will get better later on I promise you.

I remain your loving husband.
Always, Frankie

U.S. NAVAL TRAINING CENTER
GREAT LAKES, ILL.
APRIL 24, 1945

My Dearest Wife,
After last night's call, my morale has gone up. I was terribly worried about you, but just to hear your voice again made me feel a lot better than I did.

You know honey, it takes a while to make friends. I mean new friends, but it doesn't take me long. I've made quite a few already.
I remain your loving husband,
Always, Frankie

U.S. NAVAL TRAINING CENTER
GREAT LAKES, ILL.
APRIL 26, 1945

My Dearest Darling,
Honey just before I go to sleep I keep thinking of you and the times we did have together were swell. I'm sorry about the times I slapped you. When I think about it now, I could just bawl my eyes out. You know honey, never before in my life have I cried in front of any girl. You were different all the way. That's why things turned out the way they did and I'm glad about it. Another thing honey, is you should eat and get your sleep and don't work too hard in that shop. Gee, I wish you didn't have to work, but the way the situation is well there's no other way at the present time and no other thing to do, is there?
Your loving husband for always, Frankie

U.S. NAVAL TRAINING CENTER
GREAT LAKES, ILLINOIS
APRIL 27, 1945

My Dearest Darling,
Honey these 12 days away from you seems like ages already gee I only had hoped we had gotten married sooner. We had a short honeymoon but I was happy, weren't you? Well I sure will be glad when we can be together forever and have a couple of sweet kids around. That's what I'm looking forward to. Instead of starting off with double headers, we will start him off with short beers. Ha Ha.   Great kidder, am I not? Well, anyway honey, we'll see that they get the best. I'll talk more about that

when I see you again. Well I'm signing off for now till again.

   I remain your loving husband,

   Frankie, forever

   PS In about nine months I hope [drawing of a little baby.]

U.S. NAVAL CENTER
GREAT LAKES, ILL.
APRIL 28, 1945

Dearest Darling Wife,

   I've received your letters, so keep 'em coming. It makes me feel darn good inside, when I hear from you. I can just picture you with every word. The Lucky Strike Hit Parade is on now and the song they are singing now is "My Dreams are getting better all the time." Gee I hope so. Honey, things do seem like a dream, don't they? But I'm glad it's true, when I look back at my first leave, it seems like years and meeting you was like I knew you long ago. I just knew we were going to get married. Gee I'm happy about it, honey. I got plenty to look forward to and plenty to work for in the future.

   With love forever, Frankie

U.S. NAVAL TRAINING CENTER
GREAT LAKES, ILL.
MAY 7, 1945

My Dearest Darling Wife,

   I really racked down some doubles but that helped me out, because honey you don't know how I feel inside of me, when I have to leave you. Well honey, the lights are going out soon. They are all standing by here to get the straight dope from Washington on VE day, so I'm saying good night darling and I love you with all my heart.

   I remain your loving

   Husband, Frank

U.S. NAVAL TRAINING CENTER
GREAT LAKES, ILL.
MAY 19, 1945

My Dearest Darling Wife,
    Gee, I'll bet things will be wide open now. I wouldn't give a damn if they closed every place because I'm getting tired of drinking, when I'm with you then I always quarrel with you. I start 'em all and I'm sorry for it later. Well honey, I'm signing off now, with love forever, till again.... I love you and love you and love you forever,
    Frankie

U.S. NAVAL TRAINING CENTER
GREAT LAKES, ILL.
MAY 30, 1945

My Dearest Darling Wife,
    I just got off guard duty now and am now in the barracks concentrating on this letter. As I was walking around the guard post I was thinking how nice it would be to have a place of our own after this war, a couple of kids, but I wouldn't live in Cleveland. I'd like to live in the country somewhere and raise the kids healthy and strong, what do you think? Fair Dinkum. Later on I'm really going to have every extra cent possible, because we will need it.
    Your loving husband, Frankie

U.S. NAVAL TRAINING CENTER
GREAT LAKES, ILL.
JULY 25, 1945

Dear Mrs. Kucinich,
    I don't know exactly how to word what I want to tell you about Frank. Now please don't get alarmed. Well as you know Frank was

feeling pretty good and I don't blame him any because he had to leave a swell wife behind. He was aboard the train to Chicago when one of the Captains wanted to take the whiskey he had, away from him. He didn't want to give it to him, and I wouldn't have either, if I was in his place. I guess your Frankie called the officer some kind of name and they almost came to blows, mind you I said almost.

Well, the Captain took Frank off the train and ran him up to the old man. No matter who is in the right they always take the officer's word for it, and those damn people lie better than anyone can. I hate to tell you this right now. Frank is sitting in the brig. Frank said please not to worry, that it will turn out all right. I think it will.

Sincerely, Helmuth

U.S. NAVAL TRAINING CENTER
GREAT LAKES, ILL.
AUGUST 1, 1945

My Dearest Darling Ginny,
Well, when this is all over with, I just wonder how people will act in a few months or so. There will be a lot of them out of jobs. Automatically a lot of production will stop and people will be laid off by the thousands. Well it sure will be tough for some of them...
Your loving husband, Frankie

U.S. NAVAL TRAINING CENTER
GREAT LAKES, ILL.
AUGUST 15, 1945

My Dearest Darling Ginny,
Today is one day after victory and everyone's happy to think it's all over. It's unbelievable, isn't it? As far as celebrating, I didn't. We had to stand ready to go to Chicago. We're closing as soon as they give us the word today.

Did you do any celebrating? I wish I was with you. Gee, I can wish can't I? I'll bet Cleveland went mad with joy as did the rest of the world. Gee Honey, I'm going mad without you. I just have to see you soon.

Your loving husband, Frankie

U.S. NAVAL TRAINING CENTER
GREAT LAKES, ILL.
AUGUST 22, 1945

My Dearest Wife Ginny,

The days are going pretty fast and I just got another letter from you. I'm glad to hear you finally seen a doctor, it was about time. I'm glad to hear that everything is all right. I only hope I will be out that time to see our kid when it comes. Gee, I only hope it is a girl, then I'll really have something to work for.

Honey, I don't want you to strain yourself on your job. You have to take it easy, from now on. I love you honey so much, I do miss you more and more.

Well I'm signing off for now till tomorrow my dearest.

Frankie

U.S. NAVAL TRAINING CENTER
GREAT LAKES, ILL.
SEPTEMBER 9, 1945

My Dearest Darling Wife,

Gee Honey, news like that really hurts me so much. I just about went crazy. I went to the Red Cross to get a verification from them so I could get home right away.... You just don't know what a shock this is to me. It's all my fault, I guess. Well honey I guess it just had to be that way, but don't worry I love you more and more. It just hurts me not being there. I was going to take off without telling anyone but I would have meant trouble so I didn't. Honey, was there much pain? Gee I hope not, tell me everything, please, honey? I love you so damn much. I planned far ahead, too far ahead, I guess. I took a lot of things for granted.

Well, that's all for now, but God Bless my wife. I love my wife.
Your loving husband, Frankie.

U.S. NAVAL TRAINING CENTER
GREAT LAKES, ILL.
SEPTEMBER, 18, 1945

My Dearest Darling Ginny,
We really quarreled didn't we? But it don't mean a thing because
we love each other, so don't ever let a quarrel get you down. You know why
I quarrel, it's because I have to leave you every damn time. But it
shouldn't be long when I won't have to leave you.
I remain your sweetheart forever, Frankie

U.S. NAVAL TRAINING CENTER
GREAT LAKES, ILL.
SEPTEMBER, 25, 1945

My Dearest Darling Wife,
Gee, I hope I can make it home this weekend, how I long for your
love, Honey. I just have to stand it here. Well I know it shouldn't be too
long. I only hope you are not drinking Honey, because I want you to take
it easy and I only pray that nothing happens to you. God keep my wife safe
forever. Well my darling I'm closing with a heart that is breaking from
not being with you.
I love you so damn much,
Your loving husband, Frankie

U.S. NAVAL TRAINING CENTER
GREAT LAKES, ILL.
SEPTEMBER, 26, 1945

My Dearest Darling Wife:
It won't be long 'till Christmas. Gee, it really seems like years since the last one. Well I'll be 23 on the 23rd of December, an old man. Well, Honey I'm signing off now with all my love to you, so take it easy.
Your loving husband, Frankie.

U.S. NAVAL TRAINING CENTER
GREAT LAKES, ILL.
OCTOBER 12, 1945

My Dearest Darling Wife,
Well Honey, it's hell to be broke but on the outside as a civilian I'll never be broke and that won't be long from now believe me, so stand by. Well I hope, you aren't working too hard. When I get out we can really get started and will be off to a flying start, just like Mobil gas with plenty of pickup. Just keep on loving me as I love you always.
Your loving husband, Frankie

U.S. NAVAL TRAINING CENTER
GREAT LAKES, ILL.
OCTOBER 26, 1945

My Dearest Darling Wife,
I hope you still love me as much as I love you. I just go out of my head when I don't hear from you. Well you don't have to write much anymore. I'll be home for good next month.
Your loving husband, always and forever,
Frankie

Oh, my father had poured out his beautiful heart to his bride, like a songbird singing to the sunrise. I didn't think my father walked out of the dark valley of war just because his luck was good.

I think he knew love was just this side of death. It was not death in Bouganville that made Dad hard. It was life in Cleveland.

I put down the old letters. I walked from the kitchen into the front bedroom. I sat on the edge of the mattress. I turned my face to a corner of the wall, where the plaster was sagging from moisture, and broke a promise I made at Parmadale. I cried.

There were times I wasn't sure if they really loved one another, but now I knew they really did, right from the start. Dad's heart was bursting with love for Mom. He wanted so much for her, for us, for himself. It was all there, in his own handwriting. He and Mom had so many plans after Dad served America: a place of their own, a couple of strong and healthy kids, a life away from the city. What had happened? How did it come to this? Instead of living his dream he was in the hospital, and his family was without a home to call its own. He tried so hard, and all he had to show for it was a mountain of debt, a bad knee and some kidney stones.

Gary and Frank were fighting in the next room. I turned it into a three-way fight and by the time Mom woke up, I was swinging at Frank, yelling, "I'm in charge now, so shut up."

Mom settled the argument by screaming at us to stop it.

I went out of the door to Uptown to try to make some money to buy a few Christmas presents. Even if we weren't going to have a tree, we could have presents.

Chapter Twenty-Three

IT WAS THE WINTER of 1958, and a particularly nasty December night.

I was praying to do my best to make some money. I marched straight ahead, head tilted into the stinging cold, drawing the frayed collar of my thin, dark-blue summer jacket closer to my ears. My right hand maintained a firm grip on the small wooden shoe shine box. The ice-water sidewalks along Uptown between East 105th and East 107th and St. Clair were too much for my Salvation Army bargain shoes. The dampness squished its way through quarter-sized holes in the soles and climbed up the cuffs of my turquoise blue pants. The temperature dropped toward the low twenties. My feet were frozen. My hands were frozen. The cold was forcing me to act. I ducked under a neon Pabst Blue Ribbon sign and cautiously pushed open the door of the tavern.

"Hey, shut da door," said a patron whose back caught a sudden chill. I was momentarily dazzled by the rainbow assortment of bottles stacked on four shelves behind the bar. Some patrons were paying attention to the ebb and flow of beer foam. Others were watching Friday Night at the Fights.

"*N in dis cornuh, way-ying in add a hunnerd 'n seven'tee two pounds...*"

"Hey, mister, wanna shine?"

He didn't look down. He was swinging his arms in the air, watching T.V.

"Hit 'em. Throw the right. The right." His feet were moving.

On to the next pair.

"Hey, mister, wanna shine?"

A fat bartender with a big bow tie and white shirt leaned over the brown wooden bar and interrupted.

"Hey, kid whadduhya doin in heah? Dis heah's a bah."

I was too afraid to talk. Then the bartender saw the shoe shine kit, shook his head and then shrugged

"S'all right kid."

"...the only way to get a decent shave. Gillette."

DING, DING. "Here's the beginning of round three."

A customer tugged at my sleeve. "How much?"

I was so happy I had a customer, I could have shined his shoes for nothing.

"A quarter."

"A quarter? How much did the last guy pay?"

"I just got started."

I had to ask for a quarter. That's what the old black man with the shoe shine stand on E. 105th got. He sold me a shoe shine kit for fifty cents and told me don't take nothing less than a quarter.

"Well, all I got is a dime."

"I'll take it," I said quickly.

"Whatcha doin' kid, workin' yer way through collitch?" the man laughed.

"No, just want to help my mom and dad," I replied as I opened the can of shoe polish with a black cat's paw reaching across the top. I carefully applied the polish, buffed the shoes with a cloth and then stood up.

The man gave me a quarter after all. I was elated. I stepped out of the bar onto the icy sidewalk.   I began to freeze. I forgot to clutch my jacket because I was holding that quarter, making plans to buy Christmas gifts.

I walked one block east on St. Clair Avenue, past the boarded up drug store and theater, past the storefront Baptist church and the discount house, to a porcelain glazed-brick building. I crossed under a green transom with the metal numbers

10712 nailed above the doorway. The narrow hallway's railing was broken. I walked slowly up the steep brown stairs. The steam heat gave me a crisp greeting.

Inside the apartment, the bathroom window was painted black. The toilet gargled dirty water. The bathroom mirror was cracked. Mom said someone was going to have bad luck for seven years. Brown rust streaked the bathtub. The kitchen refrigerator didn't work, nor did the stove. Mom kept some food on a window sill and cooked on an electric skillet. Gary, Frank and I slept on a yellow-ringed, torn mattress. Our bed lay on a stained carpet that covered the paint-chipped front room floor in a few places. Mismatched curtains hung at the front window, which was nailed shut. Newspaper covered the windows in the bedroom where Theresa, Perry and baby Larry snuggled on box springs with Mom and Dad. I knew we had been lucky to find this place.

Mom leading a song at the USO.

Aunt Barbara, Dad and Mom just before their wedding.

A photo from one of Dad's work badges. He often wore his green khaki cap with the visor turned up.

Mom and Dad were married April 6, 1945 at St. Thomas Aquinas Church in Cleveland.

Frank (left) and Gary on the doorstep of 1377 E. 30th St.

The first grade at St. Peter's.

DENNIS KUCINICH   GARY KUCINICH   SANTA

1953

Brother Gary and I with Santa Claus.

Mom and Dad with (left to right) Cousin Richard Norris, my brother Perry and my sister Theresa.

Sister Leona, the Principal of St. Aloysius School.

A holiday visit to Aunt Betty's and Uncle Lenny's where music notes were ever present decorations.

Me and Spotty.

My first speech, at the freshman induction at St. John Cantius, September 1960.

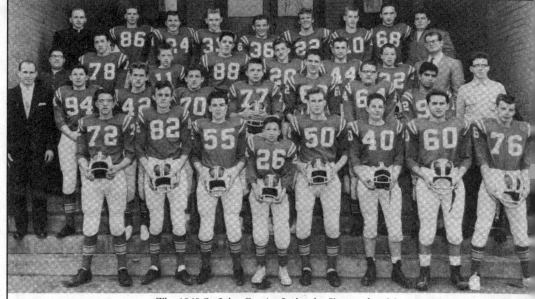

The 1960 St. John Cantius Jayhawks. I'm number 26.

Top row: Athletic Director, Fr. Duda; Bob Janas; Tom Holz; Dennis Kalemba; Jim Benedict; Dave Ostrowski; Mike Bober; John Wessel; Tom Stachowski.

Third row: Manager, Dennis Kopin; John Sullivan; Kevin Flanagan; Jack Kelly; Bob Kwiatkowski; Chuck Parete; John Greer; Assistant Coach Joe Kiraly.

Second row: Head Coach, John Chapon; Steve Klosowski; Tony Galuszka; John Kaczor; Rich Wolski; Lou Szeliga; Ken Lammermeier; Bill Quinones; Manager, Gil Flemming.

First row: Leo Gelsinger; George Varga; Joe Gilson; Dennis Kucinich; Tom Tindira; Lynn Lustig; Jim Stofey; George Sigler.

FOOTBALL

Memories are made of this. It is something our cheerleaders and our players won't forget. The joyous times and the excitement which the games provided will linger in our memories forever. Through each game, no matter if it be to a victory or a defeat, we were always steadfast and determined to the end. Although we were disappointed at times, we always looked at the best side; the effort our boys put into the game, the enthusiasm of the cheerleaders and the fans, and the fun we had in the stands together as one closesly-knit group. Our Seniors shall look forward to backing future Cantius' teams and we hope that their seasons may be just as happy and memorable as ours.

FOOTBALL SCORES

St. John Cantius	Opponent	
14	0	Our Lady of Lourdes
0	24	Newbury
16	32	St. Stanislaus
20	28	Beachwood
0	56	Elyria Catholic
6	54	Gilmour
6	46	Chanel
8	32	Norwalk St. Paul
14	36	Lorain St. Mary
6	48	Stuebenville Catholic

The 1961 St. John Cantius junior varsity. I'm number ten. Dan Backus is number 22. Richard Racela is number 32. The Coach (second row, far right) Peter Pucher.

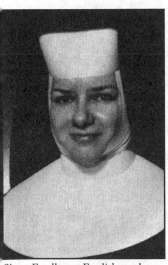

Sister Estelle my English teacher at St. John Cantius High School.

Coach Peter Pucher.

Dr. Javier Lopez.

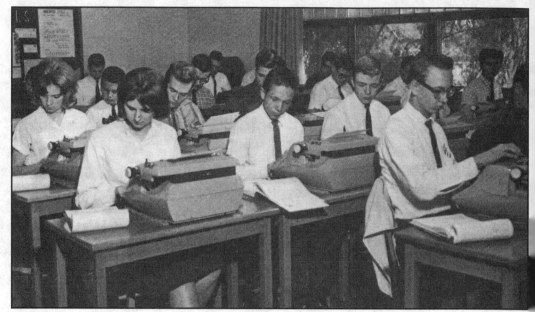

Typing class where I learned a very useful skill. I am in the center of the picture.

Working on the school yearbook with John Zapp, who became a priest.

The St. John Cantius debating team.

A picture of Dad as he saw me leave with my class for my first trip to Washington, November, 1963.

I played the lead in our senior class play, "The Mouse that Roared."

My senior picture.

The Reverend Father Francis Szudarek, pastor of St. John Cantius Church.

Graduation Day, 1964.

Chapter Twenty-Four

THE ENVELOPE ARRIVED a few days before Christmas. It was stamped "Certified Mail." The return address: Helen Lyons, Clerk of the Cleveland Municipal Court, 601 Lakeside Avenue, Cleveland, Ohio. Mom looked at the notice briefly, took a deep breath and suddenly looked exhausted.

"I'm going to rest for a while."

When she left the room I looked at the piece of paper she placed atop an ashtray.

"NOTICE TO VACATE PREMISES"

Why did the mail always bring bad news? We were going to have to move again. At age 12 I was getting much too familiar with the jargon in the legal confetti overflowing from our mail box.

State of Ohio (County of Cuyahoga) ss
(City of Cleveland)
Mr. A to Z
vs
Frank J. Kucinich

A gentle reminder.... Perhaps you did not receive our first letter.... Your account has evidently been overlooked...this bill is due and should be paid immediately.... We have verified your employment.... Unless you contact this office within 24 hours, our client's attorney will start suit and garnish your wages.... The undersigned will seek an order of attachment—order in aid of execution—to subject your personal earnings to the payment of the claim as set forth herein...I will commence action against you with garnishment proceedings....To the Bailiff of the Cleveland Municipal Court—Greeting: You are commanded to notify Frank Kucinich that he has been sued.

WITNESS, Clerk of said Court and the seal thereof at the City of

(Seal) Cleveland.

Those people who send these notices never know what it is like. How would they like it if their family was sued or put out on the street?

I started to get stomach cramps. That sulphurous smell rose from my belly to my mouth and made me sick. Evicted again! I wanted to stay in this mice-and-roach-infested place. It was our home. Mom wasn't feeling well. Dad was in the hospital and out of work. Things were becoming complicated again. I walked into the front room where my siblings were wrestling and called over the din, "Shut up. Mom's crying."

On Christmas morning my brothers and sister were in the front room playing with toys that I helped buy with my shoeshine money. They were oblivious to the upcoming move. They explored the flat world map of the living room floor with plastic locomotives routed along the cracks in the floor. Frank and Gary launched balsa airplanes which spiraled beneath the hanging plaster before they crash-landed.

If we'd had any other place, we would have left the first time the landlord told us to go. If Dad was home, we could have acted quickly on the next demand. We could have avoided men in suits coming a few days later and just carrying our stuff out the door. I gave one of the men a dirty look as I grabbed the picnic basket holding Mom and Dad's letters from atop a box he was carting away. Dad was still in the hospital. We were out of luck and out on the curb: Mattresses were piled on the couch, chairs were upside down and every-which-way, boxes and bags of tattered clothes, old pictures, a lampshade, plastic dishes. It was all set down on the curb like wreckage strewn over the sidewalk. People passed by. Some gawked from their cars. Others walked up and picked through the clutter and rags like it was a ghetto fire sale, like those of us sitting on the apartment stoop were invisible. A few people walked past the whole mess. They had seen it all before.

Uncle Joe once told me that if we were ever in trouble and needed help, to call him. I hadn't been able to take him up on that offer before, when he was in trouble and needed help of his own. Whenever Aunt Betty and I would go to visit Uncle Joe at the prison farm, he would ask us to always bring cigarettes and fried shrimp or chicken. The system had a slight lead on Uncle Joe, but he was catching up. Once released from serving time for theft, he had a regular job, hanging awnings. Joe was good-looking and he knew it, a real ladies' man. He always had beautiful women on his arm, including Aunt Gerrie.

"Hello? Uncle Joe? This is Dennis. We need help."

He arrived with a car and a small trailer and helped us haul everything away. Mom sat in the front seat with her picnic basket of memories. The youngest kids went to the backseat. Gary, Frank and I stood arguing in the open trailer amidst the wobbling furniture. We were arguing about the next move. Joe's car started and the trailer lurched forward.

The want ads led us a mile east to Brackland Avenue. It was a predominantly Jewish neighborhood with Jewish bakeries, delicatessens, newspapers and landladies.

Our new landlady felt sorry for us. She had travelled a much rougher road. She had a big scar on her arm. Numbers were tatooed near her shoulder.

"I vas in concenzentrayshun camp. Nazis did this," she introduced herself. She pointed to the scar on her arm she had received a few years before I was born.

"And they did this," she said defiantly. She lifted up her blouse halfway to the ribs, displaying a wicked buzz-saw scar cut deep in her side. "I haff no family. Nazis kill my family. I only one get out alive."

She suddenly changed the conversation and began pointing out the attractive features of our new apartment.

"You like. I paint new. This room. That room. Nice."

The lemon-yellow paint was made brighter by the sun that shone through the bank of windows in the kitchen. The new apartment had one more room than the St. Clair Avenue place, and we were only a twenty-five-minute walk from St. Aloysius. We wouldn't have to change schools. I smiled at this well-kept, beautiful refuge. I prayed we would stay here for a long time.

Our new landlady liked children. She invited us to her apartment. She served us something called bagels and lox. "I vill make good Jews out of you in no time at all," she exclaimed with a laugh.

I was so glad I could continue at St. Aloysius that I didn't mind the walk. I now lived closer to my secret love, Nancy. She had blond hair and blue eyes. Her glasses made her look intelligent. She invited our seventh-grade class to a party at her home. "Sunday Best." I had only the one pair of pants, a twenty-five-cent Salvation Army special: turquoise with black-stitched piping. It was my all-occasion pair. I wore them with a white shirt and a black string tie. My first slow dance was one of the scariest moments of my life. I held Nancy close. She didn't say anything about the pungent smell of stale after-shave coming up from my feet. I had poured heavy doses of the blue liquid into both shoes to kill the rotten odor from the water-damaged soles. As the TV commercial said, "There's something about an Aqua Velva Man."

The following day at school, some of my classmates were talking about the dance when I heard my name mentioned.

"And he wears the same pair of pants every day; to school, to church, to parties," one girl said. So what? I never really thought about it. As a matter of fact it made getting dressed in the morning pretty easy.

"They are so funny-looking," said another classmate.

"Why do you wear the same pants to school every day, Dennis?"

The question was asked in a quiet voice, but I heard it. I also heard the ripple of laughter which grew to a stream. I didn't turn to face the laughs. I just stared straight ahead at the blackboard, but I could feel my face stinging. Anger and hurt brought bad thoughts. I kept looking straight ahead. I didn't want to look at anyone else. I got up from my seat. I was going to go home. I wasn't going to come back. They could all go to Hell. Who cares if I have only one pair of pants for school? Some schools have uniforms. Maybe this was my uniform.

A hand touched my elbow as I walked out of the room. I turned and looked into Sister Leona's puzzled eyes.

"What's wrong with you, young man? Are you ill?"

I did not respond.

"What's the matter? You can tell me."

I didn't even know how to tell it. The hurt started coming up and catching my breath.

"Come, sit down."

I went back to her office. She brought me a glass of water. I fought back tears. I told her.

She looked surprised and said, "Remember, it is not what you wear on the outside, it is what you wear on the inside that counts. Never be ashamed of what you don't have."

"It's my only pair of pants. If I had another, I would wear them, but this is it."

"Well, look at me," she smiled, as her hands demonstrated her black habit, "I wear the same clothes all the time, too."

I waited in her office for a time. Sometime later, I went back to my classroom, with her reassurance. Later, I learned from one of my friends that Sister told the class it was not Christ-like to make fun of people, and that it had better stop immediately. The next day Sister Leona asked me to come to the convent after school.

"Please take these boxes home." She pointed to four cardboard boxes. "And don't tell anyone, except your mother and father. Don't open them until you get home."

I promised to keep the secret. I got some help carrying the boxes all the way to our apartment. When I got into the hallway of our building and opened one box, there was a blue pair of pants, a black pair, a brown pair and a tan pair. There were shirts, short-sleeves and long-sleeves, sweaters and jackets. There were enough boys' clothes of different sizes in the boxes for Frank, Gary and me. Sister Leona was an angel. Mom was happy.

"How nice. How very nice of her," she said.

When Dad got home he looked at the box of clothes and said, "What the hell is this, charity? We don't want charity, take it back."

I felt like I had been hit by lightning. Mom and Dad argued. Mom won. We kept the clothes. Later on in the week, Sister Leona handed me a book, *St. Joan* by Shaw.

"I thought you might like this," she said, smiling.

She had checked off some lines which read, "Dressing up don't fill empty noodle." I didn't understand.

"It isn't the clothes you wear outside that make you who you are, Dennis. It is the clothes you wear inside. And Dennis, don't ever worry about what you don't have, God always provides," she said.

I don't think Sister Leona treated me any differently than she treated any of the other students at St. Al's, but she was the second person who saved my life. I had always held the hierarchy of the Church in awe: mitered bishops and red-robed cardinals. Yet it was nuns like Sister Leona, in plain black and white garb, whose practical application of spiritual principles in everyday life affected me deeply and kept open my heart in the hard city.

Sister Leona taught us lessons about spiritual matters that were not in the book.

"Boys and girls, I have to leave the room for a moment. I want you to read quietly until I return; all right?"

"Yes Sister," the class responded as one.

Of course the minute she was out of the room, bedlam erupted. When she returned there was Heaven to pay. She suddenly appeared much larger as she straightened her stout figure and expressed grave disappointment.

Without missing a beat she said, "OK, boys and girls, take out a pen and paper and copy this poem."

Her hands flowed with practiced grace across the white-smudged blackboard, writing the verse in short sentences.

"Now I want all of you to copy this poem and memorize it."

There was a lot of grumbling, but we had no choice. I took out some lined paper, removed a leaky blue cartridge pen from the desk and began to write down the words from the blackboard:

God's Minute
I have only just a minute
Only sixty seconds in it
Forced upon me, can't refuse it
Didn't seek it, didn't choose it.
But it's up to me to use it.
I must suffer if I lose it
Give account if I abuse it.
Just one tiny little minute,
But eternity is in it.

"What does this poem mean, boys and girls?" Sister asked. No one raised a hand. Her eyes twinkled knowingly at the resistance.

"You write things down and you don't think about them?" her eyes narrowed.

She was very patient, and we were very slow to respond.

"What it means is that you are responsible for your acts. You are accountable for every minute of your lives. If you waste time, you can never get it back. No one is going to watch you every second of the day to see if you are wasting or misusing God's minute. You have to be good, even when people are not watching. When you leave this classroom, I want you to be smarter. I also want you to be good Catholics. So tonight when you go home, I want you to copy this poem fifty times and hand it in tomorrow."

FIFTY TIMES! This could take all night, I thought. Everyone was very upset about the punishment. We had to do it because if we complained at home, we would have some explaining to do to our parents. If we didn't have it done by morning, who knows what else awaited us? As I wrote '*God's Minute*' over and over, I absorbed deeply the message about the spiritual consequences of each moment. Every moment offered an opportunity for learning something, for making a choice about doing the right thing. This awareness affected my studies, sports, serving mass, guard work, cleaning after school—everything, even moving.

We had fallen far behind in paying bills. It seemed we received a notice from the court every few days.

When Dad's old car died, he tried to get a loan to pay off all of our debts and to purchase another used car. But our family's credit was bad. Dad had no collateral, no cosigner. He sometimes kiddingly referred to his kids as "my only assets, but no one will take you." He visited banks, savings and loan companies and finance companies, but everywhere he got the same answer: "NO." He was told he was a "high risk." He paid what bills he could and he borrowed money from his friends so we could eat soup, bread, bologna and cheese sandwiches.

When his paycheck came in, there was a line waiting and sometimes a garnishment notice too. His boss told him the company didn't like the extra bookkeeping and if the garnishments didn't stop, he might lose his job. He had one of the safest driving records of any truck driver. He was good at driving a truck. He wasn't so good driving away the bill collectors. He felt trapped. He was working hard five days a week, but the bill collectors were working six days a week. He was being chased by garnishments, eviction notices, lawsuits on promissory notes…everything was overdue and he had eight mouths to feed. Mom was feeling the pressure. I was afraid she would have another breakdown and then our family would be split up again.

Mom began to enter all kinds of contests, sometimes with my help, sending in hundreds of entries. In the opportunity factory of our apartment we would clip contest coupons together from newspapers and magazines, and I would deliver them to the Post Office. Mom bought Irish Sweepstakes, church raffle tickets and multi-colored punch-cards on which she pencil-punched the little holes in search of windows marked twenty-five cents to a dollar.

Mom and Dad also hoped to get a settlement for Frank getting hit again by a car.

There was a feeling of excitement that our ship would soon come in, and we watched every day for the postman, to see if this was the day our ship would sail out of his big leather pouch. The arrival of the mail was often the biggest event at our apartment. Dad often talked of more money arriving for his war-injured knee, or maybe we would finally get that award from Workman's Compensation for a crate that crushed his leg. He and Mom waited and waited for this golden cargo. We all watched every day for the postman. He always delivered, but our ship was still not in sight.

As the oldest of six children, I had to try to help. I searched garbage cans on pick-up days for deposit bottles and was sometimes able to bring a few dollars home. I looked deep into iron grates along commercial districts for loose change, sold magazine subscriptions, carried groceries from the A&P for elderly ladies, shined shoes, distributed political and real estate leaflets at a penny a sheet; swept the storeroom at Martha's Delicatessen and stacked bottles in exchange for an occasional quarter or payment in bottle caps, redeemable for hockey tickets which I resold. The job at St. Aloysius was a big help, too, because it covered the Kucinich children's book bill.

There were many ways to make money in the city, but there were never enough ways. The doctors, lawyers, television repairmen, furniture store owners, loan company agents and landlords did not get paid soon enough.

Mom and Dad held the family together, though forces were building from every direction inside and outside the apartment. They struggled mightily to preserve the family no matter what. Frank had his Ginny, Ginny had her Frank, they had their children and we had a mother and a father. What more could parents and children ask for? No matter what came: evictions, we were without a home; garnishments, we were without money; repossessions, we were without a car and household goods.

I learned not to put my faith in material things, because they tended to disappear. Instead it was more important to be with each other than to have something. At mass I thought about spirit in the material world. It seemed that life's department store carried so much illusory merchandise, so many things we didn't really need. Even when we were almost stripped bare, I learned to persevere. Tomorrow would come with new possibilities and sometimes the same problems.

Eventually a loud knock came on the door of our Brackland Avenue apartment. The man showed Mom his badge and handed her some papers. It was an eviction notice. Mom was having trouble hearing what he was saying because of all the noise we were making in the front room. We were three months behind on our rent. There were a few holes in the wall of the apartment that hadn't been there when we first moved in. I guess we were all pretty rough on the place.

We were on the streets of the city once again. No one wanted to rent to a family with six children. We couldn't afford to make a rent deposit. Sickness followed our family; bill collectors followed the doctor bills. Eviction notices immediately followed discovery of so many people in one apartment. They also followed when we couldn't afford to pay the rent, so we kept moving. I made many friends in the city at a very early age. Sadly, I left many friends behind.

This moving business felt like being inside a large top, trying to balance myself while images of house and neighborhoods spun by faster and faster until it all became a blur. The velocity increased with each move. The more we moved, the more we spun, and the more the images blurred. After awhile, all of us were just dizzy and confused. Urban nomads, we spun from house to house, apartment to apartment, neighborhood to neighborhood.

I dreaded each move. I tried to learn lessons from each one, though I could never learn enough to stop the next move. I didn't know enough to stop fast-buck artists from chiseling Dad's income. I didn't know how to stop used car salesmen and television repairmen from suing Dad for not paying for things that didn't work. I didn't know how to get Mom to quit buying multiple insurance policies on everyone in the family. I wished I knew how to discourage Mom and Dad from walking into a local tavern in the evening to buy drinks for themselves and their friends. I once overhead Uncle Frank and Aunt Marion talking about this; Uncle Frank said Mom liked to have a good time and she had been drinking and smoking since she was a kid. Marian said they should have been home more. I'm sure there were many opinions about how we got into so much trouble. I knew enough not to ask any questions.

Chapter Twenty-Five

FROM 2519 CARNEGIE Avenue, to 10650 St. Clair down-stairs, then upstairs, back to 2519 Carnegie Avenue, to East 72nd Street, to E 72nd Place, to 1377 East 30th Street, to a 1948 Dodge, to E. 33rd, off Perkins Avenue; to Uncle Pete's, to the car, on the edge of the industrial valley, to East 101st Street, to Koom Frank's on 8110 Finney Avenue, to Uncle Frank's on Kirton Avenue, to Parmadale, to Uncle Paul's in Millington, Michigan; to Hough and Crawford apartment # 1, to Hough and Crawford apartment #2, to 10712 St. Clair Avenue, to Brackland Avenue, to...? I was twelve and I knew very few people lived this way.

We drove along St. Clair Avenue in an 'as is' Mercury Dad had purchased for $65. I sat in the back seat wishing everyone would be quiet so I could read the want ads of the *Plain Dealer*, the *Cleveland Press* and the *Cleveland News*. Dad gave me strict instructions to find something on the East Side, "Apartments to rent, children allowed."

"Dad, there doesn't seem to be any places on the East Side," I said.

"Sure, there are plenty of places. There's places all over this side of town. Keep looking."

I checked "Rooms for Rent," "Apartments for Rent" and "Houses for Rent." Nothing fit. Either the places were too small or they did not accept children. "Dad, here, look for yourself. There's nothing on the East Side."

He pulled the car to the side of the road, annoyed. He grabbed the paper from me and began to read the columns I had circled.

Dead silence. All eyes watched Dad as he read. We hadn't been driving around for more than a few hours but we were all tired. This car was smaller and we were bigger. This would not be a good car to sleep in. No way.

Dad finished looking at the papers. He tossed them into the back seat.

He looked at Mom. "Enh, the kid's right. Nothing on the East Side for us."

"What are you going to do, Frank?" Mom was impatient. Maybe the baby she had been carrying for seven months was restless. If we had trouble finding a place rent with six kids, what would happen when Mom had her seventh? Would someone rent to a good Catholic family?

Everyone was quiet for a moment. All we could hear was the sound of trucks rumbling down St. Clair. Dad put his hand up to his face and rubbed his eyes, then he scratched his head. He was beginning to sweat. Things were getting uncomfortable in the car. I picked up the newspapers again and began to check the ads for another part of town that was foreign to us, except for the brief stay with Uncle Frank. I had never thought about living on the West Side because we always lived on the East Side. When you lived on the East Side, the West Side was a different world. We imagined that the people over there looked different and talked differently. If it wasn't for Uncle Frank and Aunt Marion, it would be easy to think that all West Siders were strange. Here I was, looking at columns of newsprint, hoping to find a place to live in a strange land.

"Dad, Dad! Here's one. Listen to this. This may be the one!"

"Come on, come on, kid, cut the noise, what is it?"

"WEST SIDE. HOUSE FOR RENT. SINGLE FAMILY HOME. SIX ROOMS AND BATH. CHILDREN, PETS, OK.

Wow! Dad, this sounds like the place. Will you call this number? Will you?"

Dad took the newspaper, went to a telephone in a nearby bar and came out with a smile on his face.

"The place is still available. I told him we had five kids and a dog. He said OK, but we have to go over there right now."

As the car sped across the Lorain-Carnegie bridge over the Cuyahoga River, the Cleveland skyline to the northeast was in bold relief against the twilight. Southeast from the bridge, I could see a fire burning away the inky blue night. It was that torch, that hypnotic light climbing, falling, drifting, billowing, shining yellow, green and blue. That same torch which lit up the sky when we slept in the car parked alongside the industrial valley. Things were going to be OK. Suddenly I felt good. I was sure everything was going to work out fine.

2163 W. 73rd Street became our new home. Dad borrowed money from the Teamster's Credit Union to buy furniture and to help pay the doctor bills for our new sister, Beth Ann.

"Don't anyone ever tell me about the Teamsters," Dad told Mom, as she put Beth Ann onto a bassinette in the kitchen. "We needed help and they were the only ones who came through."

Because of the Teamsters, the nine of us and our dog had a house. It was located within smelling distance of Cleveland's stockyards on a well-travelled north-south truck path. Our gravel front yard was very close to the street. We didn't have a back yard. But there were plenty of alleys in our new neighborhood, places to play hide and seek, stickball, football and homerun derby when teenagers weren't charging down the bricks with their souped-up four-on-the-floor Chevvies with the quads or Fords with bubble skirts. When we tired of playing in the alley, we would walk a mile and a half to Navy Park Recreation Center where we could play basketball, football and baseball. When I worked up the courage, I put on boxing gloves. It was so nice to have a new home in a neighborhood where we could spend all of our time out on the streets.

"Son, why aren't you in school?" the druggist at Roskey and Obert's asked.

"We're, uh, new in the neighborhood," I said as I sipped on a cherry coke that was almost but not quite as good as the ones Seymour Cohen made at his Broadway-Harvard drug store.

"How old are you?"

"Thirteen."

"Come on, you're not thirteen years old."

"Sure, in a few months."

"And where are you going to go to school?" he asked as he cleaned out some soda glasses.

"I don't know. We've been here a week or so. I guess we'll have to find one, g'bye."

It bothered me that we didn't start school immediately. I was afraid I would have to go to summer school. I was worried that the other children in our family might be put back for missing so many classes, but we were new to this neighborhood and we had to get the feel of it before we began school. I really liked living in this house.

The nearest Catholic school was St. Colman's. After we had been in the neighborhood nearly two weeks, I went to the convent and met the principal, Sister Agnes Joseph, and told her we wanted to go to school there.

"How many children would like to attend?"

"Well, let's see. There's Frank, Gary, Theresa, Perry, Larry, no, not Larry, he's too young, and me."

"Why, that certainly is a big family."

"My mom just had another one, a little girl. Sister," I changed the subject quickly, "I scrubbed floors at St. Aloysius to pay for our tuition. Sister Leona told me I did a pretty good job. I want to know if you'll give me a job here scrubbing floors. I really want to go to Catholic school Sister, what do you think?"

The proposition took her by surprise. She looked at me for a long minute. Her lower lip went up as she cocked her head and then she laughed.

"Oh, so you are an industrious one? Does anyone else help scrub floors?"

"Naw, they're too little. Well, Sister, how about it?"

I couldn't afford to beat around the bush. I wanted to go to Catholic school, to serve mass, to play basketball and do all the other things I did at St. Aloysius, but it was all up to Sister Agnes Joseph.

"I'm going to have to give it some thought," she said, and my heart began to beat fast. She studied me for about five seconds. "Yes."

"Yes!"

"By the way, what did you say your name is?"

"Kucinich, Dennis Kucinich. Actually, it is Dennis John Patrick Kucinich. 'Patrick' is my confirmation name. My mother is Irish."

"Patrick?! Dennis, we have an electric floor polisher here. Do you think you can handle the machine?"

"Sure I can. Just give me the chance. I'll do it."

An electric floor polisher? What was an electric floor polisher?

"It's pretty frisky," Sister said.

She decided to try me out for the job, right then and there. "Come with me for a minute."

The floor polisher was sitting on the dark linoleum floor. The handle came up to my neck but all I had to do, according to the instructions, was to press down on the handle. I could manage. No sweat.

"OK, go ahead."

I squeezed the handle. The polisher took off across the floor with me holding on tight. It skidded toward a large, open stairwell, careening away along with my hopes for a Catholic school education.

"Let it go! Let it go!" Sister called out urgently, just as I was about to pitch over the edge. I let it go. It stopped. My heart was pounding and I was out of breath. Well, so much for Catholic school. Let's see, Gary, Frank, Theresa and Perry would go to Gordon Elementary and I would go to West Junior High. Oh, well I tried.

Sister Agnes Joseph came up to me. She was out of breath, too, but from laughing. Not a mean laugh, but the kind of laugh that told me that maybe she didn't think much of my electric floor polishing debut.

"Dennis, you are going to do just great scrubbing and polishing the floors, but you better do it on your hands and knees. It takes longer, but it's safer."

The next day I was introduced to the class. Most of my classmates were a head taller than those at St. Aloysius. If it was something in the air or food, it presented some interesting possibilities for me. I also understood why Sister Agnes Joseph liked me. I was one of the only students in the class shorter than her.

While I was scrubbing the floors, crawling, methodically waxing, wiping and polishing, I started to think about the future. I stopped thinking about being a priest—I'd lost my vocation in sex education class. I wasn't sure I wanted to be a truck driver. There were so many possibilities for the future. I wanted to get started early, so I could really be good at something.

Chapter Twenty-Six

DAD HAD BOXED IN the Marines. He said boxing was in his blood. I watched boxing on television and knew the names of every champ. I read Joe Palooka comics about a boxer who helped people. I heard a lot about Joe Louis and Rocky Marciano, and I wanted to be a boxer. I had to face it: there was some violence inside me. The violence I witnessed at home percolated in my hands and feet and my stomach. I was ready to unleash it, but not in the street. I wasn't that tough or mean or big. What do you do when you are a kid and you feel violent? Do you look in your neighborhood for people to beat up? Do you vandalize? Do you just plain raise hell? I didn't want to do any of that. But I figured if I was going to win in life, I had to learn how to fight and learn to fight to win. There was no better place to get the training I needed than in the boxing ring.

I had it figured out: I knew all boxing champs start early, so I would start early. Every person who became a champ knew they would be a champ someday. Someday I could be the world's fly-weight champ. If I could channel into boxing all the violence I witnessed, I'd be a champ in no time flat. I'd knock them all out! I decided to train every day. Work my way up the ladder, one opponent after another.

I boxed my shadow.

Puffs of frost vanished over my head. I walked to Navy Park Gym carrying my Salvation Army boxing gloves and sang a few Irish songs along the route.

Navy Park's boxing instructor was Italian. His toothless smile spilled from flattened lips. A fringe of curly black hair hung over his punch-docked ears, a crooked nose separated soft brown eyes. His arms were solid. He crossed in front of me and tried to flip my hands into a boxing position.

"Hey? Ya wanna box? Ah, let's see ya box! Put 'em up." I stood there like a punching bag while his hands moved toward my chest.

"C'mon, put 'em up. Ya gotta hold yer hands up dare like dis if ya wanna be a fighta." Big, firm Everlast boxing gloves hung unchallenged on a nearby hook. A few little punchers were already sparring, dancing on a blue mat to the "Jab, jab, jab, jab. Left, left, left, left," choreography.

I was introduced to the other boxers.

"OK, Dennis, yer stance, yer feet, put 'em like dis." I spread my left foot slightly ahead of the right. The Italian pushed me off balance.

"Lose yer balance and yu'll get killed! Plant dose legs. Ya gotta stay on yer toes if ya wanna fight."

The stance. The feet. The jab. Timing. Bobbing. Weaving. After six weeks practicing the mechanics of boxing I was ready for my first bout. Tom had a long reach. He didn't watch where his arms swung. We fought to a curtsy…and a draw.

Jim was taller and heavier. He stepped into the ring and I put up my guard. In the time I thought through putting up my arms, standing just right, crouching like a pro, his first punch hit me squarely between the eyes. I couldn't see. My head went numb. He hit me again. I saw stars. I was eating his leather glove. I had to do something quick or I was dead.

"You win," I declared, my eyes blurred, my head hurting. I stepped back, my guard still up, before he did any more damage. The Italian took me aside.

"Hey, kid, ya don't wanna box. Hey, look at me. Look at me. I boxed. Know what happened?" He tugged on his ears, nose and slapped his cheek, as if he was giving secret signals. "Got my brains beat out. Now I can't do nothin' else."

I was listening to the voice of a thousand punches.

"Ya want dis to happen? Ya ain't gonna make it as a boxer kid, sorry."

I was heartbroken. I wanted to be a boxer more than anything in the whole world. I put my gloves in the gym bag. It was snowing outside. I walked home watching the whiteness break in flurries from the night sky. My dreams were swept along with the swirling snow.

My boxing coach was wrong. I *had* become a fighter. It wasn't that my opponent was too big; the Navy Park arena was too small, so I lost. The fight for survival takes place in a ring which could be at least as large as a city. In time, my rage was transformed, redirected. I had a fighter's instincts. I knew there were many fights ahead. I did not yet know who I would be fighting or what or whom I would be fighting for. I didn't even realize I was in training, but I most definitely was: survival training. I needed only the courage to get back into the ring.

Chapter Twenty-Seven

I CONQUERED MY disappointment about boxing through basketball. I made guard on St. Colman's CYO lightweight team. Most of my classmates and teammates were Irish. Names like Cooney, Donnelly, Flynn, Gallagher, Kilbane, McCarthy, McNamara, Moran and O'Malley were common at St. Colman's. My best friend was a Philippine-American named Rich Racela. He lived with his twelve brothers and sisters on Lorain Avenue. His father was a chef at a downtown hotel. I ate at Rich's house frequently. After dinner Mrs. Racela brought the devout Catholic family together in the living room to pray the rosary with the priest on the radio. Every Sunday the Racelas took up an entire pew at church. I usually went to Sunday mass with Rich.

After church we would board a public transit railway located in a valley behind St. Colman's schoolyard and set out on a thirty-cent round trip to discover more of the city, first to the westernmost limits and then back towards downtown. Rich and I watched our window reflections flicker against multi-story factory districts where steel was fabricated, glass was cut, greeting cards were designed, and clothing was made. We saw dozens of small machine and manufacturing shops huddling around the larger buildings. The "Big Ben" face of the West Side Market tower at West 25th Street was frowning the wrong time as the train zipped over the Cuyahoga River and the warehouse district below. Smoke drifted from the steel mills and the refineries to the southeast. Sure enough, that torch was burning over the flats, against a blue sky.

The train slowed, the wheels screeched at the rails and a voice called out: "Union Terminal, Cleveland Public Square, exit please."

Cleveland Union Terminal was one of the largest passenger depots in America. In the grand concourse, beneath Cleveland's largest building, stood the 712-foot Terminal Tower. Passengers marched to the call of the uniformed railroad scheduler, who chalked up arrivals and departures on a big board. A policeman gently nudged sleeping rail passengers and homeless men from the train station benches. The stench of urine and stories of knife attacks in the public restrooms made visiting them a real danger, but when you've got to go, you've got to go.

Our city tour led from the wide ramps of Union Terminal to Cleveland's Public Square. The heart of downtown Cleveland was empty, except for pigeons squatting on General Moses Cleaveland's proud cast-iron pose on the southwest quadrant. A robust Tom Johnson, Mayor of Cleveland from 1901 to 1909, sat facing the city from the northwest quadrant, his back to the Cleveland Electric Illuminating building. Henry George's "Progress and Poverty" was held firmly in his right hand. Anguished soldiers cast immortally in determined combat surrounded the Soldiers' and Sailors' Monument on the southeast quadrant.

The Square was bordered by department stores, restaurants, office buildings, a federal courthouse, a hotel, banks and the Old Stone Church. We walked north across a long mall which led to a view of Lake Erie and the Cleveland Municipal Stadium, where I went to seven baseball games for free. The *Cleveland Press* and the Cleveland Indians baseball club sponsored a program where students with a straight-A average were given seven sets of box seat tickets. Dad and I became very close during some of those games. We talked about everything, baseball and football and how nice it was being together.

Rich and I walked to the steps of Cleveland City Hall, assessing the large pillars that looked like giant arms holding up the building.

We returned to Public Square and the Terminal Tower, where a ride to the top cost twenty-five cents. If you had the money it was worth it, because from the forty-second floor observation deck the people on the ground looked like ants. A person could feel really tall standing at the top of that Tower. If you spent most of your life dozens of stories above the ground, you would think the little human-type creatures down there really were ants.

Some Sundays, we headed east with the train, past old factories, old neighborhoods and abandoned houses. Black persons got on and off only at East Side stops.

Rich and I exited at a stop called "University Circle" where we roamed through a natural history museum and the art museum. The Cleveland Museum of Art was the best place in town for a kid with thirty cents for a rapid ride, especially because of the mummy and the men in armor who just stood still, holding maces and axes, ready to smash anybody who touched the paintings.

I wanted to be a painter, too, but there was one thing I quickly learned in art class. I couldn't draw.

Until I began riding the Rapid Transit, I thought I knew Cleveland well. Now there was an entire city to explore. It was a city much larger than the blocks where I lived, a city that was interesting, exciting and funny. All you had to do was put your money in the fare box and the day's adventure would begin.

I liked living on West 73rd Street. I had my own bed for the first time since I was three. Not that I minded sharing with my brothers, but it's hard to be nice to them when they are sticking an elbow in your side or shoving smelly feet in your face.

Mom was happy; Dad was working regularly. Then, for some reason, we started to slide backwards. Fast.

First we fell behind on gas and electric bills. The roof of the house was leaking. Every time it rained I did the pots and pans routine under the dripping water so no one would slip. We moved out of the damp, dark and cold house into a four-room rear apartment on W. 61st Street. The new apartment was behind a rowdy bar, and the bar was above the tracks. Thankfully it was just down the street from St. Colman's.

One door of our apartment led directly to the back of the bar. We had lived in the place about two months when Dad got into a fight there. It was around Christmas. We heard a commotion in the bar, then Dad stumbled into the kitchen with white bone fragments protruding from his bloody forehead. I thought he was done for. Mom grabbed a towel. She filled it with ice from the refrigerator and put it on Dad's head. He groaned. A small tear came out of one of his eyes.

"You should have seen what I did to that son of a bitch."

Frank Jr. had seen the fight. He agreed.

"That guy suckered Dad, came up from behind, grabbed his head, poom, poom, poom! Smashed Dad's head into the bar and that made Dad real mad. Dad shook his head, turned around, sidestepped a chair thrown at him and then he flattened that guy. The guy is still there. He's on the floor."

"Dad won?" I asked. Dad was bleeding; the dog was barking; Mom was crying. Dad kept bleeding. I called the police, and they came and took Dad to the hospital. I hated this place.

Chapter Twenty-Eight

I HAD A BIG decision to make. The school year was ending at St. Colman's and I was about to graduate from the eighth grade. I wanted to go to Catholic high school; however, the tuition was just too high. I didn't think I could scrub that many floors—not in a hundred years. I applied to two Catholic high schools anyway. I was prepared for rejection.

The letter might say: "Sorry, there's not enough room." Or, "Sorry, too many kids in your family."

Instead, to my delight, I was accepted at both schools. I selected the one that was the cheapest. I needed advice, so I wrote to the person I usually turned to for advice, Uncle George. He couldn't give me advice on money matters, but he was smart. I wrote and told him I was planning on going to the same high school he graduated from, St. John Cantius High School.

Dear Uncle George,

You'll be happy to know I've decided to go to school at St. John Cantius, the same place you graduated from school. I'm sort of nervous about school. It is a big step. I'm not sure what to study. I'd like to be something someday, but I'm really not sure what. I would like to help other people, Uncle George. You always know what the score is. Please write back and tell me what you think.

Love, Dennis (your nephew)

Dear Dennis,

You've got to learn French and Latin. You must study the classics. Pay attention to your studies. You can be whatever you want to be. Francois Mariac said, "We make our lives by the experiences that we have, then we must live the lives that we have made." Good luck. You'll do the right thing. I'm counting on you.

Love, Uncle George

Whenever I had to make an important decision, I could always count on Uncle George. He had graduated from high school, the only one of seven brothers who did. Dad told me that when I grew up, I ought to be like Uncle George. If Dad was mad at me, he would say, "You'll never be like your Uncle George. There's a smart cookie." The constant negative comparisons caused me not to like Uncle George for a long time. Yet once I got to know him, I learned Dad was right. George was smart, and I learned to pay close attention to what he said. I always included a few packs of cigarettes for him in the mail I sent to the state prison at Marion, Ohio, where he was serving time for theft.

On registration day at St. John Cantius, the Sisters asked me about Uncle George.

"Oh yes, Sister, he's doing great! He's away on business."

Uncle George could have indulged himself by locking himself up in his own prison, but he didn't. He wrote lots of letters full of excellent advice. I followed it. I wished I could have given him advice, on how to stay out of prison. He needed his own Uncle George.

Chapter Twenty-Nine

SMELLY HOT TAR bubbled from St. John Cantius' sizzling parking lot. Pastor's mangy brown dog bayed by the Blessed Virgin's shrine as tennis-shoed trespassers ran by the rectory into a sun-bathed gym. I was on my way to try out for football. I loved football. I had something to prove. I wanted to prove that I was tough, that I could take a physical pounding and dish it out. I wanted to grab the ball and score, just like the sports heroes in the football novels I read. I wanted to prove I could make the team.

Aspirants of all shapes and sizes stood along the baseline of the freshly oiled basketball floor. I disappeared behind the massive person standing in front of me. I moved invisibly toward my physical for the freshman football team. Tryouts were two weeks away. I came to the front of the line. "Are you waiting for somebody?" asked the sturdy man with cropped hair. Coke-bottle glasses were set low on his nose. A sweatshirt marked "Assistant Coach" draped his paunch.

"Yes, the doctor," I replied.

"You his grandson or something?" he asked.

"No."

"You go to school here?"

"Yes. I'm a freshman."

"You, uh, going out for football?" He started to smile, as other aspiring players looked on.

"Yes."

"Well, sorry," he said. "We already have a football," he roared as the laughter rippled through the room.

I said nothing. The funny man walked over to another coach. He pointed to me. I stepped up to a scale. The doctor's posture and patience was bent with the years. He frowned at me. He recorded "eighty-nine pounds." He measured my height at 4' 9." He put his hand to his chin, regarding me with suspicion. He fidgeted for his stethoscope.

"Pull up your t-shirt. I want to listen to your heart," he grumped. "Breathe deeply. Blow it out. Open your mouth. Say 'ahhhh.'" He checked my eyes and ears.

"Drop your pants."

This had happened once before, in CYO football.

"Turn your head to the one side and cough."

Hack, Hack, Hack.

"Turn your head to the other side. Cough."

Hack, Hack, Hack.

"Again."

HACK, HACK, HACK, HACK.

He looked me in the eye, squinted, then said:

"OK, but you better do something about that cough." Maybe he thought I had asthma, though I had outgrown it.

The Coach came over to talk to me.

"You're much too small," he said.

"I can play," I insisted.

He shook his head. "You'll get hurt. I'll be in a lot of trouble."

"Look, I'll show you I can play football," I said. "Size doesn't make any difference. Come on. Give me a chance. Let me come to practice. I'll show you I can do it." I think I wore him down. He may have thought that after taking a few hits, I would quit.

"You can come to practice," he relented. "I can't promise you'll be on the team."

I stayed on, through jumping jacks, kneebends, sit-ups, push-ups, wind sprints and poundings. I got equipment. I tried on shoulder pads—they were too big. I tried on hip pads—they were oversized. I put on football pants—many sizes too large. The leather helmet was loose. I swam in a faded jersey. I was ready to do battle; all I needed was a jockstrap.

Most football teams have forty players. That's three complete teams and a few extras. It wasn't a good year for football at Cantius. Twenty freshmen tried out. The varsity team had only twenty players. After the freshmen played a few scrimmages, the coach combined both freshmen and varsity teams. Three weeks earlier I had almost been denied a place on the freshman squad because I was too small, and now I was third-team varsity.

I wanted to make an impression in my first intra-squad game. In the huddle I drew the assignment to block on an end-around play. A 6' 4" defensive end, the tallest person on the team, was absent-mindedly watching the play unfold. I pulled from my right halfback position and unwittingly threw a perfect cross-body block at him. He stumbled and fell to the ground.

"You little son of a bitch."

"Knock it off, Dave," the coach said. "You were sleeping. Good job, what's-your-name." The coach really liked that block.

I had knocked down the biggest guy on the team. That's one way to find out if you have what it takes. Throw a shot at him, come out of it alive. Then you can stand up to anybody. I had something to prove. I may have been small, but I got their attention. I certainly got Dave's attention. Size doesn't matter.

Practice was over. I was in the locker room. The door was locked.   Upper-class players crowded around me. They lifted me up, uniform and all, and put me head first into the top half of the cage. They made animal sounds. Another time they pushed me into the bottom half of a "cage." They locked it and took turns pissing on me. Sport builds character.

As the season progressed the after-practice torture continued. I was dropped by my heels into a four-foot-high garbage barrel and left blind upside down. I managed to tip it over after about an hour. A senior tossed me into the low ceiling. I broke through the acoustical tile and waited a long time in the dark and musty rafters. The school's janitor finally saw my legs dangling through the ceiling and came running with a short ladder.

"Drabina za kriltka!" he said excitedly. I didn't understand him. I dropped to the floor. Despite the hazing, I was learning how to play football and my teammates really liked me.

My first concussion came in mid-season. I hit somebody's knee squarely with my head. Suddenly the number of players doubled. My head ached. The two big juicy peaches I hid inside my helmet for between-the-play snacks were smashed, and pieces of yellowish orange mush dripped down my forehead.

"Don't touch his helmet," the coach anxiously ordered.

I groaned.

The players, expressing great sympathy, started to crowd around my inert body.

"Call the meat wagon!"

"Take him to the butcher shop," they urged as an assistant coach backed up a jeep. I was transported quickly over a jagged road to the hospital. I waited on the hospital cart for a long time. A door accidentally swung open; two female nurses were making love on a cart in the next room. I was given some aspirins and sent home.

The Big Game arrived. We played Central Catholic in Steubenville, a smoke-filled steel town. Central Catholic was one of the state's top-ranked teams. Cheers rocked Big Red stadium. The Central Catholic machine rolled out. Every one was a head taller and fifty pounds heavier than our players. We huddled on the sidelines and we prayed to win. God, did we pray. I prayed to play. The kickoff. One by one our players were carried off the field. I had a safe seat. I was at the end of the bench; third-string quarterback. The only way I would play in a varsity game was if the other two quarterbacks were hurt. The odds were against it.

Our first-string quarterback was hit by a hard-charging lineman and was injured. Then a chant started in the stands.

"Twenty-six...."

"Twenty-Six." That was my number, but they could not have been calling for me.

Then the second strong quarterback was injured.

"Twenty-six...."

"Twenty-six!" They were calling for me to get into the game, for the same reason the Romans called for the Christians to enter the Coliseum. I wanted to play, but I also wanted to survive. Held scoreless in the first quarter, Steubenville scored about three touchdowns in the second quarter.

At halftime when we went to the locker room we were already physically beaten. The coach surveyed the gnarled, mangled, dirty, dejected players. I was one of only four who had a clean uniform.

"Kucinich. You are starting the second half."

My chance to be quarterback had arrived! Along with my chance to get killed. My stomach knotted. My hands were sweating.

Out of the locker room, another instruction from the coach: "Join the kick-off return unit, too. Stay deep," he ordered.

"What if the ball comes to me?"

"Run fast. Run real fast. Don't let them catch you."

I kicked the chalk line at the ten-yard line. I looked fifty yards downfield. The whistle blew, signaling the second half of the high school gridiron version of Armageddon. The Central Catholic line moved toward the ball. The pigskin arched slightly. It was straight coming at me.

I grabbed the ball. I thrust ahead to the rhythms of grunts and growls. It was a blurry ballet of smashing heads. I was hit. The sky screamed. I sank into a twisting mass of red jerseys. The whistle chirped. People in the stands were on their feet, craning to see. Silence descended upon Big Red stadium. Had someone been killed?

Like a bug trapped in a grassy rug, I waited in pain to be unearthed. I spit out the yard marker dust. I stood erect, and nonchalantly flipped the ball to the official. I ran off the field, pretending not to be in pain. The coach pushed me right back onto the field.

"You are quarterback, Dennis!"

I had a big problem. I had never practiced snapping the ball with the first team center, and I couldn't see over his rear end.

The first play was broken up. I returned to the huddle and confronted my center. "Hey, I can't see over, uh, your, uh, ass."

"Don't get smart with me, or I'll fart in your face. Stand on your tiptoes!"

That was a very long game. We lost 48-6. Immediately after the game a few St. John Cantius footballers strayed to prostitutes in downtown Steubenville. On the bus ride home, I chinned up to the bars of the baggage rack. I climbed in with the dirty-feet smelling equipment and duffle bags. The aroma of horse liniment filled my nostrils. This was the only advantage of being the smallest football player for the Jayhawks. I pulled my jersey over my nose and went to sleep.

Chapter Thirty

THE SISTERS HAD a ceremony called "Freshman Induction" where they paraded the school's newest students in front of a full assembly. It was intended to give the freshmen a feeling of belonging; instead it provided the upperclassmen with free entertainment. The high point of the rite was a speech by a freshman. Sister Sabina was a silhouette of a nun in black and white. She gave the one hundred and twenty-five newcomers a description of the speech and asked for volunteers. No one spoke up.

"Come now. I'm sure one of you would like to do this," she said in a soft, bewildered tone. No one volunteered.

"Well, I guess I'll have to tell the principal no one wants to speak. This has never happened before. This is not a good way to start," she said reprovingly. The home economics classroom had a faint, familiar odor. The smell of natural gas overwhelmed the space where another freshman had turned on gas jets from one of the ovens. The suspect lifted eyeliner from a classmate's purse and penciled dark eyebrows, a mustache and eyeglasses onto his face to avoid detection. Tumult reigned.

I decided to offer to give the Freshman Speech. I raised my hand. Lots of sucking sounds and muttered charges of "brown nose."

Call me a "brown nose" but never say I passed up an opportunity. I didn't stutter, and I could prove it now. I was ready to give my first speech.

The gym was full. I watched from behind the stage curtains as the event progressed. It was time. I was scared stiff.

"Go on, go on," someone called from behind me. No. Can't do it. I changed my mind. No. Can't. Stage fright. Promised to do it. Have to do it. Will do it.

I approached the podium. I disappeared. The audience could see a microphone and hear a voice coming from the public address system. Maybe a ventriloquist? A voice thrown from behind the curtains? Three long minutes passed.

"...and thank you and God Bless You."

I stepped from behind the podium to murmuring. There was laughter. A low level of prompted applause. I would have roused them if only they could have seen me. My cheeks were burning. Well, who cared? This would be my last speech.

After the induction a few freshmen girls came up to me. Wonderful speech, they said. I thanked them. It would not be my last, I assured them.

Sister Theresita, a thin Polish nun with heavy eyebrows and a thick accent, asked if I wanted to be in a school play. I had visions of starring opposite a certain senior cheerleader.

"Yes."

I played a badly disfigured hunchback in a drama called *The Infanta*.

"You sent for me, Your Highness?" That was my only line.

We moved from W. 61st Street. No eviction notice this time; we left on our own and headed back to Finney Avenue. Mom didn't object. Koom Frank was in the hospital, so we were house-sitting. A large blue-grey forsythia bush flowered near the front door. The backyard looked the same. Things looked the same inside, too. The worn, grayish-green linoleum matted the kitchen floor. The faded yellow walls. I promised Gary one penny for each roach he could kill.

Things were going well enough for Dad to give me an allowance to pay for lunches and bus fare to St. John Cantius. I got up each morning at six o'clock. Dad was already awake reading the paper. He liked talking to me about the "bunch of noise" that he said made up the day's news. The street was his classroom, his truck was his school desk. The bus was my classroom; I read more books there than at home or at school. And I kept up with the news, listening to half-asleep people talk about the 1960 Presidential election as I read the morning newspaper over their shoulders.

It was an hour-long journey to school. Broadway Avenue zipped by through the windows of the Number 19. The bus drove past Holy Name churchyard and stopped across from the elementary school. It rolled past the used car lots. I thought of our car always breaking down. We went by the Laundromat; once a week I took the family wash there. It was just around the corner from Marble Avenue where Dad was born, and A.B. Hart where he left school to go to war. We passed the Olympia Theatre at E. 55th Street. Sunday afternoons neighborhood kids gathered there while parents stayed home and made love without interruption. We stopped at St. Alexis Hospital. Dad went there when he had blood in his urine. Then the mills came into view. All eyes on Cleveland's torch. That triumphant torch, burning day and night.

The bus circled railroad tracks and oil refineries. It turned a corner near the New York Central Freight Lines terminal where Dad had won safe driving awards. We moved toward the concrete canyons of downtown Cleveland, and the Number 84 transfer bus. The Starkweather route wound through the southwest side. I followed Uncle George's advice: I took classes in French and Latin. I learned the accents, inflections and greeting words of Greek, Polish, Ukrainian, Slovak, Russian and Spanish from passengers aboard the Number 84.

Chapter Thirty-One

WE HAD A NEW coach at St. John Cantius.

"We have rules," Pete Pucher said on the first day of practice in 1961. "And if you want to be on the team, you are going to have to follow the rules." He was serious and tough. "No drinking. No smoking. No swearing." He would not have fit into my family. "You break the rules, you're off the team," he said sternly. "I don't care who you are; if you are the best player on the team or the worst player, you keep the rules. You're going to learn discipline, you hear me, discipline. If you are afraid of it or don't think you can take it, you'd better quit now and nothing will be said. But if you stay on, if you want to play for Cantius, you are going to have to meet the test."

He carried himself with the assurance of a winner. He was a solid, 6'3" quarterback from high school and college championship football teams. He was a coach who hated to lose. Unfortunately, he had a team that hated to win. We lost our first game, 64-0.

At the next day's practice, he ran us around the rutted dustbowl of Tremont Field. We ran until all but three players dropped from self-pity and exhaustion. He cursed us as "a bunch of bums." When the torture session ended he lined us up. One by one we had to look into a mirror. Muddy, bedraggled reflections looked back.

"Look at this mirror, go ahead, look at yourself," he scowled. "Can you say to yourself, 'I did my best'? Go ahead, look, try to say it." His ice-blue eyes rewarded effort, drive, intelligence, heart, and teamwork. He punished arrogance, sloth and cowardice. His disciplinarian approach began to take hold. Some liked it. I didn't like it one bit, and I didn't like him. He kept me on the bench most of the time.

I was getting into frequent fights with my brothers and with Dad. We fought about everything, and they were all stupid fights. Most of them took place at the dinner table, and I felt sick after every one of them. I thought about leaving home. Sooner or later a person has to go out on his own in life. I yearned to go out into the world to find a place that was peaceful and secure. I was confident I could do it.... I'd get a job and in no time would be making more than Dad. I'd show him. I'd buy my own car and have my own place. Boy, would he be surprised.

And while I was thinking about leaving home, I thought I would leave school as well. I knew I could make it with what I knew. What more was there to learn at school anyway? I had read all the books in the world—well, at least most of the books in the Miles Park Library. I knew the football and basketball playbooks. There was nothing else I needed to know, except how to quit St. John Cantius but keep playing for the Jayhawks.

Sister Estelle, my English teacher, called me to her room after class.

"Dennis, I would like you to enter an essay contest."

"What's it about?"

"It's an essay contest for English students, and I think you would have a good chance. The deadline is in two weeks."

I might as well let it out. I wasn't going to be around in two weeks, so she shouldn't waste her time.

"Sister, I'm not going to be here. I'm quitting school."

"You're not. Don't say that," she was shocked.

"Yes, I am."

"Why, Dennis? That would be a *terrible* thing for you to do."

"I don't feel there's anything here for me anymore. There's nothing left to learn. The only classes I like are English, and I've already read the books."

"There's more to school than reading books," she said. "You haven't even begun your education. Your mind is still developing. If you quit now, you won't realize God's plan for you."

Nuns! They always brought up religion every time they tried to convince you of something. This time I wasn't buying.

"Suppose God wants me to quit school?"

She became angry. "Listen, you will ruin your life. It's such a shame. God has a purpose for you. Remember I told you so. You can't just quit," she insisted.

"I'm ready to start my life," I proclaimed with shallow confidence.

"No, you are ready to end it," she replied. "You have to stay in school. You have to go to college. If you quit, what do you think you will be able to do?" I stopped and considered her question.

"Oh, I'll get a job. Don't worry about that!"

"Doing what?"

"Oh, I don't know, stock boy, dish washer, scrubbing floors. Something like that."

"And do you plan to do that for the rest of your life?"

"No. I'll do other things, like—"

She cut me off. "Not without an education you won't. You quit high school right now and you might be washing dishes your whole life. How would you like that?"

I shrugged my shoulders.

"Why should I stay in school?" I asked. As if she hadn't told me.

"Dennis, believe me when I tell you this. You can be anything you want to be in life, but only if you get a good education. You have a good mind. It's a gift from God. God doesn't like it when we waste our talents. You have no right to waste any of your talents."

"How can a person be anything he wants to be?" Uncle George didn't want to be in jail. Dad didn't want to be in the city.

"By believing in yourself. Believing in God. Persevering, not quitting. You don't strike me as a quitter."

"I'm not a quitter!" This struck a nerve. Could I quit school and not be a quitter?

"I think you know the right thing to do. Now here's that contest entry form. I want an essay on my desk by next week." I was ready to quit school. I could have quit school on a dare. I needed someone to tell me to stay.

 "You can be anything you want to be." She's supposed to say that. She's a nun.

Her words ran through my mind for days. The essay kept me so busy I forgot about quitting. A week later I handed a final draft to Sister Estelle. In return she handed me a page from a magazine. It had a quote from President Theodore Roosevelt:

In this world we get nothing except by effort. Far better it is to dare mighty things, to win glorious triumphs, though checkered by failure, then to take rank with those poor souls who neither enjoy much nor suffer much, because they live in that grey twilight, which knows neither victory nor defeat.

Sister Estelle made a prediction. I moved to fulfill her prophecy. She provided me with a steady stream of philosophical observations. She would then question me as to the meaning.

"Here, read this."

Ah, but a man's reach should exceed his grasp. Or what's a heaven for? —Robert Browning

She believed in me. I started to believe in myself. I kept reaching. She kept pushing me. "You can be anything you want to be." This was the thought that led me to extend my reach, to reach beyond Finney Avenue, to reach towards the far ahead and begin to think about my place in the future.

"Here, read this," said Sister Estelle.

Only he who attempts the absurd is capable of achieving the impossible. —Miguel de Unamuno

I contemplated this deeply while thinking of my own life and that of the members of my community. In my sophomore year, when I was fifteen, I wrote an autobiographical essay for English class. I thought back to my freshman year and flung far into the future a new dream.

I think everyone including me in high school at the time President Kennedy was inaugurated thought that he was talking to them when he said "...a torch has been passed to a new generation of Americans...." His message meant that young people suddenly had an important role in the life of the nation. When he said, "Ask not what your country can do for you, ask what you can do for your country," I was inspired. I felt a calling to be of the greatest service to my nation.

I began my essay with President Kennedy's call in mind as I wrote: "Someday I intend to be an author, but this I consider secondary. My main ambition is and will be a career in national politics, and I'm going to aim for the very top. I want to do something for my country, and I intend to in choosing politics as my career."

Sister Estelle taught me never to quit and to reach high. There was another lesson I had to learn, but Sister Estelle was too kind to teach it to me: discipline.

Chapter Thirty-Two

I WAS GETTING AN excellent education and I was starting to get mighty impressed with myself. Even people I'd known for years seemed unintelligent. There was no reason to listen to Mom and Dad any longer. Fights that had been confined to the dinner table began to spread to other rooms. Pretty soon home was one big riot, and I was always in the middle of it.

One day after football practice, Coach Pucher invited me to a small room in the gym under the scoreboard clock.

"Things getting a little rough at home?"

I was startled. How did he know? Mom or Dad must have called him. I had to think of something to say. I remained silent. Caught.

"Sounds like you are out of hand, boy. You are going to have to shape up," he said.

I began to contend. "Coach, you don't understand. Listen."

"No Dennis, you listen." He knew details: Getting into constant arguments with Mom and Dad, refusing to let them know my whereabouts. They told him I stayed away from home on weekends. I squirmed and looked at the door.

"And you have a 'chip on the shoulder' attitude. What do you think you are headed for, besides trouble? Just who do you think you are?" he demanded.

I could not look at him.

"I'm going to straighten you out, boy. If you are going to play ball on my team, you are going to learn some things about discipline. You are going to learn obedience. You are going to learn responsibility." This was the stern coach speaking.

This was awful. I couldn't say anything. I couldn't argue with him. I may have been ready to drop out of school, but there was no way I could drop out of sports. He didn't tell me what he wanted me to do. He showed me.

At the next football practice he came up with a new drill. He lined up the entire team for tackling practice. He lined up individuals from the first team, backfield, opposite the tacklers. Each backfield player had to run the entire gauntlet of tacklers. Boy, did they take punishment. He flipped the ball to a husky fullback who ran about five yards and then, BLAM! He was hit hard at the knees. The lineman wanted to prove how tough he was. The fullback paid.

"All right. All right. Get up. Get up," the Coach ordered. "All right, Stachowski. Get back to your position. Here's the ball. Run."

"Hit 'im. Hit 'im. HIT 'IM," he urged each successive tackler. Stachowski was called the "Bull." He was the strongest guy on the team. Until he ran the gauntlet.

One by one the ball carriers lined up. One by one they went down, again and again. I was one of the tacklers. I got in a few licks. You rarely got a shot at a first-string back in practice: his blockers would run you over. This was fun. I really threw my shoulder into the tackle. I was suddenly glad I wasn't first team. Soon the drill would end, practice would be over and I could go downtown to Kresge's for a soda.

"Kucinich! Get up here!"

Coach's snarl startled me. Hey, I'm not on the first team. If I have to go through this you'd better play me more often, I thought to myself.

A whole line of tacklers lined up. The backfield I had just nailed joined the parade.

"Get ready." The coach looked very mean.

This guy is a real bastard. I'll show him. I'll run his goddamn line. OK smart-ass coach, give me the ball. Bring on your candy-ass tacklers, bring 'em all on. I lined up facing the tacklers. You get in that line too Coach. See if you can knock me down.

He threw me the ball. I tucked the ball securely inside the gut of my five-foot, one-hundred-pound frame. I lunged forward.

"Hit 'im. Hit 'IM. HIT 'IM," he screamed. One by one, they took their shots. The first few tacklers hit me hard. I could handle it. A few more tacklers.

I was tired. The tacklers were fresh and they just kept coming. One after another. I was pounded. I felt weak. "HIT 'Im, HIT 'IM, HIT 'IM!"

I should have known this coach wasn't right. Last game, we came in the locker room with a 14-0 lead. We had a chance to win. We were feeling strong. The Coach scowled at us. "You're losing," he yelled. "I tell you, you are losing. Losing. Do you believe me?" Coach! It was one of the few times all year we had a lead. We weren't losing it. He was. "Yes, Coach."

"Yes Coach. We are losing, Coach," we all responded.

"Then go out there. Get that ball," he demanded. "Score. You are behind 14 points." It was wild. We scored. The offense came off the field. The Coach still insisted: "You're losing!" He called out to the defense. "Get the ball. Get the ball. You are losing." They got the ball. He screamed at the offense, "You're losing." They scored. This worked pretty well. We won 36-0, but something about it was wrong.

Like this gauntlet. He wants to kill me right here on this crummy field. No ambulance, no doctor, no hospital, no priest, no prayers, no services, nothing. Hey Coach, bring the shovel, bury me in my uniform OK? My brain felt like jello splashing around inside a shelled coconut. I was hurting. I couldn't remember the time or the day. There was no reality except pain and the Coach.

"All right. All right. Break."

Then he brought out the mirror.

"Did you do your best?" His eyes met each player's, challenging each of us: "Did you do your best?" He pronounced each word for effect. I got to the front of the line. I looked into his cruel, flinty eyes then I looked into the eyes of an old man. Panting, profusely sweating, dusty-faced and beaten. It was me.

"Kucinich. Did you do your best?"

He pinned me with a real hard look. I knew what he wanted me to say. I wasn't going to say it.

"Yes," I said with the last ounce of defiance I had left. I took another look at the mirror, just to check. "Yes." He didn't say anything else. The punishment ended. I struggled up St. Tikhon hill.

"Whadya do to get the Coach so mad?" another player asked.

I shrugged. It was called practice. The Coach was practicing to break me. A few days later he told me to run a few extra laps.

"When can I stop?"

"Just keep running." So I ran and ran.

I wanted to drop. I kept a lemon hidden inside the top of my helmet. I took it out and sucked on it. It helped keep me from fading. I slowed. I tried to catch my breath. He saw me.

He shouted: "You're dogging it! Kucinich! Come on, move. MOVE."

I was glad to see football season end. I played about ten quarters during the entire year. I looked forward to basketball season.

Different sport, same coach. I was on the junior varsity team. I was glad to play. I liked basketball. I had grown to 5'1'. I practiced long shots.

After our first practice, the Coach called me to the sidelines. He told me I had to stay late. What for!? Oh, no, not this again.

"All right, double calisthenics. Let's go. Hit the floor."

Push-ups, come on, up one, up two, up three, up four, up five...

Push-ups, jumping jacks, sit ups, squat-thrust, wind sprints. "All right, all right, that's enough. Come here." I was standing in front of him, at center court. He looked around the gym.

"OK. SEE THAT WALL? RUN UP THAT WALL!"

"Do what?" Run into a wall? I stood there.

He had a way of looking down at me. He twisted his chin. He squinted his eyes. He looked mean. He pointed to the wall.

This was not like football. This was worse. Tacklers have a little give. I could have quit football. I didn't play that much, but I stayed with it. The thought that I might play was all I needed to endure. I had played in all the basketball games. I wasn't going quit. Why was he doing this? What had I ever done to him? There was no one to complain to. I took a deep breath.

I ran towards the wall. I hit it at full speed. My foot landed three feet up the wall. My second foot touched above the first. I stood sideways for a split-second.

"All right, come back here. Do it again."

Each time I landed on my feet, or on my face. The Coach hated me. I hated the Coach. The secret was poorly kept. I anonymously put a copy of *The Coach Nobody Liked* under his door. He saw me the next day and mentioned he read the book. He also told me I would learn discipline even if it killed me.

He told me he had a book too, one he wanted me to read. I laughed to myself. He could do anything to me when it came to sports. There was no way he was going to get me to read one of his books. Besides, what did he know about other than football, basketball and baseball?

A week later. "Did you read that book, Kucinich?"

"Uh, what was the title, again?"

"The title," he paused, very irritated, "is *Message to Garcia*."

"Oh."

"Read that story, Kucinich."

Time passed. It was two days before a game. He asked me about the book again. Of course I hadn't read it. Why should I? He was the coach, not an English teacher.

"Uh, no, Coach," I said quietly. "I haven't read it. Didn't have a chance to go to the library."

"If you don't reach the book, don't come to the game."

He wasn't kidding. He was threatening me again. I had to be in the game. He wanted me to read the book? OK, I'd read the stupid book.

"I'll read it tonight."

"*Message to Garcia*?" I inquired of the librarian at the Cleveland Public Library's Main Branch. She located a reference copy. She set it on the counter. It was a reed-thin edition. I was embarrassed that I had delayed reading such a small book. It was set during the period of the Spanish-American war.

A man named Rowan was sent to Cuba by President McKinley. His mission was to locate an insurgent leader, Garcia. Rowan carried a "Message to Garcia" from the President.

Elbert Hubbard wrote: "Rowan took the letter and did not ask, "Where is he at?" By the Eternal! There is a man whose form should be cast in deathless bronze and the statue placed in every college of the land. It is not book-learning young men need, nor instruction about this and that, but a stiffening of the vertebrae, which will cause them to be loyal to a trust, to act promptly, concentrate their energies: Do the thing—carry a message to Garcia."

One day before the game. "Kucinich, did you read that book?"

"Yes, Coach."

"What does it mean?"

I knew. I remained silent.

"It means this: When you tell someone you are going to do something, even if it is just a promise to read a book, you do it. A promise is a responsibility. Carry out your responsibilities."

I stared at him for a long moment.

"Sorry, Coach. I should have read the book sooner."

As I was leaving the office, he called out after me: "Kucinich!"

I turned. "Do you think you can take a 'Message to Garcia'?"

"I'll try, Coach."

He curled his lip. "You'd better try, Kucinich, because I'm going to keep after you."

Whatever it was the Coach was trying to teach me, I was learning. He let me stay after practice to shoot baskets with him and a few varsity players. The Coach would not let us play for pennies or nickels. Instead he had us play for each other's heart, our courage, our pride. When you won a game like that, you knew you really won something.

Chapter Thirty-Three

I WAS CALLED TO a meeting with the principal. I was gently reminded that I had a tuition bill due.

"Pastor wants to know what I am doing to see that the tuition is paid. How are you going to pay this bill?" asked the principal.

I didn't know. I was worried. It was spring. I had not found a job. I owed the school about $200.

"Dennis, you have an obligation to pay this bill."

"I know, Sister. Please give me more time. I want to pay it. I *will* pay it."

Two hundred dollars is a lot of money. Oh sure, Uncle Paul was managing a hardware store. He let me help him Saturdays. That was good for about $4 a month. Uncle John's wife hired me to cut the grass twice a month, so I earned another $3. Aunt Betty gave me a few dollars here and there. I used up all of the money. I spent it on books. I checked with the operator of the bowling alley at Broadway and Harvard. I offered to be a pin setter. He said I was too small.

"You get hit by one of those balls, we got a problem," he said. I checked the whole business district. No one needed any extra help.

I asked my neighbor, Gene Wolchko.

"Gene, I've got to find a job or I'm sunk."

"You should have said something sooner. I work at Beechmont Country Club. I'm a caddy. I'll bet I could get you in there." The course would open soon.

"Really? That's great. What does a caddy do?"

"Carries people's golf clubs. Watches where golfers hit the ball. You'll have to get up very early. We leave at quarter to five in the morning. We'll have to hitchhike up Harvard Avenue."

"Hitchhike?!"

There were no buses at that time. It was about six in the morning. A light blanket of stars lay over the golf course. Wildlife scurried across the still tees and greens. Three middle-aged men, two black and one white, stirred from their slumber. They had slept overnight in the caddy shack. They would be first to caddy that day.

Gene introduced me to the caddy master. Vic was as tall and as thin as the stockade boards that kept the caddies out of view of the membership of Beechmont Country Club. He looked at me. His dark glasses moved down his nose. He looked puzzled. Then he turned to Gene.

"Think he can carry a bag?" he asked.

Gene nodded and looked at me to answer the question. Could I carry a golf bag? I didn't know.

"Carry a golf bag? Sure, I can carry anything," I said, unconvincingly.

Vic looked amused. "Well, if you say so, son. You don't look much bigger than a golf bag, but let's see."

Vic picked one bag from a rack. It was a dark green leather golf bag with tags which read "El Dorado Country Club."

Vic placed the fully loaded bag on my shoulder. "There, how's that?" he asked, smiling.

"Fine."

I struggled to stand up. My shoulder strained. The bag weighed so much that I left deep footprints in the grass. How could anyone carry these things around for three, four, and five hours in the sun? The bag began to slip. The strap was too wide, my shoulders too narrow. Please Mr. Caddy Master, please don't laugh. I really need this job. I set the bag down three times. I brought it back up three times.

"See, no problem at all. I can handle it."

His arms were folded. He didn't want me to be a caddy, I could tell.

I felt sick. I was glad I remembered how to get home.

"That bag is too heavy for you. Try this one."

He handed me one that was as light as a feather.

"That's a lady's golf bag. How does it feel?"

Hey, I am a man. I came to carry a man's golf bag. I didn't know women played golf here. My options were limited.

"Oh, it's just fine. No problem."

"Good. Welcome aboard. I'll put you on the list. Wait in the caddy shack until I call your name." I wasn't sure how all of this was going to work out.

I went into the shack. Some caddies were still sleeping, others were reading books. There were circles of boys and men playing Tong or Morra. They were high school seniors, college students and old men. They were black, and white, Italians, Poles, Slovaks, Irish and a Croatian. We were all there to make money. We ignored the racial and ethnic jokes that flew through the air. A caddy carrying one bag made a minimum of $2.50 for eighteen holes. This took half the day. Many of the golfers at Beechmont were good tippers. If one liked you, you could make $3.25, even $3.50. I'd pay that tuition bill off in no time.

The first time I was assigned to a golfer she looked at me and then told the caddy master she wanted someone older. I felt bad.

I had an awful time carrying the golf bag. Members knew it. Most didn't complain; they were curious about me.

"Aren't you too small to be a caddy?"

"Aren't you too young to be a caddy?"

"How old are you, sonny?"

"Dennis? Oh, you mean like 'Dennis the Menace'?" I just nodded and smiled my way through it. What did I care? I was making money.

I had the shoulders of a squirrel, but the eyes of an eagle. My sharp eyes saved me. I could follow the small white ball for three hundred yards. No one I caddied for lost a ball, unless it went out of bounds—even then sometimes I still found it. I gained a reputation as a good caddy as I carried clubs for a full round of 18 holes. Within a few months I was working 27 and even 36 holes a day. I earned as much as $7 in one day. I saw the sun rise and set at Beechmont Country Club. I was the first one out and the last one in. One day I caddied for 45 holes and made $10.

I was so tired when I got home I fell asleep with my clothes and shoes still on. I'd wake up the next morning and know for sure I was in the Great Indoors of Finney Avenue: a beery, stale-cigarette, steel-mill smell; the sulphur dioxide perfume wafting into the house to meet my morning's first breath. The golf course smelled different, clean and green. My thoughts were of home, though, when I walked hours and hours up and down the fairways and into the rough of Beechmont Country Club.

I thought about my brother Frank. He tried so hard in school. I thought about Cousin Mary Ann, who had run away with a man from Tennessee. My brother Gary was developing into a great athlete. Brother Perry seemed lost in the shuffle. He cried most of the time. Larry and Theresa and Beth Ann all seemed so scrawny. Would they ever grow? Things didn't change much for Mom and Dad. I thought about Koom Frank, who made sure we had a home. I thought about Uncle Steve, who told me that we were all reincarnated from somebody or another. He spoke to me of the soul living on after the body dies. I wondered about the big chart in his room. It had colored strings crossing a dark blue felt. The lines zig-zagged along map pins.

"This red string is my life. See? It ends here."

He was pretty close to the end of his string, and he was only thirty-seven years old. What he said bothered me. As I kept walking one hole after another, my legs began to feel very strong. Up one hill and down another. I thought about Sister Estelle, how she said I could be anything and what that meant for a career in national politics. I thought about Coach Pucher. The football season was drawing near. What surprise would the Coach have in store? I thought about two books that inspired me, Moss Hart's *Act One* and Harry Golden's *Only in America*. I wondered if I could achieve my dreams. I began to weave the fabric of those dreams. Step by step down the fairway. Through the rough. In the traps. My skin began to bake. My eyes became heavy with sun. My nose peeled. That sulphurous mucus kept come up from my belly. God, it hurt. Mind over matter. I walked and walked. I thought about everything. But I kept my eye on the ball.

"Caddy?! Where did my shot go?"

"It's over there, sir, just up ahead."

The old duffer started off the tee early. It was the only way he could avoid holding up the play behind him. He refused to take an electric cart. His spindly legs looked odd dropping through the fine creases in his new plaid Bermuda shorts. I followed him closely on the greens. He dragged his feet. He tore up the smooth surface. I repaired the ground quickly with the point of a golf tee. I wondered if he was going to make it through the round—he was that old.

"I'm glad you saw it. I lost it in the sun." Twenty-five yards later we stood by his ball.

"What club do you think I should use?"

"Well, you are in the rough. I think, maybe a seven iron." The divot went ten yards, the ball about forty. But it was on the fairway." That was a good shot, Sir."

"Eh, well, I can't hit 'em like I used to, that's for sure." He glanced at me and then he looked ahead while we walked toward the next shot. "How old are you, son?"

"I'll be sixteen in October."

"Sixteen! I wish I was sixteen again. I'm seventy-five years old."

He stopped at his ball. He took a wood out of his bag. He hit a shot about ninety yards. It was his best stroke of the day.

"Sixteen! I'll tell you something, I'm worth a lot of money. I worked for all of it. My sons will get it when I die. I'm a happy man. Life's been good to me, but I would give it up to be young again, like you. You don't ever want to get old, sonny." He looked up the fairway towards his ball. "Oh, to be young again. I'd give up everything. You should be happy, you have your youth."

The round ended. He did not give me much of a tip.

Chapter Thirty-Four

I TOOK A DAY off from caddying. I had a routine physical examination for football. I felt great, except for the knife-like pains in my belly. What they can't see in a physical can't hurt you.

The doctor frowned when he put the stethoscope to my chest.

"Has anyone ever told you that you have a heart murmur?"

"A what?!"

"You have a heart murmur. I can't approve of you playing football. I'd advise you to see a heart specialist. I'm sorry."

I felt sledge-hammered. A heart WHAT?

"Sure, doctor, I'll, uh, see a specialist." I was so perplexed I didn't ask any questions about the consequences of his diagnosis. All I remembered was that he said I couldn't play football.

I felt very depressed the next day at Beechmont and I guess I looked it.

"Dennis, what's wrong with you? Are you feeling well?" Mrs. Violet Ludwig Mendes looked at me with her big brown eyes. I caddied for her many times. There wasn't a nicer member in the whole club. I wished she hadn't asked. It made me feel bad all over again. I guess I wasn't too good at concealing my feelings.

"The doctor said I have a heart murmur." Deep breath.

"I can't play sports." Very deep breath.

"Is there anything I can do to help?" The nicer she was the worse I felt.

"I, don't, know."

"Well, I have an idea. A good friend of mine is a heart specialist. As a matter of fact, he is a member here. I'll bet if I asked him, he would see you."

On the golf course there is a rule: You don't talk to the members unless they talk to you. Mrs. Mendes always talked to me. She always asked me how things were going. She asked what I was studying in school. She knew I liked to play sports. At the eighteenth green she asked me to wait at the caddy shack. Minutes later she called me forward. She had arranged an appointment.

Dad was sitting at the kitchen table, drinking and crying about Uncle Steve. "Why the hell did he have to do it? We would have helped. He didn't say anything to anyone."

"Dad, what's wrong?" I forgot about my heart murmur. "Uncle Steve, poor Stevie, my brother killed himself."

Dad wasn't much for talking. I walked across the tracks to Aunt Ann's and Uncle Paul's, where Steve had lived. The tiny home was nestled in trees at the bottom of a hill next to Calvary Cemetery. It was just in front of railroad tracks. Paul and Ann were in the kitchen. Paul had his arms folded. His cheeks were hollow; his dentures rested in a cup on the sink.

"Dennis, you need to know what happened here," he said. "Your Uncle Steve has been very sick. He couldn't stand it any longer. He took an overdose of sleeping pills. Stevie was a hard-working man. He was a good uncle and a good brother. But he's dead. That's that."

Aunt Ann stared at Paul. She left her untouched cup of coffee to lead me upstairs. We stood inside Steve's room.

"He died here, last night," Aunt Ann said.

The bed was clean and neat. It invited a good night's sleep.

"They took Stevie away late in the evening. But I could still hear him this morning. He was crying. He was moaning. He was asking for help. His soul is restless. It hasn't been released. We have to pray for him. The poor man. I was worried he would do something." Her voice broke into sobs.

There, on the wall, in a wooden frame, was Steve's cosmic chart. "See that red string? It ends here," he had told me. A black map pin was securely set at the end of the red string. He used sleeping pills to cross the black map pin and escape into the expanse of dark blue felt. "This life of mine is almost over," Steve had told me. "But mark my words, I'll be back. I don't know what I'm coming back as, but I'll be back. Uncle Steve will be around."

Life had become too hard for him. On his bookshelf I saw many volumes he had loaned to me. Books like Dale Carnegie's *How to Win Friends and Influence People*. And there was *The Tractenburg System of Mathematics*. Steve had his own math system, which he used each day to handicap the horses at Thistledown racetrack.

I had my appointment with the heart specialist after Steve's funeral. The doctor listened to my heart. He put his stethoscope down and he looked at me.

"Oh, yes, I can hear it. You do have a murmur." Then he put me through a number of tests. We sat down for a talk. "Son, you have a heart murmur. There is some scarring of the mitral valve. This can cause you a problem later in life. You may have had rheumatic fever. Did you ever have a sore throat? Soreness in your joints? A high fever?"

Sure, all the time. I was always sore and thirsty after caddying 36 holes.

"Ever have a serious infection of any kind?"

"No." I had a lot of cracked teeth. Some were infected, and sometimes it was painful. My gums often bled. But that was normal. No serious infection.

"Doctor, can I play sports?" I asked apprehensively.

"No son, I'm sorry. I'm going to place you on a prevention program. I want to make sure no further damage is done to your heart." He gave me some penicillin pills. He handed me a signed slip. "You take this to the Health Department at City Hall. They will refill it for free. It's a government-sponsored program."

"Doctor, I'm thinking of going into the Marines after I graduate."

"I'm afraid they won't take you with that heart murmur. You'll be classified 4-F. I'll write a letter for you to take to your draft board. You'll have to make other plans. I'm sure it will work out for the best."

"Doctor, are you sure?"

"I'm sure," he said through a tight-lipped smile.

"Oh." I took a deep breath. He patted me on the shoulder.

"Really, you'll be fine. You'll probably live past 80." This was terribly bad news and now I had to pay a big doctor bill. I suddenly knew how Dad felt so many times.

"Doctor, how much do I owe you?" St. John Cantius would have to wait for the money.

"Don't worry about that, either. Mrs. Mendes is taking care of the entire matter. Good luck, son."

When I got home, Dad was listening to the baseball game on the radio. Flies were zooming in and out of the kitchen through the holes in the screen. He was looking in the refrigerator for something.

"Dad, I was just at the doctor's. He said I had a heart murmur and I couldn't play sports. He said because of this heart murmur I couldn't even get into the service. I can't be in the Marines."

He came up empty-handed and closed the door. His eyes were expressionless. He was silent. He had a look that suggested that his thoughts reached back to another time. He refocused.

"Can't be in the Marines, huh? Eh, no big deal. I wouldn't worry about it." He went back to the refrigerator and pulled out a beer. He took a swig and sat down. "No big deal, no big deal at all," he said. He looked out the screen into the sky. I could tell he was very hurt, but he was tough. Marines don't cry.

I showed up at football practice and passed the word to some of my teammates that I wouldn't be able to play. Then I spoke to the Coach.

"The truth is, Dennis, I would have had to cut you anyway. All the other backs are bigger and faster. There just wouldn't have been any room for you," he said matter-of-factly.

I wasn't going to be playing football, no matter what. Well, that's life.

"By the way," Coach continued, "if you are interested, you can still be a part of the team. I need someone to keep statistics. It would be a big help. You could be our official team statistician. What do you say?"

"Really? Great! Thanks, Coach. Sure, I'd do a good job. I'd love to keep the statistics."

After practice, the coach made the announcement. A number of players congratulated me as if I had just run a good play. A few others held their chests, laughed and dropped to the ground with faked heart attacks.

Chapter Thirty-Five

DAN BACKUS AND I were best friends. We laughed at each other's jokes. On dates, I served as his front-seat look-out while he wrestled with an endless number of coeds in the back seat of his father's 1961 white Ford Fairlane. Meanwhile I sat clueless and chaste in the front seat with a date who looked out the window. As a result of my friendship with Dan I nevertheless gained a measure of popularity. The girls could say (without mentioning me) that they sat in the front seat of the blonde, blue-eyed football hero's car. At 6'3" and 195lbs., Dan could kick a football seventy-five yards, out-rebound most basketball opponents and throw a baseball ninety miles per hour—*and* he was a good student. Some people are just good at everything.

Dan lived in Parma Heights, ten miles from St. John Cantius. On school days, we coordinated our inbound transit so we could meet at the West Side Market's restaurant to share coffee, doughnuts, homework, troubles, jokes and dreams, all to a popular juke box song, "Our Day Will Come."

The brightest evenings at Finney Avenue were those when Dan arrived. His car was a vehicle for exploration. When we visited his girlfriends, their Catholic mothers were always pleased that "nice boys" preferred to come to their home to see their daughters. Better that than their daughters participating in unvirtuous gyrations in the back seat of a car.

On weekends, I lived at the Backus' home. It was very quiet, there was plenty of food, and I had my own room. No fights, no roaches, no rats, and no mice. I returned to Finney Avenue on Sunday nights, sometimes after fierce, break-even pinochle games that lasted as long as twenty-six straight hours.

Dan's street was pitch-dark as we crossed Metropolitan Parkway Drive to walk the last quarter-mile to his home. The varsity basketball team had just won another game. Dan starred. I kept track of the baskets and fouls, since the heart murmur had ended my own playing days. The basketball game was history, and we had other things to discuss.

"Think you'll get a sports scholarship to college, Dan?"

"Maybe for football or baseball, but my Dad doesn't want me to play football. He thinks if I go for football I'll hurt my knee and I'll be washed up, with no college, no nothing. Baseball is it. Major league scouts are already watching me pitch. I can get a scholarship for baseball. Yup, I'll bet on it." He could pitch.

As a senior he struck out eighteen batters in a seven-inning game. He threw three no-hitters in a single season. And he finished the season without an earned run average. I fully expected him to pitch for the Cleveland Indians one day.

"You going to college?" he asked me.

"Nobody in my family ever went to college. That would sure be something. I can't even imagine it. Sister Estelle keeps telling me 'You have to go to college, you have to develop the skills God has given you.' Maybe I will, maybe I won't. I think I will if I can ever get the money."

Dan and I tied for eighth-place academic ranking out of the eighty-eight students in our high school class. I was unlikely to get a scholarship based on grades. I sure wasn't going to get one for sports. What I did best was to write about people who played sports. I was St. John Cantius' correspondent to five Ohio newspapers and one radio station. I called in the box scores. It was easy for me to be accepted by the "in" group. I was able to get the names and pictures of athletes in the sports columns of the dailies and the school newspaper, where I was sports editor. The players appreciated my writing about their exploits, and I appreciated being invited to their parties.

It was almost as if the touchdowns, field goals and home runs counted only if they were recorded in black and white. I didn't understand how much publicity meant until Ed Chay, a sports editor at the Cleveland *Plain Dealer*, named me the *Plain Dealer's* "Correspondent of the Week." Upperclassmen, even their parents and kids from other schools congratulated me, as if I had done something important. Writing about sports was the next best thing to playing. But colleges sent out scouts to prospect pitchers, quarterbacks and fullbacks, not sportswriters.

Maybe I can make enough money as a caddy. Then I will be able to have enough money go to college, I thought.

"After college, I'm going to play pro ball and then maybe be a coach someday," Dan declared.

Gosh, he's going to college; then professional ball, then coach. And I'm going to be caddying at Beechmont. Suddenly, I remembered the old men who slept in the caddy shack. I paused for the longest time. We drew near to Dan's home. I tried to think about the past, present and the future all at once. That can be hard on a kid's brain. While weighing possibilities against the odds, I remembered what Sister Estelle said: Once I set my mind to something, I could be anything I wanted to be. I looked up in the night sky. Perhaps somewhere in the spaces between the stars there was an answer, or maybe it lay inside the vast unexplored regions of my self. I was seized with an impulse, an intuition, to speak a strange thought. It had nothing to do with sports or college. I said it aloud to my trusted friend as we continued our walk.

"Dan. I can't really tell you why I know this. But I just know it will happen. I'm going to be the Mayor of Cleveland by the time I'm thirty years old!"

He did not disappoint me. He laughed. "What do you know about being mayor?"

"Well. I once met Mayor Ralph Locher at a Cleveland Indians baseball game," I replied. "What's more, in tenth grade I chose as my goal in life a career in politics 'aiming for the very top.' Well, you have to start somewhere. I'll start locally."

"Yeah Dennis, you're going to be Mayor of Cleveland, and I'm going to be John Glenn," he guffawed.

His dad's car was sitting in the driveway. We paused under the basketball hoop of the garage before entering the house. I looked up at the stars, searching for more inspiration.

"Holy Smokes! Did you see that?" I pointed up to the sky as a star plummeted through the heavens. I made a wish. I had once read that when you wish upon a star, you should never tell anyone what you wish, otherwise the wish may never come true. I tucked this star away until I needed it. Dan and I were still looking up when I said, "I'm telling you, I know I'm going to be Mayor of Cleveland. Just you watch." He shook his head and snickered as he pushed me into the house.

Chapter Thirty-Six

THE LOGICAL FIRST STEP on the route to becoming Mayor of Cleveland was through the student council elections, so I became a candidate for president of the St. John Cantius student council. I made up signs: "Kucinich for President," and circulated a platform that included total freedom to publish in the school newspaper whatever one wanted. I shook a lot of hands. I got a lot of guaranteed support.

The good Sisters were not happy with the prospect of my election, especially because I printed articles in the school newspaper without their approval. My sense of humor was, well, different. I had been known to throw my voice inside inanimate objects or outside the classroom window, "Sister, Sister, come here, outside!"

I'm sure many would never forget "Letter Sweater Day." St. John Cantius' athletes were invited to wear sweaters with decorations of their athletic prowess to classes. I hung back to make sure I was the last student to enter the class. I walked in with a straight face. My 5-foot-tall, 105-pound frame sported a sweater I borrowed from Scott Sikorski, a 6'5," 280-pound athlete. The class went wild with laughter as they saw me in a sweater that appeared to have a long train.

The good Sister was writing on the blackboard. Distracted by the uproar, she whirled around and cuffed me sharply on the head. Exaggerating the blow, I fell to the ground, my fist banging the desk making it appear that my head had bounced off the floor.

Classmates (accomplices) carried me, in the manner of medics, out of the room. I returned ten minutes later, holding my head, which was wrapped in bandages I borrowed from the gym's medical kit. Later that day the Principal sent me home and said I needed a letter from a Doctor before she would let me back in school. I came back to school the next day, claiming a miracle had occurred. I was known as the prankster, the instigator—nothing vicious, just fun.

Yes, many of the Sisters had my number, and it wasn't Number 1. They supported the candidacy of a Polish straight-A student, a friend of mine. The Sisters constantly reminded students how nice he was and how smart he was. The mention of my name brought eye-rolling and silence.

Election Day. The students did the voting. The good Sisters counted the votes. The Sisters announced the results. I had lost by three votes. There was no recount. The ballots were destroyed. I thought the election was fixed. I went to Coach Pucher to complain.

"You lost. That's it. You are going to have to learn how to accept things."

"Come on, Coach. Do you think I really lost?"

"I said, Dennis, accept it. Forget it. Come on now. The bus is ready to leave for the game." Then he looked away. He was smiling.

Coach Pucher left St. John Cantius at the end of the 1963 school year. He went on to a bigger school, a bigger team and bigger victories. I was really sad to see him leave. He was the third person to save my life by teaching me the importance of discipline and keeping my promises.

Chapter Thirty-Seven

SOME THINGS YOU don't tell anyone. I'd never want the Coach to know that Dan, Phil and I broke one of his rules. No way. So we didn't talk much about the night we drove over to the East Side, off Cedar Avenue, and entering a broken tenement building on a dark August night to visit "Hungry Helen."

Her wares were well known by many young Catholic initiates with virgin girlfriends. She was a legend, this ebony goddess who held services on an overstuffed, squeaking, queen-sized bed veiled by glass-bead curtains and illumined by red boudoir lamps. Hungry Helen was receptive, unlike her neighbors, who acted like we didn't belong in the area.

Phil was first. Helen was eager, bidding. Phil turned to Dan and me, and, with a lost, screwed-up look on his face, he asked: "Hey, either of you guys got any money?"

Dan gave him four dollars. I gave him three hard-earned bucks from caddying eighteen holes.

The bed moved slowly up and down, creaking like a bandsaw cutting slowly through a two-by-four as the radio played the blues. Slow moans rose above the music and the creaking. I whistled the St. John Cantius High School alma mater until Dan hit me in the shoulder. Phil came out of the room, zipping up his pants. The apartment's water pipes strained as the lady filled up a pan she kept at the bedside. She stepped from behind the glass beads.

"All right, which one of you fellas is next?" Her breasts were bulging over her low-cut dress she had just put on again. Her large red lips parted again as she looked at me impatiently: "Say, what's this? This here ain't no nursery school, fellas. You somebody's little brother here?"

I was ready to make a run for the door when Dan came to the rescue.

"Yeh, he, uh, he'll uh, he's okay. He's old enough. I'll vouch for him. He's just short for his age."

She was suspicious. "Well, come on! Come on! I ain't got all night. Who's next?"

What was I doing here? This was a terrible idea. Hey, I just came to watch, do I have to pay? Dan hedged. The lady was upset. She opened the door of her apartment.

"Look boys, if you don't want nothing, get the hell out of here. Don't waste my time. This is a business." We had no further business so we ran down the stairs, jumped into Dan's car and sped westwards home. Dan and I pressed Phil about when we would get back the money we loaned him. He smiled and said, "Are you kidding? Right away! She was fantastic!" We hooted and hollered at his antics. As the school year drew to a close he still had not paid us for his encounter with Hungry Helen.

Chapter Thirty-Eight

THE SUN SHONE DOWN on Finney Avenue on my Graduation Day. The birds were chirping, the roaches were playing tag, our dog Spot was in the backyard arguing with a neighbor's cat. I waited in the front room for Dan to arrive and drive us to the gym where our class would assemble. I was wearing a metallic-thread purple-and-black striped jacket that was Uncle Lenny's favorite for cold days at the track. Family members stole peeks at me, as if I were leaving on a journey never to return.

Dad was dressed in a white shirt, tie, dark pants and a light summer jacket. He wore his best for this day. He stood near me. I could feel the weight of his gaze.

"Kid, I just want you to know that I'm proud of you. Sometimes your old man doesn't show it, but he is."

Wow. The last time he said that to me was when he got up at 5 a.m. to see me off on a trip to Washington, D.C., a senior class excursion which Aunt Betty had paid for. On that morning, he was the last parent to wait for the bus to leave. He walked alongside that bus, smiling, waving, saying, "I'm proud of you kid," even as the bus was pulling into the street. I knew he meant it.

This was my Graduation Day and I wasn't going to cry, no way. Not after everything I'd been through.

Mom walked into the living room. She was holding the collar of the tattered light green robe she wore while sleeping. She coughed hard, as she had every morning for the last few years. I hoped she would feel better in an hour. I wanted her to go to church with Dad and Aunt Betty.

"He's growing up, Frank. He'll be leaving us soon," she said, "but I hope not too soon."

"Like hell he is," Dad corrected her, "he'll be staying right here at home with his Mom and Dad. He's graduating. But he is still our kid."

He looked toward me. I didn't say a thing.

They had both tried hard and given a lot of love to make this day possible. Sure, they drank and fought. That didn't mean that they loved us any less. It didn't mean they were satisfied with giving us anything less than they could. Maybe the past dozen years hadn't been easy for me, but they were a hell of a lot harder on them. It was a miracle that they'd managed to hold the family together. How many kids were lucky enough to leave for their graduation with both parents watching them get their diploma? I mean, when I considered it, it was really something: Mom and Dad looking at me and what I represented as their hopes and dreams for the future of the Kucinich family. They were proud of me—well, I was proud of them too.

"Honk Honk," Dan arrived in his car, and we sped to St. John Cantius.

As I put on my cap and gown inside the gym, I thought about Sister Estelle and how proud she was of me too. It was because of her that I was the first-place winner for sportswriting in a statewide writer's tournament. I was also the first runner-up in the Cleveland Indians batboy essay contest. I thought about Coach Pucher and how he almost killed me right here in this gym; about how close I had come to quitting school. Now here I was graduating with awards for drama, journalism and—get this—perfect attendance for four years, including the time Dan and I slept overnight in the basketball locker room because we were concerned we wouldn't be able to get back to school in a heavy snowstorm. No clogged lungs, no hot stomach was going to keep me from going to St. John Cantius.

This was the biggest day of my life. After this, I could go out into the world and make my own way. Graduation!

I was put at the front of the graduation line, still the shortest in the class. Girls were crying. A number of boys had tears in their eyes too, less from emotion than the bottle of Seagram's Seven Crown whiskey they had just shared in the john. It was the last illicit pleasure they could sneak at school.

As the line stepped from the gym to the school yard, I was taken aside by the principal. She looked chastened. Her eyes were downcast. She leaned in very close and whispered in my ear.

"Pastor wants to see you. Now."

"Uh, how about after Graduation?" I said. "I'll come after the ceremony."

"No. He says he has to see you now."

I didn't know the Pastor. I understood he was nearing retirement. The only thing I remembered about him was that he made the parish janitor tear down his own house with a crowbar to save demolition money. He had also come over to the gym a few times during basketball practice to tell us to shut the lights off, even before we had finished our evening drills.

I rushed around the corner to the rectory's side door entrance. The Pastor's old dog gave an apathetic growl as I rang the buzzer.

Father Francis Szudarek, the Pastor of St. John Cantius, opened the door without saying a word. He had a short-cut fringe of gray hair. His face was full. There were deep creases at his mouth. He wore a short-sleeve black shirt. I followed him to his study and watched as he sat down. He pulled a long clothbound ledger from a drawer in his desk. He looked stern as he opened the book. He surveyed columns of figures, carefully moving his eyes up and down the rows as an accountant would.

"Listen, Kucinich," he said in an altogether unfriendly manner. "You are almost two years behind on your tuition. I can't let you graduate."

"What?"

"You can't go into the church. They won't call your name. You won't get your diploma. Not until you pay your tuition bill."

He pushed a piece of paper under my nose. "$225" was written on parish stationery. That's what I owed. With the help of my caddying job, I had paid the first two years and three months of my tuition. I had planned to pay the rest off after graduation.

"We run this school like a business. You owe us money. You are going to pay it. Do you have any money on you?"

Well yes, I did. Aunt Betty had given me $20. I took the $20 bill from my pocket and tried to give it to him. He pushed my hand aside.

"That's not enough," he said curtly.

"That's all I have," I said as I put the $20 back into my pocket.

"Pastor," I tried to speak as softly as I could. "My mother and father are in that church. I have other relatives there too."

"Well, then get the money from them."

"They are in church," I continued, "and they came to see me graduate. It's important to them. I don't care if you want to keep the diploma until I pay you, but I just have to be in that procession. I have to graduate."

"You should have thought of that before today," said the Pastor, as his mouth closed tightly.

"Father, would I have paid you for the first two years if I wasn't going to pay for the second two years?" His nose was pointed straight down into his ledger.

"Go ahead, look in your book. Check the payment record. You'll see that in the summer of 1963 I paid for my sophomore year. This summer I intend to pay for both my junior and senior years. I'll be able to do it. Now I can carry two golf bags at once. I'm making more money."

"Good. Then you will pay for your diploma."

"But what about church? What about Graduation?" I asked with exasperation.

"You can't go," he said with a stone face.

My approach obviously wasn't working. I became angry. He had every right to insist on payment, but I had shown him my payment record. Why was he doing this? What would my class think? I could see my friends asking me as I got old: "What ever happened to you on Graduation Day?" "Where were you?" "Why didn't you graduate?"

Oh, this was not going to be pretty. I had waited for this day and worked hard for it. Besides Uncle George, I was the only person on my Dad's side of the family to complete high school. And the Pastor won't let me graduate? Just because he didn't believe I'd pay my tuition? I imagined people in the church looking for me, holding up the procession, wondering where I had gone.

I tried another tack, acceptance...sort of.

"Father, let me put it to you this way. Let's say I don't graduate today. Let's say you don't give me a diploma." His eyes narrowed as I continued. "Then, if you really believe I'm not going to pay, there's no reason for me to pay, is there?"

His hand tightened to a fist as he put it to his mouth. I detected an opening.

"See," I said. "There's the guarantee you want. I graduate, I pay. I don't graduate, I don't pay."

He placed both hands on his desk and rose silently. The meeting was over. The church organ began to pipe. Pastor glowered at me. He was disgusted.

I grabbed the small white piece of paper with "$225" written on it from his desk. Remembering the words from all the legal stuff that landed on Mom and Dad's door, I wrote, quickly:

I promise to pay the sum of $225, by 10/1/64
Signed, Dennis J. Kucinich

I held up the note, tightly in both hands and showed it to the Pastor. He studied it for an instant and then reached to snatch it.

"Give it to me! Get out of here! Go graduate!" he growled, flicking his hand dismissively.

Pomp and Circumstance was playing as I raced through the churchyard to the front entrance. The procession had already moved into the church. I darted up the aisle and reclaimed my place at the front of the line as the procession reached the front of the church. My face was red. My pulse was pounding. I was out of breath, but by God I was about to graduate!

Chapter Thirty-Nine

I WAS SEVENTEEN YEARS old. I had given this moment a lot of thought. I had things to do with my life, and this was my time to do them. Graduating was not going to be enough. I had to go out on my own. I had to leave home.

I dreaded having this talk with Mom and Dad. I knew they would not want me to go, but I plunged in when I saw Dad sitting bare-chested at the kitchen table reading the newspaper.

"Dad, I'm moving."

"Moving?!" He scrunched his face and put his down his paper. "Where you going to go? You live here," he said.

"I'm going to go out make it on my own Dad."

"Whaddaya mean? You've got it made here, kid."

"I've already made up my mind, Dad. Scott's parents are renting me rooms above Brayton Avenue."

"Oh really?" he said. The impact of what I had told him was beginning to settle. He got up from his chair and took a step towards me, his temper rising rapidly.

"So we're not good enough for you anymore, huh?" He said. Mom heard his rising voice and came into the room.

"C'mon, Dad...."

"C'mon yourself. You would just walk out on your old Dad, huh?"

"That isn't it Dad, it's just that...."

"It's just what? Look at your mother, she's crying. Don't you care about her anymore?"

"Yes I do. I care about everyone in this house," I said.

"Listen, you little shit, once you walk out of that door, you can just keep going. I don't ever want to see you in this house again. Do you hear me? Never!" His eyes widened. His voice was strained. He turned his back and walked into the living room shouting to no one in particular, "Move away from home! He's only seventeen! What the hell kind of noise is this? We raise him and now he just runs out on us?"

Mom called after him: "Frank? Frank?" Then she came close to me.

"Dennis, you know this will hurt us very much. Why don't you just stay here? Please? Things are OK between all of us. Stay here. Please?" Her eyes were brimming with tears.

I noticed a slight graying to her temples that I had not seen before. I weakened for a moment. OK, I'll tell her I'll stay. OK, just stop crying and tell Dad to calm down. I'll stay on Finney as long as you want me here. I'll….

"No. I can't stay. I love you both. But I'm moving."

It was an awful time. I felt like I wanted to throw up. I went upstairs to put my books in boxes and clothes into shopping bags, which I planned to pick up later.

I went back to the kitchen.

"Will you come back to see us?" Mom asked gently as put her hand on my arm.

"Come back?" Dad chimed in. "Like hell he can come back." Then, facing me directly, he pointed to the door and said: "See that door, kid? When you leave don't let it hit you in the ass! Hit the road."

I walked past Dad's glare and Mom's sobs through the door and out on to Finney Avenue. I glanced at my brothers and sisters playing in the back yard. I patted our dog Spotty on the head. I opened the gate and walked down the street to catch the bus at Broadway and Harvard Avenues. I was scared.

I was on my own in the big city. It's not as though I had never been on my own before, but those times I always knew, or at least hoped, I would be back home with Mom and Dad. This time was different. I knew I was not going to go home again. As I travelled downtown to transfer to the Number 84 bus, the city suddenly seemed enormous. My new place was only a few blocks from St. John Cantius High School in the Tremont area. It was upstairs at the Sikorskis, whose son I played sports with at St. John Cantius. The drug stores, the bakeries, the supermarket, the football field down the hill, familiar landmarks I had seen almost every day for four straight years, all looked different somehow. This was my neighborhood now.

Mrs. Hazel Sikorski gave me the keys to the upstairs apartment at 815 Brayton Avenue. I walked up the narrow stairs. The door opened to a kitchen, which had a refrigerator, a Magic Chef oven, a white table with yellow vinyl-covered chairs and a small sink. A bed and a dresser filled a room off the kitchen. A small bathroom was in the back. The front room had a large red and gray velvet couch with a matching end chair. Three rooms and a bath all to myself! This apartment was about the same size as the place near Hough Avenue where seven of us had lived for a short time.

The Magic Chef oven was better than the one Mom used at Finney Avenue. I didn't know anything about cooking, so it really didn't matter. For the first week I shared dinners with the Sikorski family. The dreaded moment, however, eventually arrived. I had to learn to face the oven, chest to burners, cook or starve. I decided upon a compromise: TV dinners.

I quickly understood that I should have taken Sister Sabina's home economics course, but it was not available to boys. There were no instructions on the cardboard container concerning how long to stay on the telephone when the chicken TV dinner was heating in the oven. By the time I ended my phone call my first try at cooking ended in ashen chicken and a kitchen filled with acrid smoke.

Now I was the one getting bills in the mail. I had to find a better job. Caddying at Beechmont covered my expenses, but it was no way to make a living. When it snowed, the golf course closed.

I began reading the want ads, hoping to find some kind of work closer to my new home. I wanted work that would give me a chance to learn. I wanted a job where I could help people. I answered an ad for an orderly at St. Alexis Hospital: "No Experience Necessary. Will Train."

I applied and got the job. I was issued white pants and a white shirt. It was my work uniform as an orderly. I may have looked like I was ready to receive my first communion, but I was there to clean bedpans, scrub floors, deliver trays, and distribute water pitchers. I didn't like the bedpan routine at all.

Hospital work caused me to take a different view of life. I listened to patients' life stories, learning about their families, their jobs, and their hopes. I also learned that the closer some people came to losing life, the harder they fought to keep it. I quit thinking of myself at work and began to think of them. I was working to help people get well. I was also working to make money.

Hospital work instilled me a feeling of the urgency of each day. Time is short. Live each day to the fullest. Get everything you can out of every waking hour. Hospital work also gave me a hernia.

I had been working on a surgical patient ward. Mr. S. had undergone major abdominal surgery. A bandage covered most of his belly. I ran to his bed to catch him before he fell to the floor. He weighed about 100 pounds more than me, so there was little I could do except cushion his fall. I felt a sharp pain in my right side as we went down. Mr. S. was fine, but I had a tear in my groin, a hernia. I knew because I took care of patients with hernias, and now I was about to become one.

When I returned to work after surgery, I was in better shape than ever and wiser about what patients go through in surgery. I began to work fifty and sixty hours a week, at $85 for forty hours. I worked another twenty hours a week overtime. And I opened my first savings account at Cleveland Trust bank.

I visited Finney Avenue. Frank Jr. was in the field behind the house. He had a shovel. A small pile of fresh earth had been turned. Mom was in the kitchen, sitting in her chair, crying. Perry, Larry, Theresa, Beth Ann, and Gary were all in tears.

"I told him not to come with us to the store. But he followed us to the corner anyway," Theresa sobbed.

"We were inside Seymour's Drug Store..." Mom was so distraught that she stopped talking.

"Spotty got hit by a car. He got killed," Gary said. "I carried him home in my arms."

"No! Oh, no! What? Where? Oh, no!" I turned to face the wall. This dog had been through so much with us. He was the tenth member of our family. He was there at dinner, although under the table. He refereed arguments, barking so furiously when things got out of control that we lost track of what we were fighting about as we turned our attention to him. When I was home, I cleaned up after him and I fed him.

I'd thought of taking him with me when I moved to Brayton Avenue, but that wouldn't have been fair to my brothers and sisters. And it wouldn't have been fair to Spotty, because he loved being around people all the time. I had expected that he would just go on and on. I sometimes pictured him as an older dog, sitting by the side door, snapping his jaws at the flies trying to get inside the house, laughing as he regarded the craziness in the kitchen.

I walked to the backyard, climbed that old rusty fence, joined Frank in the field above the gulley. Frank was crying as he dug a few feet down. "You know, Den, he played in this field all the time. He didn't belong in...that street...Spotty belongs right here now, looking over the Gulley." We placed Spotty in his grave. Frank patted the ground with his shovel. He put some rocks on the fresh earth. Suddenly I felt terrible about having left home. Maybe if I hadn't left this wouldn't have happened. Frank and I said some prayers for Spotty. Then we surrendered our little dog to the wild lilies and the crickets, the birds and the stars above the Gulley.

October 1, 1964 was fast approaching and I had a promise to keep. I had saved up enough money. After work one day I stopped at St. John Cantius convent to see the Principal. She gave me a warm welcome.

"What can I do for you, Dennis?"

"I have a matter I want to settle, Sister." I reached into my pocket and pulled out an envelope with $225 in it. I gave it to her.

"It's for my tuition."

"I knew you would pay. I just knew it," she said excitedly. "I told Pastor, 'You don't have to worry about this one. He's good. He'll pay.' When Pastor told me what he told you, I, well, I was very sorry about that, but I couldn't say anything to him. After all," she said confidentially, "he is the Pastor. My, my, you paid off the whole thing. Well, that's wonderful. God will bless you for this."

She gave me a receipt. I shook her hand and walked away with a sense of accomplishment.

As I arrived at work, the nursing supervisor at St. Alexis Hospital informed me of a job opening for a surgical technician trainee. If I wanted it, I could learn to assist the doctors and nurses during operations.

"It's extra responsibility and it's more pay. I think you are ready for it," she said.

I had been trained to assist as a "scrub" on all surgical cases. The presence of God is palpable in the operating room. He makes His decisions right there. When the surgeon is doing the aortic graft, God is there. When the pathologist brings back the biopsy report, God is there. I developed a keen interest in medicine and gave real consideration to becoming a doctor. When the schedule of surgical cases and the assignments were listed, I went home to study *Grey's Anatomy*. I wanted to know everything I could about surgery. I asked frequent questions as operations came to completion.

One elderly surgeon reproved me as he motioned to an exposed abdominal cavity. He demanded to know why I hadn't finished sewing up the patient as he directed. I explained that I was a technician, not a surgical resident. The surgeon was taken aback as the rest of the operating room team tittered with amusement. The supervisor, Miss Josephine Tercek, put me "on call" frequently. Some weeks I worked eighty-eight hours. I slept on a recovery room cart, listening to soft music on a transistor radio. While I waited for a case to be called, I had a lot of time to think. Naturally I thought about things at Finney Avenue. Frank Jr. quit school and enlisted in the Marines on his seventeenth birthday. Gary excelled at athletics and street fighting. Theresa was getting interested in boys. Perry locked a cat into a freezer at his friend's home. Larry found a part-time job at a hardware store after he put a baseball through its window. You can leave home but home never leaves you.

At the operating room table I had to focus:

"Scalpel, sponge, hemostat, sponge, hemostat, hemostat, hemostat, retractor; scalpel, hemostat…suction, hemostat…tie, tie, tie."

No procedure was ever routine. I began to understand the kind of hours doctors must commit to their patients, and decided against becoming a doctor.

Miss Tercek became a confidante. I talked to her about things happening at Finney Avenue, family-type matters. Somehow she always knew when things were bothering me.

"Dennis, you have to keep looking ahead. You have to go to college. You are going to have a great future. You have to make something out of yourself. You can do it." She seemed to be far more certain about me then I was.

The elderly ladies who showed me how to fold linen in the surgical stock room encouraged me every day think about my education. Everyone working within the clean green walls took an interest in me. They encouraged me to think big. They showed an interest in my future. I was their boy.

I had paid my own and my siblings' way through Catholic grade school, and my own way through high school, but I needed to make serious money to be able to afford college. I took a second job, as a copy boy in the city room of the *Plain Dealer*. Ed Chay, the *Plain Dealer* sports writer who had hired me to work *part-time* in the sports department and encouraged me to enter the Cleveland Indians' batboy essay contest years earlier, called and told me there was an opening for a copy boy. He told me that I should apply right away. I did. I told Miss Tercek that I was taking another job.

"You're leaving us?" she asked.

"No. I intend to work two jobs. Eighty hours a week."

"Now how are you going to do that?"

"I'll start work in surgery at 7:30 in the morning. Work ends at 4:00 p.m. I'll start at 5:00 pm at The *Plain Dealer*. I'll work until 2:30 in the morning."

"You really think you can take it physically?" she asked.

I worked out every morning. I felt so good, if I had wings I could fly. Sure, I had stomach pains once in a while, when I'd feel fire lick its way through my intestines. I put it down to eating TV dinners six or seven times a week.

"Are you kidding? I'm in real good shape!"

"Oh, you are?"

"Yes. Miss Tercek, remember, some weeks I put in over 80 hours."

She nodded her head. "But you think you can do a good job in both places? How many hours of sleep do you need?"

"Three…four…aw, who likes to sleep anyway. Sometimes I just go for days without sleep and you'd never know it."

"You better be sharp when you come in here in the morning," she admonished. "You really want to do this, don't you? You really think you can handle two full-time jobs."

"Watch me," I said. After all, I had caddied Beechmont, sun up to sundown, once.

Chapter Forty

"Boy!" WHEN THEY called, I had to take the news from the reporter to the city editor, from the city editor to the copy desk. I took the marked copy from the copy editor, placed it in the plastic pouch and sent it up to the composing room, where the news was set into type. I was a conveyor in the city room where news is made, just like steel is manufactured in a mill and cars are produced in auto plants. News is made in the city room by reporters and editors, because if they don't report it or print it, it is not news. I also helped to make the news by running errands for coffee, tea and broiled hamburgers with ketchup, skip the onions. "Yes sir."

The city room might appear to the untrained eye to be a disorganized fire sale of papers, desks, typewriters and hooks presided over by chain-smoking, hard-typing, hard-driving, hard-drinking young men and women on the make, and older men and women on break. Watch and listen carefully, however, and see and hear the first movement of the City Room Symphony of the Streets of Cleveland: the dissonance of murders, fashions, bombings, business promotions and demotions, wars, births, deaths, shootings, strikes, burglaries, utility rate increases, stabbings, politics, fires and the weather. All of that and more as the performers sit at their desks and type.

"Boy!" The more often they called "Boy," the closer I knew it was getting to that pitting of man against white space, the deadline. The deadline produces the mentality that produces the news copy that becomes the reality of the city. When the newspaper comes off the presses, it *is* Cleveland for many people.

"Boy!" The thing I didn't like about this job was the assignment to pick up photographs of Cleveland-area soldiers killed in the war in Vietnam. I drove the white Dodge with the words "Plain Dealer" written on the doors to personally pick up the art. I found myself in an older neighborhood. I pulled up to the address. The house was a single-story wooden-frame home, like the homes in the Finney Avenue neighborhood. The wooden steps creaked beneath my feet as I walked onto the warped planks of the porch. The curtains in the window were yellowed. A single blue star was affixed to the upper window. The screen door rattled underneath my knock.

A younger brother or sister would open the door, revealing a threadbare carpet in the living room. The father and mother were sitting on an old couch, their arms locked in consolation. Their son's service portrait was set proudly atop a small television. Portraits of Jesus and John F. Kennedy were on the wall of the living room. I offered my condolences. I am offered something to drink. I decline because I have to return to work. Is there a picture they would like me to take back to the *Plain Dealer* to be published in the morning paper? They review a small family scrapbook and decide none of the pictures are suitable. They then walk to the television. One parent takes the picture off the set as a priest might remove a sacrament from an altar. The picture is brought to me. "Please take this, but bring it back soon because we want to place it atop his coffin." They hand me the picture, tell me how much he loved his country, that he was fighting for what he believed in, that they were so proud of their son, he was a hero, and it was an honor to have his picture printed in the newspaper. I thanked them. I again told them I was sorry.

I drove away from their humble home, speeding out of the neighborhood that looked all too familiar, wondering about my brother, Private First Class Frank J. Kucinich, Jr., USMC, on patrol in Da Nang, South Viet Nam. I worried about Gary, who quit school and was waiting for his seventeenth birthday so he could become Private Gary J. Kucinich, USMC. Mom and Dad kept a picture of Frank in his dress blues on top of the television set. I carried the same picture in my wallet. I made many such art runs, and each time I thought about Frank and whether one day I would have to bring his picture from home to the office to be printed in the newspaper.

"Boy!" I hardly noticed that I was working eighty hours a week, I was so busy. I took on extra duties at the *Plain Dealer* assembling weather and Great Lakes shipping data, filing wire service copy, assisting the composing room editor, and answering phones. The telephones linked the city room with the streets of Cleveland. It was through answering the phones that I came to an understanding that many people were calling the newspaper because they had their own stories to tell. Not because they wanted to be in the news, but because they needed help, and the newspaper represented to them a public court of appeal.

When I was answering the phones at the *Plain Dealer* city room, I was more than a copy boy. I was Ask Andy, Miss Lonely Hearts, Ann Landers, City Hall and the editor, all in one. I listened to stories of loneliness that made me feel ashamed of my own fears of being alone. I heard the sounds of suffering that made the rumbles and twitches in my belly seem insignificant. I heard hard luck stories that made those of my family seem ordinary. I learned of another city within the city which seldom saw print, where tragedy does not strike families or individuals just once in a lifetime, but every single day. Countless nights on the telephone brought to me a city of pain, agony and desperation, where men and women whisper their plights into plastic mouthpieces. If you can hear the people, you can feel the people.

There were so many people out there who needed help. I knew that referring them to a reporter, to an agency, to a priest or to a counselor was never enough. Sometimes I hoped it was enough that someone listened, someone who represented authority or power, even though it was only me, the lowest-ranking office worker at the *Plain Dealer*.

"*Plain Dealer* City Room, can I help you?" I asked.

It was an old man calling. He was threatening to take his own life. He said he had a handful of pills, and he was going to swallow them. "Because I have nothing to live for," he said with a chilling resolve when I asked him why he would want to do such a thing.

I felt startled to discuss the end of his life with him. What if I were in his shoes? What if I called a newspaper to tell them what he told me? What kind of advice would I want? To kill myself? No way. I couldn't imagine that anyone would really want to do it. Maybe they toy with the idea until someone talks them out of it? Maybe that was why hc was calling the *Plain Dealer*. He didn't want to commit suicide. I didn't think that Uncle Steve had really w anted to die. He had blamed it on Karma or something. This old man could be somebody's uncle, too.

"You don't want to kill yourself, Mister. Listen, we can get you some help. Don't do it," I pleaded with him.

I mean, Jesus, there are enough things that come at you from all sides in this world, there are enough forces out there which try to destroy a person without a person trying to destroy himself. "Listen, Mister, no, wait, don't do anything. What's your address?" I knew if I could find out where he lived I could get over there and try to stop him from killing himself. I couldn't put this call on hold and ask someone else for advice, because he might hang up, or the call could be lost. If I handled this wrong, he just might do it, right then. He refused to give me his address. I persisted.

"Look, you don't want to kill yourself. There are people here who will help you. I'll get you help." After all, I, Dennis Kucinich, was the Voice of the *Plain Dealer*, as were other copy boys named Andrzejewski, Juniewicz and Brown.

"I'll come over there right now. Please give me your address," I said, trying to restrain my great concern. He relented and told me where he lived. "Please don't take those pills, Mister. I'll be right over. I'll get you help."

"I'm too old. I'm sick. I have nothing to live for, I'm alone," he said, and then he hung up. I never considered for a moment that it might be a prank. I didn't think to ask the police to go there first, because if the man wanted the police there, he would have called them. Besides, I told him I would come and I knew I could get there fast. I took a *Plain Dealer* car and roared down Superior Avenue toward E. 55th Street.

I was prepared for anything. I didn't want to find him sprawled on the floor in a coma as the drugs began to take effect. I just wanted this old man, whom I didn't know a half hour ago, to be alive. I was hoping that maybe I could help to save him. He was at the brink. I didn't know why and I didn't have to know why. All I knew is that he called and he needed help and it was either me or.... What if Uncle Steve had tried to call someone on the night that he took those pills? I arrived at the tenement house. It was hot in the hallway.

The stairs creaked as I walked upstairs and knocked on the door of Apartment 31. I could hear him sobbing. He was still alive, but had he taken the pills? Without further invitation, I entered the room. He sat in a wooden chair, his head resting on the porcelain-top table nearby. His right hand was clenched. I put my hand on his shoulder.

"I'm from the *Plain Dealer*. Did you take any pills?"

Dozens of bottles of pills, some containing prescription sedatives, huddled around a pair of salt and pepper shakers in the shape of an old man and an old woman. If he had planned to take his life, he had plenty of substances to help him.

I shook his shoulder gently. "Did you take any pills?"

He slowly opened his right hand. Nearly fifty multi-colored pills tumbled from his grasp and onto the table. I moved the pills out of his reach and telephoned for a police ambulance.

"There's a man here who needs help. Oh, I'm from the *Plain Dealer* newsroom. He called there and said he was going to kill himself. I'm with him now. He had a lot of pills in his hand when I got here. He really needs to go to a hospital."

Twenty-five minutes later I could hear the police car urgently drawing near. As the policemen led him out of the apartment, the old man looked at me for a moment, a stranger to a stranger, no name. I was just another copyboy at the *Plain Dealer* who was trying to do his job answering the phones. Answering the phones can be a very serious business.

On the way back to the *Plain Dealer* I thought about that old man and what we had in common. He lived alone. I lived alone. My friends would ask me, "Gee, Dennis, you live alone, you're on your own, what's it like?" And I'd tell them, "It's great being by yourself. You have complete freedom. You can come home from work and have the entire place to yourself. There's no one there to tell you what to do. You can come and go as you please. You can go to sleep at whatever time. There is never any noise. You can read without distraction." In other words, I hated it. Whenever I felt alone, a kind of paralysis set in. I couldn't think about anything other than the fact that I was all alone.

When the feeling hit I'd grab the phone and call up people I never would have called in a million years, just to talk with someone. The fact is, when you are alone, no one cares when you come or go. In the evening it is not the strange clatter in the house that frightens your soul. It's the sound of silence. I never knew that family life at Finney Avenue had been the background noise of my life. It took me a long time to get used to silence.

Chapter Forty-One

WHEN YOU ARE NINETEEN years old, it is easy to become casual about life—casual except when you see the beeping cardiac monitor, the expanding and contracting respiration bag, the surgeon's race against the clock to maintain the rhythm of life. Except when you hear the telephoned pleas for help and witness the dynamic, dramatic chronicling of life reporting on itself. Then you learn that there is not enough time anywhere.

In the quiet hours in my apartment, I could hear the Big Ben spring-alarm clock beating loudly, warning me that time was running out, time was conspiring against being and striving. "Get on, get on, Dennis, there is is much to do and so little time to do it in." Sister Leona had said it eight years ago: "I have only just a minute, only sixty seconds in it."

"Brevity" is what I heard when I awoke and when I rested. I was happy; working hard at two jobs. I was helping people.

"You like to help people? That's nice, go to college and you can learn how to help more people," Liz Jacobson, a fellow "copyboy" told me as we stood behind the pneumatic tubes, sending copy to the composing room.

This elderly Jewish lady never talked to me about anything but poetry and college. Every time I saw her, poetry and college. It was enough to drive me nuts. Everytime we stood together behind the tubes she would press a volume of Keats, Browning or some other Romantic poet into my hand and tell me, "Read it, you'll like it," or show me one of her own poems, just completed, with the meters measured.

"This," she would say, "is rhymed iambic pentameter."

Her poetry was good. But what had I done to deserve this endless prodding from her: "Go to college, go to college, go to college"? Hey, I wasn't interested in college. I was learning every day. While she measured her poetry between copy shots, I read Webster's Dictionary. I was educating myself. College?

Oh, sure, I wanted to go at one time. I think everyone I grew up with wanted to go to college, especially after we were told from the seventh grade on that that was the only way we could beat the Russians after they sent Sputnik into orbit. That all seemed far away now.

I earned two paychecks. I was adding to my bank account. I was helping Mom and Dad a little because they moved from Finney Avenue after Koom Frank's attorney had his will probated, took charge of his estate and told my family they would have to leave the house. They moved into an apartment above a bar on Harvard Avenue, near Jones Road. I had a new apartment at 829 Brayton Avenue, just down the street from my first place. At $25 a month it was a dream, with an extra room and private views of both the steel mill and my landlord's pigeon coop.

I had it made: My own apartment, a girlfriend, a stereo, a new bedroom set with a leopard-print bedspread that I bought from Uncle Joe for $65, and I was saving money to buy a car. I had to deal with the challenges of living alone, like buying my own food, cooking, washing clothes, paying the utility bills, worrying if working two jobs was enough, and facing terrible fears about life being so short. The last thing I needed was this frail, grey-haired lady looking up at me through her small red bifocals and lecturing me in soft, nasal tones as if it were her mission in life.

"You have to go to college, Dennis." Jeez, after a while, working the tubes with Liz was like having asbestos in your underwear, it was an itch that no amount of scratching could stop. I couldn't see what difference it would make, but Liz would not let up on this going to college business.

I told her I could read a few extra books a week, her response, "Go to college and then you'll know what you are reading." I told her I could takes notes on what I read and discuss books with friends. She said, "It doesn't matter; in college you will develop real analytical skills." I read where I could get a college degree through the mail. I pointed out the promotional material. She laughed and said: "That's not a real degree, you have got to go to a real college for years to get a degree."

Eventually Liz Jacobson got to me. I enrolled in courses at Cleveland State University. For a time I staggered my hours so I could work at the *Plain Dealer* and St. Alexis while going to school part-time. Liz would not relent. "You're wasting your time, going part-time. If you quit the hospital job, you can go to school full time during the day." She did it again. I left the operating room to attend college full time. On my last day in surgery, Miss Tercek, the old ladies in the linen room, the technicians, nurses, secretaries, janitors, anesthesiologists and surgeons I worked with regularly all came up to me to wish me well, as if I was going off on a long voyage.

"Hey, don't worry," I told them, "I'll be back to see you."

I felt pretty important my first day in college. I thought about how I would be the first person on either side of my family to get a degree. I organized a schedule so I could go to school and work full time at the *Plain Dealer*. I canvassed tables of books for the courses I had to take and had no idea when I would get the chance to read them. In my first classes I learned I was about to delve deeply into English literature, philosophy and communication. I quickly decided I wanted to read the same books the professors read to teach the class.

When I walked into the city room after a full day of classes at Cleveland State University, I didn't expect anyone to say, "Hey, there's Kucinich, he's going to college, he's heading places," and no one did, except for Liz Jacobson. "Now watch. You are really going to go places," she said. Gene Maeroff, an assistant city editor, looked up from his copy momentarily to notice I carried a large briefcase stuffed with books.

"Oh, so you're going to college?" he presumed. "That's good," and then he continued working.

Once word got around the office that I was a full-fledged college student, I gained new respect. Reporters let me sit in on their dinner drinking sessions at the Rockwell Inn, where they talked about their long-lost loves, the agony of reaching thirty years of age and the wars in Ireland, Vietnam, Cleveland and the Middle East. As journeymen and star reporters drank one round after another they talked of another Cleveland, an HFR-HOLD FOR RELEASE Cleveland web of corruption. They spoke with great animation about conflicts of interest, thefts in office, price-fixing, and other offenses so close to finding their way into print; stories that were only a confirmed source, an affidavit, an inside-tipster away. These stories seldom saw print. It was the stories that had not been written, or that they did write and never saw published, that kept tippling journalists at the Rockwell in a semi-controlled beer, scotch and martini-tranquilized rage.

I listened to their stories of political intrigue and sexual conquests with great interest, but I did not join in the drinking as a matter of principle. Every time I wanted to drink I thought about Finney Avenue and a dozen other places where the bottles and woes were piled high. I preferred to find some other way of dealing with my problems, like talking them over with my girlfriend, with whom I planned to elope, or with Sister Estelle, over a telephone at the far end of the city room late in the evening. When that failed, I would sit in a rocking chair in my living room and read Emerson or try to fall asleep hoping that problems would be gone when I opened my eyes. No, I wasn't into liquor, but I was curious about it; to me a martini was just a glass of water.

When a group of reporters nursed their martinis through a dinner hour, I inquired, "If it looks like water, does it taste like water?" Of course, I was offered a sip. I didn't know there was a right way and a wrong way to drink a martini, so I drank the four ounces of gin and vermouth swiftly. The reporter pointed at me:

"Jesus! Did you see that? He drank that martini right down! Holy shit!"

A second reporter chimed in, "Hey, you aren't supposed to drink them that way."

"Big deal, it looks like water to me." I didn't know what a martini was supposed to taste like, but I didn't particularly care for it. Of course, the first reporter ordered another martini and asked me to repeat the performance. I obliged.

"Jesus Ka-Rhist!" He shook his head, stomped his feet and rocked back in his chair.

There was one more encore and we walked back to the city room. About a half-hour later I began to feel light-headed. By late evening the tale of my adventure into martiniland made the rounds of the city room. One reporter refused to believe I could drink three.

"Why, you little shit," he said as he worked at his typewriter from the re-write desk, "no way would you be able to drink three martinis. You wouldn't even be standing here. You'd be on the goddamn floor barking like a dog."

I knew he was egging me on. Why did people do that to me? The last time that happened was at an all-you-can-eat chicken drumstick dinner. On a bet, I ate twice the amount of chicken drumsticks at Woolworth's downtown lunch counter that my two gluttonous buddies ate. 2 x 43 equalled 86 drumsticks, which was a lot for someone who weighed just over one hundred pounds. I ate over the protests of the kitchen help, until I kept pointing at the sign that said ALL YOU CAN EAT and said I hadn't eaten all I could eat. Then there was the twenty-seven pieces of blue pike filet at one sitting. Of course I didn't want to eat fish for years after that, but don't bet me that I can't do something, unless you want to part with those coins you are jingling in your pocket.

"Oh yeah? Hey listen, I drank those three and I could drink another three on top of that. It's nothing. It's no big deal." He rolled his eyes. He knew a mark when he saw one.

The next evening's dinner at the Rockwell Inn, the bet was made. The bidding started with five martinis in a half-hour, the reporter would bank the house. He would also pay for the drinks.

Other reporters joined the table. There was nervous laughter when I suggested that I could drink more than five.

"How many can you drink?"

I looked at the four ounces of gin, no ice, and calculated, "I can drink ten martinis."

There was a commotion heard across the room. Printers, who set the type for the paper, and mailers, who worked the press room bundling stacks of newspapers, turned from their stools. Six reporters put their money on the table. Five, ten, twenty, thirty dollars in fives and ones were laid before me. There was a jostling for positions at the table. People stopped watching the television and came over to see the Rockwell Inn's Human Sacrifice Special, forty ounces of gin in one half-hour. When the hoots and whistles stopped, I called for silence. I drank down the first one, then number two and number three in the two minutes. I sipped on the number four, watching an image on the television at the other end of the bar.

The fifth one tasted awful, like rotten celery. I looked at the eyes that looked back at me. They were certain I had to stop. There was no way this guy can keep it up, they were thinking. They began to smile.

"Watch him, he's quitting."

That was just what I needed to hear, the siren call of the daredevil. These guys had no idea that I was after the world record. I didn't know or care who kept the books, but they had told me it was impossible for anyone to drink ten martinis, so I had to prove them wrong. Twelve minutes had elapsed. I waited another minute, got my bearings and put down the sixth martini. A hush fell over the small group as I swallowed the seventh. My throat burned a little. I could feel my jaw becoming slightly numb. My neck felt like someone was sitting on it. I began to yawn. I looked at the clock. Sixteen minutes. Fifteen minutes to go and I had to drink three more martinis. Whoa! I took a deep breath, grabbed the eighth glass, threw it to the back of my mouth, sloshed it around my teeth like a mouthwash, then gulped it down. Suddenly the faces around me seemed grim and blurry.

"Jesus Ka-Rhist! He might do it!" I heard a distant voice mutter. The eight glasses were lined up one by one around the border of the table, the table....

"Uh, where's the next one, come on, where is it? Let me have it." Number nine went down at twenty-one minutes. I looked at the clock. I couldn't tell what time it was.

"How much time do I have?"

"You have nine minutes," someone said in a solemn voice.

I looked around the table one more time. I could see clearly now. They were not laughing. They were taking notes with their eyes, the way reporters are trained, because one more martini and they would lose $30. I smiled at them, toasted them with the last martini and then....

A copy boy friend of mine told me later that I downed the tenth martini, scooped up the $30, shook hands, promised a betting tour of local nightclubs which one enterprising reporter wanted to manage, walked to the men's room and tried to throw up. But there was no way I was about to give up that gin, at least not immediately. No, I had to be led home and assisted up the steps of my apartment, where a friend pointed his index finger at my mouth, leaned me into the business end of a toilet and forced a few martinis from my yellow recesses, up my esophagus and into an American Standard porcelain jigger. He put me in the bathtub, which I think was full of cold water, and let me sit there for awhile, then he got me up and walked me around my apartment.

"I want to go to sleep," I complained, "Let me go to sleep."

"You aren't going to sleep until you walk this stuff off."

"Jesus!"

He kept me up for a few hours and then my cousin Ray came over to take me to Thanksgiving morning breakfast and then a high school football championship game at Cleveland Stadium. It was freezing. I sat in the stadium stands with only a t-shirt covering my chest. I have no idea who won the game. Later I ate a big Thanksgiving dinner and drank a lot of water, which made me drunk all over again.

Two weeks later, my friend, whose first name was also Dennis, put a news clip in my mailbox in the city room. It told the story of another drinking binge. It was headlined:

BOY, 18, DRINKS FIFTH, DIES

I almost accomplished in a single night a feat that took members of my family a lifetime to achieve—to drink themselves to death. Needless to say, that was the last drop of hard liquor I touched. I called my friend Joe Boland and renewed my membership in the Pioneers, an Irish temperance group that had signed me up when I was in the eighth grade at St. Colman's.

Chapter Forty-Two

WHY WAS MY APARTMENT'S phone ringing so late at night? It had to be bad news. No one ever calls at 3:30 in the morning with good news.

"Hello, Dennis? This is Scott." It was my out-sized friend from St. John Cantius.

"What are you calling me for so late?"

"I'm at work, at Republic Steel. I'm on a break. Listen, you won't believe the deal I found out about. A friend of my mother's wants to sell a 1951 Chevy for $125 and, get this, it has only 18,000 miles on it. It's in A-one condition. I'd buy it, but I already have a car. I think you ought to buy it. My mother says the same thing."

"Scott, I've been saving for a car. I have the money right now. I want to see it." This *was* too good to be true. I had my one true love, and I needed a car to complete the arrangements for our secret marriage plans. The wedding plans were set in motion from a phone in the Home Economics and Food department of the *Plain Dealer*, which was empty in the evenings. I didn't mind giving up my dinner hours. I was in love, I could eat tomorrow when we would be on our way, in our very own car, to Michigan, to marry.

"Dennis, Dennis! Are you there? Hey!"

"Yeah."

"Listen, if you want the car, meet me in the morning."

"OK, Scott, and don't tell anyone about it, please? I mean, I want a chance to buy it."

Sight unseen it was a bargain. But to see this car was to fall in love with it. I was five years old when this sleek black beauty with bright chrome sparkled off the assembly line. Scott opened the door and I moved to the soft beige cloth front seat and looked at the odometer—18,000 miles exactly. I adjusted the rear view mirror and I was already on the Happy Valley Highway. This was not simply a car that would speed my intended and me to our rendezvous with a preacher in a small church in the Michigan woods. This was a wall-to-wall carpeted family car, a car you could drive to church and have heads turn as you tooled into the parking lot. It was such a formal-looking car you could probably lease it to a funeral home.

"Well?" Scott asked, "What do you want to do? You want to buy it, or you want to just sit in it?"

"Buy it! Why sure, here's the money."

I reached into my back pocket and pulled out one hundred and twenty five dollars, in denominations of five. It was the easiest car purchase I ever made. The most difficult one had been a few months earlier, when I bought a 1963 Pontiac Tempest that broke down the minute I drove it off the used car lot. I learned that day what "as is" meant. Fortunately, I had caddied for the new car dealer who owned the used car lot, so he gave me back my money. I vowed then and there never to buy another car, but I could easily break that vow today, so my dearest and I could take our vows tomorrow.

I made several phone calls to a courthouse in Detroit to confirm the information I had read in the World Almanac concerning Michigan's requirements for legal marriage age, blood tests and waiting period. She was seventeen years old. We were both sure that her mother would never approve of an early marriage, so we wanted to surprise her, as in "Hi Mom. We're home. We're married."

Our marriage would be made in heaven and we had a sweet black chariot to carry us along the Ohio Turnpike to Michigan. We made sure that no one would miss us on the day of our departure. We both scheduled a day off from work. I would miss only a sociology test.

It was such a glorious day that we sped along at sixty miles an hour to make our love legal. She never looked better, aglow in her cotton jeans, her reddish-brown hair flowing in the breeze that followed our charging Chevy. The Ohio Turnpike never looked better. Ah, History. Here's Fremont, Ohio, home of President Rutherford B. Hayes—yes, Ohio is the mother of Presidents. She touched my hand.

"Hon, do you notice anything?" I looked at her. She had a puzzled look in her blue eyes, a frown on her angelic countenance.

POKA, POCKA, POCKA, POCKA. I squinted suspiciously toward the loud sounds coming from behind the dashboard. I looked into her eyes, the eyes of love, the eyes of someone who knew as much about cars as I did.

"What is it?" she asked with great calm.

"Uh, sounds like the carburetor, or something, whatever that is. It'll be okay. Don't worry." I tried to reassure her as I slowed the car to fifty.

POCKA, POCKA, BLAM! TSSSSSSSSSSSSSSS...

The car was suddenly without power. It coasted while I guided it to the side of the road. She looked out the window as the scenery of Fremont, Ohio drew near. The car came to a stop. I looked at my watch. Well, maybe if I can fix it I can get us on the road and we will get to the marriage license bureau in Detroit before it closes. The day was young. I patted her on the hand and went to the front of the car where I lifted the hood to begin repairs. Nothing under the hood of the car made any sense to me, but I wanted to look as though I was trying. I loved her so much as she sat there, perspiring in the afternoon sun which beat down piteously on the roof of our black love express.

Oh joy, a highway patrol car. I hope he doesn't ask how old we are, or where we are headed to. He turned on his flashing lights and pulled behind our car. His badge glinted as he walked up.

"Need some help, kid?"

"Yeah, uh, I think my car, uh, it won't work."

"So, you want a tow, is that it?"

"I just want to get the car fixed. I don't want a tow."

"The only way they'll fix it around here is if they tow it in. You want me to call someone?"

"Oh, all right." This was going to cost money, I was afraid.

"I'll call Whitey's Garage. They'll be here within a half hour." Then the highway patrolman smiled knowingly. "Kid, I hope you have a lot of money."

As a matter of fact, we didn't. We had enough for gas, for lunch, for the blood tests, for the marriage license applications, but that was about it. This was strictly a low-budget elopement.

"Money? Oh, sure, no problem. Just call them."

Maybe it won't cost that much, I thought, as she and I rode to Whitey's garage in the cab of the truck, our black dream machine in tow. Maybe they'll fix it right away, I'll give them our lunch money and we'll still get to Michigan in time.

"Ya wanna wait in the office?" a mechanic asked us, as the tow truck set down our car in Whitey's lot.

"Can you tell me how much time it will take, Sir?"

"Yeah, I won't be able to look at it for twenty minutes."

"Twenty minutes!?"

"You got somewhere to go, kid?"

I looked at her. I envisioned our car, travelling along the Ohio Turnpike. We could be in Toledo right now. Somewhere to go, yes! We have to be in Michigan in a few hours. Our lives depend on it. Come on, Mister, fix this damn car. I nodded. I saw two customers arguing with a man about the price of repairs. A half hour later the mechanic asked me what I thought was wrong. I described for him the noises, the slowing car; the loss of power.

"Sounds like you blew the engine, kid. I'll have a look. It's gonna take quite a while. Why don't you go get something to eat and come back in about an hour or so?"

I wasn't hungry, I was sick. I looked at my true love. She was tired but totally patient, for this was a relationship made above. We waited inside the hot, oily garage. One hour and a half later, the mechanic walked away from the car. He had the look of a doctor who was about to tell someone the bad news, news that is usually followed by tears.

"Kid, the engine's shot. It's going to cost you about $125 to fix it. I'll need to buy a used engine."

Time had run out. There was no way to get to Michigan. We were trapped in Fremont, Ohio, the home of Rutherford B. Hayes and Whitey's Garage. I didn't have $125. Even if I did, he told me it would take a couple of days before he could get the car running. We had to be back in Cleveland this very night. Her mother would be expecting her home by ten o'clock. Hey, how was I supposed to know that the car, which was owned by the proverbial little old lady who only drove it on Sundays, had never been driven faster than thirty-five mph? How was I to know that I had to break in the higher speeds gradually? Who knew on its high-performance maiden voyage that the engine would blow up? Oh God. How could this happen to me on one of the most important days of my life? And she is so understanding. Oh, well, true love will try again. I will save up and buy another car, reclaim the bliss and then this day will just become an awful memory.

"Mister, I don't know if I want to buy another engine. I just paid $125 for the car."

"Kid, it's gonna cost you to leave this car here. There's a storage charge."

How can things get so complicated in one day?

"Okay, I get it. I'll send someone to pick it up for me." I knew I could ask Uncle Paul for help. He had a small jeep rigged with a tow bar which he used to tow his brothers' cars to various garages around town. He would pick up my car for me, I was sure. There is nothing to do at Whitey's Garage in Fremont, Ohio when you don't have a car, except to leave it for the Greyhound bus depot.

"Two one-way tickets to Cleveland, please."

Well, there went our money for the blood tests and for the

marriage license applications, but at least we would be back in Cleveland on time.

Oh, that was a long bus ride home. She and I covered years of knowing each other. We went over every single aspect of our relationship while a black woman sang Negro spirituals from the back of the bus. We talked about what her mother would think of this whole thing. We talked about destiny. She felt that God was sending us a message: DON'T GET MARRIED! And that's why the car broke down on the Ohio Turnpike. Who's to say what God wants us to do? Is God a mechanic, a used car salesman? Maybe, if He was sending us a message, it was DRIVE A FORD! I didn't know; I hadn't gotten that far in my philosophy textbook.

The depth of our relationship helped us withstand the test of the bus ride from Fremont to Cleveland. As the bus pulled into the Cleveland terminal, I looked at her to thank her for her patience and understanding, but she was sound asleep. We had just enough money for a cab ride to her home.

Later on that week, we talked again, me from the back of the city room, she at home, and I learned something else had broken down on the Ohio Turnpike, in Fremont, Ohio: our love.

"It's over," she told me. I was numb. Had I time to cry I would have, except I had a philosophy term paper due in thirty-six hours and I had to read about fifty books for the topic I chose: Immortality and the Theosophical Concept. I was broken-hearted but had no time to cry.

Uncle Paul towed the car home that weekend. "Dennis, it ain't worth nuthin' but scrap. I wouldn't buy another engine for it. If I scrap it I can get you enough money to cover Whitey's towing and storage charge."

If anyone knew cars, it was Uncle Paul. He had been in the scrap business for years.

"Uh, OK, Uncle. Thanks a lot for helping me."

Nope. I wasn't going to get upset about this thing any longer. I sat alone in my apartment thinking about the loss of love and the fragility of relationships, and about a previous girlfriend who refused any more dates after she found out that I cleaned bedpans for a living. Now, all the plans for another future, gone, along with my new car. One hundred and twenty-five bucks, gone. It was all very depressing, but I decided not to worry about it anymore. After all, tomorrow's another car.

Chapter Forty-Three

"GOOD EVENING, *PLAIN Dealer* City Room, can I help you?" It was another one of those nights answering the phones, taking messages and dispensing advice. At one time or another it seemed as though the entire city was calling.

Some nights I received a collect call to my heart.

"City Room, can I help you? Uh, listen, Theresa, I know Gary's going into the service. I'm sure he'll be OK. He can take care of himself. Well I know, yes, but if he doesn't get along with Dad, maybe it's just as well. He'll stay out of trouble once he's in the Marines. Oh? They are fighting right now? Listen, just stay out of the middle of it. I'll stop by on the weekend."

"Good Evening. This is the *Plain Dealer* City Room. Can I help you? Yes. This is Dennis Kucinich. Oh yes, Mr. T., I know, I understand, but what can I do about it? Yes, I know your son and my brother, Perry, are good friends. Gee, that's awful. I'm really sorry about your cat, honest. Perry isn't well. I'll talk to my parents. Hey, hold the line a minute, would you?"

"*Plain Dealer*, City Room, can I help you? Yes. This is he. That's right, they're my parents. Uh huh? They are fighting? You live in the next apartment?! Gee, I'm sorry. I really don't know what to do about it. You are going to call the police? I'll call and ask them to quiet it down."

"City Room, can I help you?"

"Flen Dilluh Shitty Room? I whanna talk wit da edditta. Ya heah me, da edditta? Ree gotta guy whrose gonna rhun forrr shitty gounsel, n'es gonna win pie golly."

Oh, Jesus, it was thirty minutes after midnight and there wasn't even a full moon. I was tired. I didn't need this call—the slurred language, the blurred polka music in the background, a boozy late-night political plot—but a customer's a customer.

"Can I help you?"

"Yeah, hyam ear at Hotz's Bar n'dere's dis guy, ya see, e's gonna rhun for whatsis an ees gonna win, got dis down?"

"Oh, sure, I'll take a message for the political writer. Can I have your name or his name?"

"No, wait, gawdammit, ees a next gounselman from, from, you know what I mean now, don't get schmaart."

"What's his name?"

"Oh shit, I gan't tell you now. Bud ees gonna rhun gainst Beeleenskee, you know, Gounselman Beeleenskee."

Beeleenskee was actually Councilman John Taras Bilinski, a 62-year-old Ukrainian fellow who had been in Cleveland City Council for eight straight terms, or 16 years. He represented Ward Seven, which included St. John Cantius High School and Brayton Avenue. He was my councilman.

The man in the bar was interrupted by other voices. Someone turned off the polka music and yelled, "Hey, hang up the goddamned phone!" Then there was a click. Strange call, a draft candidate from a bar, where, as A. E. Housman could have put it, "Malt does more than Milton can to justify God's ways to man." Politics.

Of course I had been interested in politics since Kennedy's Inaugural in 1961. That's why in the tenth grade I knew I wanted a career in national politics. I'll bet there were a lot of young people who were touched by President Kennedy in that way, and because of him we began to pay closer attention to what was happening in politics. When he was murdered that changed. After Kennedy was killed, many of us stayed away from politics until some of our friends began to die in Vietnam, and then we got interested again. I was concerned about Vietnam and about the deterioration of the inner city, which I'd had the chance to experience from the front steps of every apartment and house the Kucinich family had lived in.

How I would start a political career? That was a mystery to me. I knew that some people were born into political families. My family wasn't political. Dad took me to a few union meetings where he got a colored button each month for his green work cap, a token for paying his union dues. And he always supported Eddie Lee for business agent to Teamster's Local 407 after Eddie made sure our family had gifts for Christmas a couple years in a row when Dad was broke.

Kucinich wasn't a political name, although there were probably a lot of bill collectors around town who knew it. Like the one who called me at home and said he was trying to find Uncle Joe because he owed a furniture store $250 for a bedroom set. My family didn't have the money to pay the bills, let alone to get into politics. I understood that some people bought their way into office. My friends didn't have any money, or those who did kept quiet about it. Neither was I a member of the powerful Ward Seven Democratic club that elected Councilman Bilinski. The ward machine was made up of elected precinct committeemen and women who were part of a network which dispensed favors, ran the ward elections, counted the ballots and helped Mayors and Municipal Judges win with big turnouts at the polls on Election Day.

In the City of Cleveland, a councilman is a big deal. More than a legislator, he or she is the personification of local government: a vendor of patronage, a protector of the peace, a cleaner of streets, a filler of chuckholes, a picker-up of garbage, a flusher of sewers, a purifier of the air, a cutter of red tape, a janitor at large and the sovereign of the ward machine.

I knew generally what a Councilman was supposed to do. I didn't really know if Councilman Bilinski was doing it. I read both Cleveland newspapers several times a day, and when news accounts were written of council debates, I never saw his name mentioned. "Quietly effective," his backers would say. I didn't understand how any representative of an old neighborhood could be effective at City Hall if he kept his mouth shut? A councilman who never said anything publicly about people's problems—why would people vote for him? Politics was hard to figure.

Legend had it that councilmen would sit at their phones day and night, to take calls which told of people's needs and hopes. Calls that were a lot like those I received at the City Room of the *Plain Dealer*, night after night. I contemplated. Hey, I'm already doing the kind of things a councilman does, answering the phones and trying to help people, but if I couldn't win a student council election how could I win a city council election?

Councilman Bilinski's tenure was remarkable for at least three reasons. First, he was supported by the strongest Democratic ward machine in the city. Second, he maintained a serene silence during all council meetings. Third, he was re-elected to the council, twice, after pleading guilty to a reduced charge of failing to file his federal income tax returns, a matter which he likened to failing to pay a parking ticket when his opponents called for him to be ousted. "You wouldn't kick a faithful servant out of office for getting a parking ticket, would you?" How can you figure out a councilman getting re-elected twice after being nabbed by the government for not filing his tax returns, especially when he helped his constituents prepare their own filings? Not that we don't all have our faults, as his precinct committeemen pointed out. People on the Number 84 bus said he was a good man. "He's a doer, not a talker."

Councilman Bilinski drew a large number of opponents in previous elections and vanquished them easily with the help of the ward machine. It was predictable that the first call I would receive about a challenger to the councilman's upcoming re-election effort would come from a neighborhood bar, because most pretenders would have been pretty drunk to think they could beat him. Politics!

Sports was easy to figure out. I loved to write about sports. The Cleveland Indians had folded fast in the American League pennant race. The Cleveland Browns were beginning their preseason football drills. I wanted to get back to the sports department someday as a full-time sports reporter. That would be the life, to get paid to go to baseball, football and basketball games. I wanted to join the reporters' staff at the *Plain Dealer*, but the managing editor told me that a full-time reporter's job would hurt my college grades, so he refused to hire me when there was an opening at the police beat.

"Hey, I'm already working full time, answering phones in the City Room, and I'm making the Dean's List at Cleveland State. What do you want? Come on, give me a break," I told him.

You have to make your own breaks. When you are twenty years old and you are answering the phones late night at a major newspaper, you hear nothing but stories from people who have had the worst possible breaks in life. Most of them believed they never had any control over what happened to them. I wondered about that, but the more I read of philosophy and English literature, the more I figured that we all have a lot to do with what happens to our lives. Mom and Dad made their choices. I made my choices.

Take this guy who had just called from a bar. It was his choice to put a candidate in a council race, spur of the moment, Fate doing somersaults. I stared at the rewrite desk for a moment thinking heavy philosophical thoughts. Reporters spend years and years at that desk, endlessly writing and rewriting. Did I really want to do that? Did I want to spend my time writing about what was happening, or did I want to spend my time making things happen? Politics. Hey, if a candidacy could begin from a bar on the South Side then it could certainly begin from a desk in the City Room. Maybe this was my moment to launch the political career I had been planning since my late teens.

Or maybe I'd better keep these ideas to myself. If I told anyone that for one second I was thinking about running for council, they'll think I've gone power mad, or drunk too many martinis again. Especially as I was only twenty years old. Heck, most people my age with any self-respect were marching on the administration buildings of college campuses or demonstrating in the street against the war. I didn't even have time for that. I had taken a few communications courses, not much preparation for standing up and speaking out.

In many ways it's a lot easier to play it safe and let someone else go out front. If you don't get involved then nobody raps you. You can just go your way and other people go theirs. Get involved in politics and right away you become a target. Hey, if I got into it really well, before long people would be marching to protest me. Yeah, politics stinks if you ask me, but when you are sitting in the quiet of the City Room and it's one o'clock in the morning, you end up thinking about your future. You know that at some point you are going to have to take some risks and do things you ordinarily wouldn't think of doing—like Bob Manry, the *Plain Dealer* copy editor. He talked of sailing the Atlantic in a small boat, and he did! If you are going to make any kind of mark in this world, you have to be willing to take a chance. Most people twenty years of age would never think of running for City Council while working full time and going to school full time. But I had wanted to be of service to people for such a long time.

If someone phoned in a question to the city desk and I didn't know the answer, I often turned to the assistant city editor, Gene Maeroff. He sat at a large desk directly behind my phone panel. He looked smart with his black-rimmed glasses, and he was smart. When his sharp eyes focused on their news copy, some of the reporters had conniptions. His dark crew-cut hair added to his no-nonsense aura.

It was very late at night. The city room was practically empty. The only sounds were teletypes ticking and the wheels of destiny whirring.

"Hey, Gene, how old do you have to be to run for City Council?"

"Who wants to know?" He did not look up. He was all business, marking copy.

"Me," I answered, so quickly I surprised even myself.

Gene set down his papers and looked at me keenly. "Are you interested in running for city council?"

"Yes…." My God what was I saying? Had I *really* thought this out?

"Are you old enough?" he smiled. "You have to be twenty-one."

"I'll be twenty-one a month before the General Election."

Gene's hand moved to his chin. Would he take a red crayon, the kind he used to edit copy, and draw a line through my fledgling career?

"Well, what do you think, Gene?"

"I think you can do it," he said emphatically.

He was not known to have an endless capacity for humor, so I knew he meant it. That was all the encouragement I needed to embark on a wondrous journey. I was ready to run, but I didn't know where to run to.

"You should go to the Board of Elections to find out the correct procedures," Gene advised. "I think you will need a few hundred signatures to get your name on the ballot."

"I'll do it tomorrow." I had just declared my candidacy in the news room of the Cleveland *Plain Dealer*, at a time when the presses were shut down and the bars were closed. City Council...Hmmm. Councilman Dennis Kucinich, I could see it already. Where's the Board of Elections? Where are those petitions? Who could I borrow the money from to pay the filing fee? Bring on John Taras Bilinski and bring on those candidates from all the bars in Ward Seven.

Look out Cleveland, here I come!

Chapter Forty-Four

"HELLO, SONNY, ARE you waiting for someone in particular?"

"I want to take out petitions for City Council."

The Board of Elections clerk had a quizzical expression on her face. Wasn't it obvious? I had been standing at that high counter for ten minutes, while she repeatedly squinted in my direction.

"This is the 'Petitions Counter,' and I want petitions," I said confidently.

"For whom?" she asked.

"Me."

"Oh," she tilted her head slightly and smiled, "You must be mistaken, Sonny, you have to be a registered voter, and…."

"I am. I just signed up."

"You are? You can't possibly be old enough."

"How old do you think I am?"

"Fourteen. Certainly no more than fifteen years old."

I knew I looked young, but fifteen? Huh! There had been a time when looking young was an advantage, like when I rode the bus for nothing because they thought I was under seven years, or got into the movies for the children's ticket price, but this was serious business. I planned to run for City Council. Fifteen? This clerk had no way of knowing that for the past few years I had worked two jobs, sometimes ninety hours a week. I was now working full time and going to college full time, and as a result I was getting old as fast as I could.

I would turn twenty-one on October 8, 1967, four weeks before the general election. Fifteen? I didn't want an argument, just petitions. It's a good thing I had my birth certificate, driver's license, social security card and 4-F draft card with me. She obviously wanted proof. I took the papers from my wallet and spread them on the counter. She walked away, as I called after her.

"Lady, I'll be twenty-one before the General Election, and the law says...."

She was out of earshot, flitting around the office from desk to desk, getting the attention of other clerks, pointing at me and making faces, as if I had passed her a threatening note: "THE PETITIONS OR ELSE!"

A gregarious man with ruddy features came up to me. "You want petitions?"

"Yes sir!"

"Are you sure you know what you are doing?"

"Yes sir!"

"Well," he chuckled, while motioning to the clerk, "OK, give him the petitions."

"This doesn't seem right," she said to no one in particular, as she handed me eight petition blanks.

"The Board can rule later on whether or not to accept his filing, if he can get the required signatures," the man who I understood to be a supervisor told the clerk. I took a deep breath and very neatly put the petitions into my briefcase. I could feel the curious eyes following me as I exited. Gosh, who knew it was this hard to run for council? Now I had to get signatures from people I didn't even know.

J.C. Daschbach, a salty old reporter at the *Plain Dealer*, heard I had taken out petitions at the Board. He said I shouldn't have any trouble getting the signatures. As a joke he had once taken a petition to Public Square to advocate that a certain personality be hanged, and people lined up to sign for the lynching.

"People will sign any damn thing you put in front of them," he assured me.

The only thing I needed to know was how to conduct a campaign. My Dad had an old marine buddy who was now an

assistant to a local Congressman. I remembered meeting the man
at a Labor Day picnic in 1960 where Senator John F. Kennedy,
candidate for President, spoke. Dad said the man, Joe Kaselak,
never forgot a name or a face. I was about to find out because I
decided to call him for advice. I didn't know of anyone else
connected to politics. When I called him for an appointment, he
didn't act like it was a big deal.

"Sure, I know you," he said. "I met you about seven years
ago, with your family, at a Labor Day picnic." We arranged a
meeting for the next day.

"Yeah, I've known your father for many years, even before
you were born," Kaselak said as he greeted me in the reception
room of Congressman Charles Vanik's Federal Building office.

"How's he doing?"

"Fine. They've just moved from Harvard and Jones to East
71st Street, above the Mello-Tone Bar. They're doing all right."

He guided me to his desk in an office plastered with
pictures of his boss with major political figures like FDR, JFK, LBJ
and Truman. He took up a chair in front of an American flag.

"Now, what can I do for you, Dennis?"

"Mr. Kaselak, you're the only person I know who knows
anything about politics, and I'm trying to find out what I should do.
I took out petitions to run for City Council and I've never been in
a campaign before and...."

"And you want me to tell you what you have to do to win?"
Mr. Kaselak cut to the chase. "Well, Dennis, a lot of people have all
kinds of theories about how to win elections, but most of those
theories are wrong. It's actually easy to win elections."

I was attentive, on the edge of my chair. "All you have to do
to win that council seat is to knock on every door in Ward Seven,
and you'll win."

"Don't I need a lot of money? For signs, literature, bumper
stickers and...."

"Don't you worry about those things. Just knock on the
doors. Let people see you, let them get to know you, they'll vote

DENNIS J. KUCINICH

for you." I looked deep into his twinkling blue-grey eyes. I may have been hypnotized.

"No kidding? Just knock on doors and I will win?"

He put his hand down on his desk, "Guaranteed! It works all the time."

"Guaranteed? Wow! Mr. Kaselak, gee, thanks."

He got up from his desk and put his arm around me. "Son, you just go out there and hit every door, find out what people have to say. Once you know what they want, tell them you want to help them. Just remember Old Joe when you get to the top."

So that was it. I had the petitions from the Board of Elections and the Secret of Political Success from a professional politician. I was ready to knock on that first door and take it one step at a time, house by house. When it was over, I could see it: VICTORY. On a Saturday morning I paced my apartment, trying to work out what to say to people when I went to their doors. It is one thing to imagine running for City Council. It's quite another to ask people to sign their names on a petition for someone they never heard of. One of my speech professors recommended practicing speeches in front of the mirror, so I stood in the bathroom and faced myself.

"Hi! I'm Dennis Kucinich, and...I'm Dennis Kucinich, I'm running for City Council, and...Hi! Could you sign this petition? I'm running for City Council and my name is Dennis...." Gosh. This could take longer then I thought. I had to show I wasn't afraid to get signatures. I had to want to be a councilman. The worst anyone could say is "no," and I didn't even want to think about that. What could they have against me anyway? They certainly didn't know me.

On the other hand, maybe they'd like me. "Hi! I'm Dennis Kucinich. I'm running for City Council in Ward Seven, and I'd like you to sign my petition so I can get my name on the ballot." That was it, short and simple. I was ready. I fixed my tie, placed the petitions on a clipboard, and marched down the stairs. I could hear my heart beating.

I headed for the first door I ever knocked on to ask for a vote. The implications overwhelmed me: the outcome at the first house could determine not just this election but my entire political career. The rest of my life could be decided right here, at this modest single-family home which leaned precariously away from Brayton Avenue towards St. Tikhon Hill. If the little old lady who lived in this house said, "Yes" and signed the petition, then the whole thing would turn out great. But if she said "No" I was finished. No chance, goodbye politics. But maybe she would be glad to have a visitor, I mused. I didn't think many people stopped by to see her; she had thrown her Christmas tree out only few weeks ago, in July.

I knocked on the rickety screen door. She peeked through the curtains. Her face looked as weather-beaten as her house. She opened the door and stood akimbo in her blue duster, a babushka covering her stringy grey hair. Her bifocals were badly scratched. I began to work up the courage to begin my short speech, to tell her of my desire to have her signature, to represent her in Council, to stand up, to speak out for her. "Hi, I'm Den—," but she quickly turned away.

I waited, perplexed. In a few moments, she came back, extending her right hand as if to shake mine. Ah, success, without even saying three words, the election was in the bag! "Guaranteed!" as Joe Kaselak said. I reached out to shake her hand and she pressed a coin into my palm. A quarter?

She shrugged her shoulders and said: "I thought I already paid you for the paper." She thought I was her paperboy! Oh Jesus. I could hear my heart beating again, making lots of noise. How to tell her that I planned to be her next councilman?

"No Ma'am, there must be some mistake." I reflexively smoothed back my cowlick. "I'm Dennis Kucinich and I'm running for City Council. I want you to sign my petition." I offered her the clipboard and a pen. She wrinkled her nose.

"Are you sure you aren't the paperboy?" I held the petition up and gave her a weak smile. Just like J. C. Daschbach told me, she signed.

"Aren't you too young to run for City Council?" she asked.

"No Ma'am, I'll be twenty-one before the election."

"Well, you sure don't look it. Can't you grow a beard or something?"

Thaddeus E. Kopinski, another *Plain Dealer* copyboy, had told me people didn't trust candidates with beards. Besides, it would probably take me a few years to grow one, and the election was this year. Kopinski had also told me it would be easier to get signatures if I wore older clothes when I walked door to door, so I was in one of Uncle Lenny's hand-me-downs. It was old-looking, it drooped and was very warm.

This going door-to-door was real work. Joe Kaselak did say that's the way to win, and he should know, his boss never lost an election as congressman. I canvassed for signatures the next few Saturdays and at every house people looked at me and asked the same questions:

"Aren't you too young?"

"Aren't you actually doing this for your father?"

"This is for Councilman Bilinski, isn't it?"

"What's this name on the petition?"

It was rough going.

"Bilinski put you up to this, didn't he? Well you go back and tell him I'm not falling for it," was the response of the Councilman's opponent from the previous election, attorney Michael P. Socha, when I went to his W. 14th Street law office to get a signature. He had a handwritten note penned on cardboard taped to a lamp on his desk:

"Bilinski, you can't get under him
Bilinski, you can't go over him
Bilinski, you can't get around him
Bilinski, you'll have to go in the backdoor."

He was unconvinced when I tried to explain I really was running for City Council. He believed that Councilman Bilinski had sent some kid to his door to torment him about the last election and the next election, and he was not about to be fooled.

"Listen, tell Bilinski not to waste his time sending people over here, will you?"

Most people had trouble believing that I was running for council. Still, true to the J.C. Daschbach rule, many people signed my petitions. I filed. The Board of Elections met to determine whether or not I would be permitted in the contest. Five elderly men sat around a large table facing each other, their stomachs growling. I hoped they would make a decision on the merits, not on their bellies' relationship to the approaching lunch hour. Two Democrats, two Republicans and the director batted my political future back and forth for a few minutes. The question on the table: Can he run if he isn't twenty-one right now, but will be twenty-one by the General Election?

"Aw, we might as well let the kid run," said one of the Democrats, looking nervously at his watch.

"He has my vote on this matter."

One by one, the members agreed.

"We have approved your candidacy," said the chairman solemnly, an extremely thin man with an undertaker's demeanor.

"You mean I can run?" I echoed with a mixture of great appreciation and fatalism.

"Yes," said a white-haired bear of a man emphatically. "Run young man, run. Run like hell! Meeting adjourned."

There was a commotion and some laughs. They headed out for lunch; no one noticed me anymore.

I overheard one board member say, "What the hell is John Bilinski worried about? He's just a kid, and he won't get two votes for Chrissakes! He looks like he just started high school."

Chapter Forty-Five

I NEVER THOUGHT OF myself as being *that* young, because I felt pretty old. I had seen a lot of life for a person of twenty years. If my age were measured in experience, I felt at least thirty, maybe thirty-five. I just couldn't change looking young. Yet that was all anyone ever wanted to talk about.

"What's a nice kid like you doing in a race like this?" The *Plain Dealer*'s political writer, Jim Naughton, asked me when he "requested" an interview with me for the morning edition.

"An interview? Why?"

"I think our readers would be interested in why a twenty-year-old college student would ever consider running for City Council. Somehow I just can't picture you puffing on a big cigar." He offered me a stogie and I declined. He proved his point.

It was surreal to be interviewed in the city room, to have the blond, crew-cut political whiz reporter calling me "Mr. Kucinich" one minute and "Boy" the next.

"Mr. Kucinich, why are you running for city council?"

"To be a voice for the people."

"Do you think you have a chance to win?"

"Yes! I'm going to knock on everydoor."

"Isn't it a bit unusual for someone so young to want to be a councilman?"

"I think I can bring to council an energy and an enthusiasm which is not currently there."

Naughton appeared to enjoy the interview. I was very nervous. I watched reporters take down other people's words all the time. Now my words were being written down. I wasn't sure what to expect. I thought the city editor was kidding me when he told me the interview with Naughton was worth Page One. Aunt Barbara and Uncle George had made the front page when she was killed by gas fumes. Uncle Pete and Uncle Paul were in the news when they were arrested for stealing wire from railroad cars, back when both were in their early twenties. I had some clippings from an out-of-town newspaper about Uncle John and Uncle George drawing prison sentences for interstate theft. But me? Page One? The only thing that approaches the magnitude of Page One is the first sports page, and my only plausible chance of making the sports page was being a professional jockey. That dream had vanished when I made it to 130 pounds and 5' 6."

The city editor made it a point to send me upstairs to the composing room for a proof of Page One. I grabbed a copy from a printer and ran to the empty stairwell to study it. I first saw a picture of a rather serious-looking young man. The headlines on the story in the bottom corner of the page:

PROTEST WITH A GUITAR?
NOT THIS CANDIDATE, 20

Well, this is it. I was about to enter public life where everything I said and did would be observed, though not necessarily reported; and when it was reported wouldn't necessarily come out exactly the way I wanted it. The name KUCINICH was being introduced on a city-sized stage. I waited with irrepressible excitement in the mail room as the first edition came off the presses. I was startled early the next morning when radio and television stations began calling. Hey, I hadn't won the election; I had only filed petitions, but it was all over the news:

"Twenty-year-old Dennis J. Kanitth...Kootsinish... Krusinski ...Kuckkinnick...Q-snitts..." Oh, how they diced the name. It was awkward to correct the interviewer's pronunciation, but if I didn't it would be only a few hours before I would be the only person in town who was pronouncing it Ka-sin-itch. By mid-morning the same story was running on all stations:

"Twenty-year-old Dennis J. Kucinich became a candidate for City Council in Ward Seven yesterday. He could become the youngest councilman in Cleveland's history."

History? Let's put this in perspective. All I did was to file petitions for City Council, now here I was standing in front of 829 Brayton Avenue, transfixed by the television camera's lens and lights, like a deer at night frozen in the glare of car lights. I tried hard to act casual. I tried to forget that hundreds of thousands of people were going to see and hear what I had to say. If only I could have remembered what it was I wanted to say! The tall, thin man placed a microphone uncomfortably close to my face.

That evening in the city room, a number of *Plain Dealer* reporters and copy boys gathered around a small television to watch the six o'clock news.

"One of the most interesting races for City Council is in the Seventh Ward, where veteran incumbent John T. Bilinski is being challenged by a twenty-year-old, Dennis J. Kucinich. Kucinich had this to say when asked if he was too young to be a councilman: 'No, I don't think I'm too young to run for Council. This city needs new ideas, uh, uh, uh....'"

When the poet Robert Burns wrote of *"some power, the gift God could give us, to see ourselves as others see us"* he certainly wasn't envisioning a person watching himself on television for the first time and feeling the the sting. I didn't know I actually looked like that. I had no idea I sounded that way. Uncle Lenny's sport coat was a little loose around my shoulders. The television newsman didn't care about any of that:

"Kucinich, who turns twenty-one this October 8th, would be the youngest councilman in Cleveland's history, if he wins. This is Joe Mosbrook, Channel Three News."

There they go again. Youth. Is that all everyone wanted to talk about? I had all kinds of ideas for the ward, but did they want to hear those ideas? No. They wanted to talk about my age. I didn't want them to keep stressing it. As far as I was concerned, the less said about age, the better. I tried to convince newsmen that I was a concerned candidate who happened to be young, just as mayoral candidate Carl B. Stokes was telling Clevelanders that he was a concerned candidate who happened to be black.

No matter what I said, the news media kept mentioning my age and anchormen would raise their eyebrows or express astonishment in introducing or closing the story. Vexed, I was only vaguely aware of the pats on the back and other motions of encouragement I received from my City Room cheerleaders. I called Aunt Betty right away. She always knew how other people would look at things. She would tell me the truth about those television interviews.

"Dennis, it was awful. You must have said 'uh' fifty times. Aren't you taking speech in college? You better work on it some more before you go on television again."

"Gee, well, uh, thanks Aunt Betty. Look, I have to go now." It was a good thing the election was still four months away. Why couldn't I have an Aunt who would bullshit me once in a while, like my Uncles did?

"Dennis, you can't go, I have to talk to you about something," Aunt Betty said. "I'm sorry Dennis, I didn't know you were going to take it this far. I hate to tell you this, but you can't run for office," she said with real force.

"What?! What are you talking about? Of course I can run. I'm old enough. I just filed the petitions," I said, dumbfounded.

"You can't run because if you do the media is going to find out about your uncles."

"My uncles?"

"Yes. You know your uncles have been in a lot of trouble over the years and it is all going to come out. That won't be good for you or for the family. There are lots of reasons why people decide not to go into politics," she said. "Your family is your reason."

"Aunt Betty, if they bring up my uncles, I will have to deal with it, but I can't let that stop me from running. I can't be expected to pay for their mistakes."

"It's going to come up. I really wish you would not run."

This was very hard to hear. Here was the one person in my life who had helped save me time and again. Now she was asking me not to run. I thought about it. I knew she had my best interests at heart. I knew she did not want the family or me embarrassed. I also knew that my life had changed. I had made a commitment to run, and I was not going to go back on it.

"Aunt Betty, I love you, but I have to run." This created some distance between us for a few days.

The public response to my announcement taught me that people pay attention to the image, not the content, of the news. Classmates at Cleveland State University suddenly 'knew' me from television and newspaper pictures. They didn't remember much of what was said or printed, but they recalled the pictures that made it clear that I was a young candidate; that they did not forget.

Though at work I helped put out a newspaper every day, I had never given much thought to how the news affects the person who is written about. One story is just like another—until you are the one who gets his or her name in the paper. Then the news article takes on a life of its own. News stories can do all kinds of things to people. The power of the press is not in the mind of the editor, it is in the mind of the person written about. If you think an article helps you, it does. If you think an article kills you, it does. There are always readers who will reinforce self-fulfilling prophecies. If you don't ever read the newspapers or watch television, you can be spared the agony, but you won't know what is being said about you. In politics it always helps to know what's being said, true or not.

My campaign was underway and I tried to take a leave of absence from the *Plain Dealer* in order to campaign full time and be assured of a job on my return. The Editor denied my request. I was informed that "politics and journalism do not mix." I was glad to have that clarified. I enrolled in a work-study program at Cleveland State and worked out an arrangement with the supervisor of the copyboy staff, O.B. Henderson, to take September and October off for "classwork." So, in effect, I was granted an unpaid leave by a clerk when I couldn't get one from the Editor.

Prior to beginning the campaign full time I went to the Cleveland Public Library to do some research about city government. I saw Bill Miller, a *Plain Dealer* reporter known for his intellect and endless humor. He also had a considerable taste for German beer and weinerschnitzel. Miller motioned for me to come over.

"Dennis, did you hear about those hearings at City Hall on the charter amendment to reduce the size of City Council?"

"I read something about the fact they were going to have hearings."

"Well, they are going on right now. I was in City Hall on a labor matter and I peeked inside the hearing room. It's all councilmen talking. Nobody else is there. You ought to go down there. If you have something to say on the issue of Council reduction, you might get on the news. Hey, you're running for City Council. Show people you are ready for it."

"I thought you had to be a councilman to talk at those hearings."

"No. Any citizen can go to the hearings and say whatever they like. Not many people do. It's one of the things that's wrong with the system."

"What should I say?"

"Say whatever you like. How do you feel about the issue? You must have an opinion one way or another of whether council should be reduced."

I nodded. He may have sensed my hesitation. Things were happening fast. I felt as if I needed more preparation. Here was an opportunity. This was a moment when I had to decide if I really wanted to be elected councilman.

"It's a good idea, Bill. Thanks. You are right. I'll go down and see if I can have a say."

"Give your opinion. More people should do that. Since you are running for council you have even more of a reason to go down there. The hearing is on the second floor of City Hall, in the committee room. Tell them you want to say something on council reduction. They'll be shocked. You'll be surprised at what happens."

Bill Miller made a lot of sense. If I wanted to represent people, I might as well begin now. I turned around and walked downtown towards City Hall. Come to think of it, I hadn't heard much about Councilman Bilinski during all those years I went to school at St. John Cantius, and I was in the neighborhood every single day. Maybe he wasn't necessary to the council; maybe other councilmen weren't needed either. Boy, would they be surprised if a council candidate came into the committee hearing and advocated that same council be reduced in size.

I entered the City Council Committee Room for the first time. Smoke drifted over dozens of empty chairs in the spectator's section, and swirled inside television lights illuminating a long wooden table. Fifteen councilmen sat on both sides, talking to each other for the benefit of a group of reporters.

One by one the councilmen attacked the idea of council reduction. I asked a clerk how I might testify. His eyes widened when he looked at me.

"Sign your name on this yellow pad. Also your address and who you represent."

Who did I represent? I signed in: Dennis J. Kucinich, 829 Brayton, representing Citizens of Ward Seven. Well, it was sort of obvious I was there to represent myself, too.

After I signed in, I became less sure that I wanted to speak. I surveyed the members of Council in debate. The smartest politicians in Cleveland were at that table. For every elected official in this room there were at least ten people who had been sent to their political graves. These guys hadn't gotten here by being pushovers or patsies for smart-assed council candidates who were trying to make a name at their expense. If I tripped up I might make a fool of myself and lose the election right then and there. Still, this was an amazing opportunity for the people of Ward Seven to see and hear more about my candidacy and what I thought about an important issue.

The chairman looked at the single name on the yellow note pad.

"The chair recognizes a Mr. Ku, Kucin...."

"Kucinich, Dennis Kucinich," I offered.

"Yes, Mr...you may come to the microphone here."

"I live in Ward Seven and...."

"Direct your remarks to the Chair, please."

"Yes Sir, Mr. Chairman. Mr. Chairman, I live in Ward Seven and I think that the people are not getting their money's worth from the Council."

A dozen men wearing nice-looking pallbearer-type suits leaned forward. Some began to fidget.

"I think you ought to give the people a chance to vote on this issue. The people know which councilmen are worth the money. I favor reducing the size of the council...."

I continued for a few minutes until I was interrupted by a straight-shouldered, dapper, pencil-thin man in a green sharkskin suit, Councilman George L. Forbes from the Glenville area. I had heard his appeal to the Chairman, "Let me at him. I want to have a little fun," and it made me nervous, so I began to wind up my testimony. I hadn't expected that a councilman would ask me questions.

"Mr. Kucinich, is that how you pronounce your name? Mr. Kucinich, now wait a minute here, now wait a minute. Did I understand you to say that you want the size of Council reduced?"

"Yes."

"Direct your remarks through the Chair," ordered the man who held the gavel.

"Yes. Mr. Chairman, Mr. Forbes."

"Now, Mr. Kucinich," I didn't like the way he said my name, "aren't you running for City Council?"

"Mr. Chairman. Mr. Forbes. That's not why I am here."

"But you are running for City Council, aren't you? Answer the question."

"Mr. Chairman. Mr. Forbes, yes I am."

"You are running for City Council and you want Council

reduced? Is that right?" As he had restated my proposition he began to laugh.

"Mr. Chairman. That's right," I said.

Forbes rocked back in his chair. His grin became a glower. "Well I'll be damned!" he exclaimed. "Isn't this something? You come in here with this kind of shit...."

The Chairman interrupted him. "It's all right, George, he's just a kid."

"Hey, I don't care. He's coming in here. He's talking about legislation which may put me out of a job." He became emotional. Television cameras and radio microphones were turned on. Reporters woke up from their naps.

"I don't believe that Council should be an employment agency," I responded.

A few councilmen straightened in their chairs.

The presiding member hit his gavel and cautioned me, "Direct your remarks through the chair. You weren't recognized."

Forbes acted as though he had been wounded by my remark. "Wait a minute, Mr. Chairman. I can't let him get away with that. He wants to be in this body but he wants to cut off a part of it." Forbes shot a look of disbelief toward me. "Man, you aren't here yet."

"I will be." I could not have been as certain as I sounded, but the Chairman banged his gavel, again called for order and reminded me to direct my remarks through the chair. Forbes laughed, shook his head and waved at me. "I think I'll just leave him alone," he said to the Chairman.

The story of the exchange with Forbes made both daily newspapers and a weekly City Hall political column:

"FROM THE MOUTHS OF BABES... Dennis Kucinich, 20-year-old Ward 7 Council candidate who looks like Alfalfa of 'Our Gang' comedy fame, gave Councilman George Forbes a critical case of forensic hay fever this week. Forbes blundered into a debate with the college boy candidate during legislation committee hearings, provided him with a forum he would not otherwise have had, and ended up literally talking to himself. Demolished in the set-to, Forbes agreed with amused observers that he should have left Dennis the Menace alone."

Alfalfa? Dennis the Menace? Why did the reporter have to write that? The sarcasm aside, in my first appearance in a public forum I was being credited with besting the sharpest debater in the Council! After that exchange I felt confident that I could discuss the issues in committee like a councilman, but I knew I had to research the issues more thoroughly. I began clipping and filing newspaper articles and magazine stories about government. I had to be ready in case I was ever again thrust into an unexpected debate. I wanted to always be prepared.

Chapter Forty-Six

GOING DOOR TO DOOR, I found that everyone had a problem; every household its own story.

I started at Valley View Public Housing Estates, where old tires and junk cars rolled crazily through a maze of brick buildings. A burned-out shell of an old bus rusted in four-foot-high grass, a perfect summer place for mosquitoes and rats to breed and for starving dogs to come to die in the winter. It was also where the children played. In the courtyard of the estates, there were no grassy lawns, only concrete and hard dirt and hard faces staring at interlopers, usually insurance men and process servers. I felt out of place wearing a white shirt and tie, but if I took off my tie the people inside the apartments would never believe I was running for Council. They might think I was casing their home to break in.

I began at an apartment with a small flower basket hanging at the side of the door.

"Magyar?" she said when I introduced myself. "I Hungarian," she squared her shoulders and stood up straight to her high-heeled height of just over five feet tall. Her heavy black eyebrows climbed softly above clear blue eyes. As she opened the door wide I could see that she wore an elegant green silk dress. Her black hair was pushed back and pinned with a rhinestone comb. Her face had hundreds of fine, delicate lines intersecting like frozen milk.

"Problems? I asked. "Anything I can help with?"

"I no go out. Not safe here. Lose husband."

"Your husband died? I'm sorry to hear that."

"He die two years ago. He make pianos. Come in, please. Nice, no?"

I entered her suite to see a crystal chandelier above a resplendent baby grand piano, an secret enchantment hidden away from the menacing outside world.

"What would you like me to do for you, if I am elected?"

"Police, please. Not safe here. Kids beat up old people, take money. No take piano, too big," she said. She shook my hand. I knew I had one vote.

On summer evenings, the police drove through the projects cautiously, their black and white cars spurting through narrow streets. They nervously eyed rooftops of the apartments, awaiting the first rifle "crraack" which would confirm the rumors of an arms cache gathered to launch an assault on police. Once out of the projects, the law stopped briefly to bless the towering cupolas of St. Theodosius Russian Orthodox Church, where on Sundays the parishioners prayed for the deliverance of Mother Russia and themselves and then bolted the double wooden doors shut for the rest of the week.

Across from Valleyview on Thurman Avenue I met an elderly Polish couple who shook their heads in disgust when I asked about the red and green "Black Power" slogans painted onto their white garage.

"They paint, they ruin. I no lock door; they break in house. Son a beetch! I catch, they get," the man produced a Minnie Minoso-signature Hillerich and Bradsby and clapped the baseball bat's trademark in his palm, while his wife smiled approvingly.

"If I get elected, I'll get the second district Juvenile unit in this area to help you," I said.

Homeowners in the Ward wanted my help to stop the destruction of property, the theft of cars and the break-ins which were committed almost exclusively by young people who seemed to have nowhere to go except into someone else's home at midnight. People desperately wanted to stop the crimes. They wanted to protect their property, because ten years ago the city had told them that Urban Renewal was coming. A massive urban renewal program was still in the offing, with its promise of millions of dollars in improvements for the area—in truth a chance to sell and get out.

On West Fifth Street, a jalopy with a red, white and blue George Wallace for President bumper sticker embossed with an American flag was parked on a barren lawn next to a wreck with a Day-Glo orange-and-black Stokes for Mayor sticker on its rear window. I walked up the crumbling steps, checking the notes I had taken from my last stop. Looking up just in time, I avoided the gap near the front door, an express fall into the basement.

"My father is sleeping," said the grape-jelly-faced little girl in the oversized dress.

"OK, don't bother him," I said as I handed her a card. The last thing I wanted to do was wake up a sleeping voter—a sure way to lose a vote. She walked back into the house and suddenly a lanky, angry man came crashing through the broken screen door, holding in his clenched right fist my crumpled campaign card.

"Wait jest a minute. Hold it right thar. Don't move," he turned toward the house quickly, then spun around to stare at me and snarl, "If yer a goddamned Reepublikkin, git the hell off mah steps afer ah git mah gun an' shootcher assoff!"

"I'm a Democrat!" I gasped in self-defense.

"Well, good for yew!" he became expansive. "Ah comes from Logan County, West Virginny, an' we doan 'low no Reepublikkins." I was still hearing his words about shooting me, visualizing him running into the house, coming out with his gun and blowing me away, then asking if I was a Democrat or Republican as I stared vacantly at the sky.

"Hey boy, yew thar? Go ahead, yew got sumthin' to say?" he called me away from my grim thoughts.

I nodded.

"Well, go ahead, gimme your spiel!"

He folded his arms in a self-satisfied manner and smiled as

I gave him my 'spiel' and walked away, grateful that I had chosen the right political party. I had become a Democrat on the advice of Saul Stillman, a senior politician who was recommended by a friend. I met with Mr. Stillman in his downtown office. He asked me what my father did for a living, where I went to school and how my parents voted in elections. After I answered his questions, he gave me his verdict.

"Dennis, it really doesn't matter so much which party you belong to, as long as you try to help people, but I think you would be better off in the Democratic party."

That was good guidance I got from Mr. Stillman. He knew a lot about politics, too. He was the Chairman of the Cuyahoga County Republican Party.

After meeting the fellow from West Virginia, I decided to ask people first thing to which party they belonged.

"Are you a Democrat?" I asked a cheerful-looking old lady, whose large ears and big nose added to an air of merriment about her. "No! Imma nodda Demokrat!"

"Then are you a Republican?" I inquired, expecting her to answer yes.

"No! Imma nodda Reypoobleekan!" She was emphatic.

"Well, then, you are an Independent." Non-partisans were the easiest to convince of the need for change.

"No, Imma nodda Indepen'."

Exasperated, I demanded, "Well, lady, then what are you then?"

"Imma Greek!" she exclaimed proudly.

I thought it paid to ask people their party, but I gave up after that exchange. It was more important to get them to talk about their problems, so I could learn what I needed to do to help.

Most of the people I spoke with wanted additional police protection. To hear some Southsiders talk, they would prefer an armed encampment, an occupying army of men in blue to protect them from the war that was being fought out in the Professor Avenue commercial section. A Ukrainian butcher kept a meat cleaver hidden in a napkin near his cash register. A Polish druggist kept a gun locked in with his painkillers. A Slovak baker swore she would move soon, she was so afraid of being robbed. First-generation Americans limped along the sidewalks, tapping their canes along the surface of streets named College and Literary, which intersect with Professor Avenue. Expectant teen-aged mothers daydreamed in front of dime store windows, slinging their first-born over their shoulders.

Everywhere I walked I could see young and old coming into contact with a threatening environment. One young couple lived in terror in their small house on the edge of the industrial valley. From their front window I could see the magnificent arches of the interstate highway bridge soar toward the Terminal Tower. From inside their living room, I could hear jukebox music blasting from the bar across the street.

"They're shooting guns there all the time," the young mother motioned toward the bar as she breast-fed her baby. "There's teenage girls going in and out of there all the time. I think they're turning tricks. I think the owner sells drugs in there too."

Her husband, a truck driver, shook his head as she spoke. His temples were pulsating rapidly.

"Listen, Mr. What's-your-name, I don't know if you can do anything about all this, but if you can, I'm all for you. I don't want anything to happen to my family. I don't like having to worry about them when I'm on the road. They cause us problems," he pointed in the direction of the bar, "and one day I'm going in there with my shotgun and I'm going to..." His voice trailed off as his wife assured him that something would be done.

I had potential constituents here. They really needed help, "If I win the election—I mean, *when* I win the election, I'll try to shut them down, I'll go after their liquor license," I vowed. That seemed to give them some satisfaction. I shook his hand and on the way out of the door I asked, almost absent-mindedly, "You are registered to vote, aren't you?"

"No we aren't," he said. "We don't believe in voting for any politician. They're all crooks and liars."

"Oh," I said. "I see." As I crossed under the freeway to another precinct, I wondered how people thought I was going to be able to help them if they didn't care enough to vote to help themselves.

Neighbors whispered disapproval of the circle of light-brown-skinned men who clutched dollar bills, waved their hands wildly and miming the deadly strut of fighting cocks pecking each other's eyes out. But the neighbors themselves did not want to get involved. They didn't even call the police to complain. They especially didn't want anyone to know they had told me.

"If I win, I'll get the vice squad to come and shut them down," I promised. I left the alley and walked past an awnings manufacturing company that had closed up shop, eliminating fifty jobs. A few streets away, someone had hung a cat from the rafters of an abandoned dairy sitting on a hill above the Animal Protective League.

On Jefferson Hill, a young Appalachian boy had ridden his bike underneath a ten-ton tanker climbing up from the flats. Neighbors pointed out the family home.

"Over there, the one with the broken chimney and falling steps."

I watched as police and firemen pulled the dead boy and his twisted bicycle with training wheels from beneath the double wheels of the truck. I was stunned. I thought how his parents would feel. Everywhere in the ward, kids played in the street all the time. Why their child?

They might ask the same way I asked, "Why my brother?" Larry had been hit by a taxicab a few days earlier. He chased his baseball into the street near my parents' new apartment above a delicatessen on Harvard Avenue. He was struck and thrown about thirty feet by the impact. Larry was in critical condition with broken ribs, punctured lungs, a broken collarbone and numerous internal injuries. He lay semi-conscious in the brightly-colored pediatric ward of St. Alexis Hospital. I went there every night to sit with him, to hold his hand and ask "Why?" Nothing is more frightening than to see a child face death.

I wanted to go to the home of the boy who had just been killed in the accident to express my condolences, to let the family know that other people did care about what happened to their child. In the same way I hoped other people cared what happened to Larry.

The door was open. I called into the living room. The mother was sitting on a torn couch, bottle-feeding a year-old baby.

"Lady, I heard what just happened to your boy. I'm awfully sorry."

She shrugged her shoulders and looked around her living room. "Wahhl, ah am, too, but I got eight others to worry about here. I told him to stay away from that hill. He shouldn't a been riding on that hill with that bike." And then she hugged her baby tight and burst into tears.

During those four months I spent going door-to-door, I learned that my neighbors kept their secrets closely guarded. Their battles were not always the great tragic moment. Their daily struggles were tidily deflected in clear-waxed linoleum floors, freshly painted window sills and gutters that didn't leak. Their hearts didn't tell of the phantom pains of chopped-off fingers and thumbs discarded in superior punch presses; of crushed limbs or brandings from splashing liquid ore; of blinding grinder sparks; of coal-encrusted lungs gasping for breath.

Something about this neighborhood felt like home to me —the agony that working people tuck away in their guts, the awareness of machines smashing mens' bodies, enraging their spirits but leaving them partially deaf and dumb to the punctuations of gun shots, tires screaming on the pavement, fire engines shrieking at the pyres of mom and pop delicatessens; steam shovels yawning at the rubble of residences cleared for freeway and neglect. This neighborhood was dying. In its final hours, it had been drawn and quartered by freeway developers, bound up in ribbons of abandoned railroad tracks and dumped on the banks of the fetid, terra cotta Cuyahoga River, which was brimming with rats, debris and industrial chemicals that burned the eyes and caught in the throat.

Yes, I thought, as I walked door-to-door, this area had been given up for dead. When this neighborhood of poor and working people died it could be anointed in sulphur dioxide and fly ash, laid out underneath a panorama of throbbing smokestacks and dozens of inspiring steeples trembling with dirges in thirty languages. Then insecure pensioners, young Catholic grandparents and hungry widows could pray the Rosary every evening for the repose of its soul. That is what I remember the most: walking the Southside in the early summer evenings, listening to the radio Rosary drifting from behind locked screens. The silhouette of the old people against their lamps, crossing themselves with arthritic fingers, praying for peace, for the faithful departed, for the strength to endure deferred hopes; praying that family, church, neighborhood and life itself would retreat no more and would stand still in time, preserved and safe, a dream-sculpted frieze.

They knew their neighborhood was dying, but they did not want it to happen. They wanted it to live without robbers, murderers, rapists, burglars, rats, vandalized homes, overflowing catch basins, uncollected garbage, barking dogs, chuckholes, air pollution and the thousands of other insults which assailed the eyes, ears, nose and spirit every day on the old block. They told me so. The people were not of the alleged silent majority. It's just that they had too few listeners, so they remained silent rather than share their concerns with people who didn't care. I discovered that when you take the time to listen to people, when they know that you care and that you want to help, they are not silent at all. They know what they want. They are speaking all the time—their thoughts and words lack only public articulation, acknowledgement and action.

City Hall represented a system of decision-making which they knew little about, and over which they felt they had no control.

I heard it over and over, "You can't fight City Hall."

People didn't know what local government was supposed to do. Not that they didn't care, but people had more pressing problems of their own: bills to pay, children to feed, deep personal concerns.

As I walked from one door to another, the soles of my scuffed shoes baking on the burning pavement, I recognized the people's discomfort, their suffering, their heartbreak as my own. I had seen and heard the same stories before, from our neighbors in houses on streets like St. Clair, Hough, Carnegie, Broadway, Finney and Lorain Avenues. It was stunning to meet the past on the way to the future.

A campaign that began almost impulsively became serious, and I began to change with each step, each knock, each person I met. I became even more resolute when I saw people wanting to believe that as a City Councilman I could perhaps make a difference in their lives. In the evenings, as I reflected on what I learned door-to-door, I began to understand the people's hopes and I was overwhclmed at their suffering. I came to believe that I *must* make a difference for them. I began the campaign wanting only their votes. Now I wanted to be their voice, to stand up and to speak out on their behalf.

In four months of going door-to-door, I met thousands of people and during that long walk I made the most important discovery of my life: *You are alive when you reach out.* It is in extending your hand that you affirm your existence.

Chapter Forty-Seven

I WAS WINNING THE 1967 city council race until Election Day, a cold first Tuesday in November. As dawn colored the industrial horizon a smoky grey-blue, Councilman Bilinski's ward machine workers were already queued up outside the voting booths, carrying shopping bags, wearing heavy overcoats stuffed with sample ballots, frozen smiles hanging from come-here-I've-got-something-for-you faces. Voters moved toward the polls toward the flurry of broad gestures, the knowing winks, the pats on the back, the Pentecostal political tongues wagging in Polish, Ukrainian, Russian, and Slovak.

"How's your mother, father, brother, sister, uncle, aunt, godson, grandchild?"

"Heard about the wedding, funeral, baptism and so and so's in the hospital, that's too bad, how are you?"

"Don't forget our Councilman John."

At the doors of Ward Seven throughout the campaign I'd heard two opinions of Councilman Bilinski. One came from people who thought he had disgraced the Ward by his tax wranglings and because he was disbarred from the practice of law. Others saw him as a sort of Ukrainian Robin Hood, who took from rich Uncle Sam and gave to the poor pans and paniis. This group of people loved him because he went to their baptisms, weddings and family funerals. Some in the Ward spoke in awe of the Councilman getting their brother or father or selves out of jail by putting up the bond money out of his own pocket. He got people jobs. He did free legal work for some and helped others get driver's licenses.

This portly man with a shock of white hair may have had trouble with his own income tax returns, he may have run his office out of his pockets, but when it came to politics, he never got anything mixed up. He knew his people and the people knew him. What's more, his ward machine, the Seventh Ward Democratic Club, was the best in town. The club knew exactly how many votes it had. It registered to vote many of the people on the same day they became citizens. The machine could speak the people's language, any language. I felt like a stranger in my own ward when I saw the machine in action on Election Day.

Inside the polling places, Bilinski-appointed election workers checked off names of voters who were slow to respond to the Call of the Vote. At one polling place, the Gray Wolf Tavern, it was customary (though illegal) to buy drinks for prospective voters.

A white Dodge station wagon with god-awful twin amplifiers worked its way though the streets. The recorded foghorn Voice of Doom drifted through the walls of the single and double-family wooden homes: I sat in my kitchen, eating a quick lunch, yet the Voice found me, the slow, deep staccato monotone enveloping me in an ethereal shroud.

"This is your friend, A.G. Sobbota. Today is Election Day. Vote for John T. Bilinski, your councilman. Do not be fooled by a young, inexperienced student who just moved into our neighborhood. Vote for your friend and mine, John T. Bilinski. You know John T. Bilinski. He knows you. Do not be fooled by a young, inexperienced student."

I stood outside a polling station all day, and I was convinced from all the hands I shook that absolutely everyone voted for me, or at least they said they did. I saw some of the literature that the Councilman's poll workers pulled from the shopping bags. It was about me, and it wasn't very nice. Old country politics had come to the new country. "Bolshevicki!" one poll worker derisively called to a Kucinich supporter who held one of my red and white signs.

As election night drew to a close, about ten of my campaign supporters gathered in a tiny office in front of a print shop across the street from St. John Cantius Church and High School. When the results were final, it became clear that Election Day, 1967 belonged to Councilman Bilinski, who maintained a victory margin of 500 votes.

"We haven't been defeated. We've only been detained," I told my dejected friends. Then I placed a call to the one politician in town who was supporting me from behind the scenes, State Representative Patrick J. Sweeney. I told him about the results.

"That's closer than anyone has ever come to defeating him," Sweeney said. "If we had known it was going to be that close, we would have gotten you more help!"

Yes, I had television coverage of the kind that Councilman Bilinski never received. I had newspaper endorsements and brightly colored campaign cards, but John T. Bilinski had the people. I was getting a college education at Cleveland State University, but John T. Bilinski was the political doctor of Professor, College and Literary Avenues, and I was his student. He knew the people. I was just starting to know them. In knocking on thousands of doors I was learning how to win, but first I had to learn how to lose.

Chapter Forty-Eight

SEPTEMBER, 1968. MY stomach was a volcano, with juices shooting lava-like up my burning esophagus and spewing chunks of undigested food in fiery waves of blood and sulphur-colored mucus over my retching tongue, out of my mouth and onto the white kitchen floor. I was shaking. I rushed to steady myself over the toilet. My watery eyes bulged and my guts gushed again. I could feel the acid searing my insides. I could smell that old rotten eggs odor and it made me want to vomit again. I felt so weak. I couldn't stand any longer. I knelt in front of the toilet, wondering what was gnawing at my bowels and praying for the convulsions to end. Again the foul mix blasted up and out of me. I hit the floor, doubled up on my side, pulling my arms tight around my rioting midsection. I tried vainly to control the pain by rolling back and forth in the small room, rocking between the toilet and wall; back and forth, rocking and vomiting, rocking and vomiting, rocking and vomiting blood and mucus. Oh No! Not this again!

It had happened in May, too. I had been riding with Dan Backus on the way to a baseball game when a powerful twinge in my left side sent me deep into the passenger's front seat. I felt sick to my stomach. I pitched forward, burrowing underneath the dashboard. I felt so stupid. I was supposed to be sitting in the stands at Edgewater Park watching Dan pitch Class A ball, not gazing into the glaring lights of a hospital operating room, watching with astonishment as doctors raced to remove my appendix before it burst. I had had plans that did not allow for such rude interruptions, which is why I ignored the pains whenever they grabbed at me. No time for pain. Mind over Matter. Think hard, concentrate, pray and it will pass. Well, that was the way it was supposed to work: Mind over Matter. I knew I could get up off the bathroom floor. I knew I could stand up, walk to the kitchen stove, and make a cup of tea to settle my stomach and I'd soon be sound as a roach.

Before my appendix had revolted, I had planned to travel to the state of Oregon to campaign for Robert F. Kennedy for President. I had already severed ties with the *Plain Dealer*. City Room editors had been touting me for a summer reporting job, but senior editors rejected my application so I rejected them, typing out a two-word resignation letter: "I quit." It was a painful moment. The *Plain Dealer*, where I had learned so much from reporters and the public, where I had come into touch with an intellectual and political life, had become a dead end. I departed abruptly, saying only: "You'll be writing about me."

Yeah, they'd be writing about me all right; writing about me writhing in front of a toilet on the bathroom floor. What the hell was I doing on a bathroom floor? This wasn't supposed to happen. In June I was supposed to be in Oregon campaigning for Kennedy. I was not supposed to be in bed watching the Oregon and California primary returns come in, while convalescing at Dan's house under the care of his mother, Anne.

When I left the *Plain Dealer*, I made up my mind to be a participant in events, not a spectator. I had begun to believe that one individual could make a difference and help to make this a better world. A passage in Robert Kennedy's campaign book, *To Seek A Newer World*, said it for me and inspired me to help in his campaign:

"Each time a man stands up for an ideal, acts to improve the lot of others or strikes out against injustice, he sends forth a tiny ripple of hope. And crossing each other from a million different centers of energy and daring, those ripples can create a current which can sweep down the mightiest walls of oppression and resistance."

Yes, I was supposed to have been in Oregon, organizing to help Robert Kennedy become President, not in bed in Cleveland watching him declare victory at the Ambassador Hotel in Los Angeles. He was going to end the war in Vietnam and put a stop to the wars being fought in the streets of America's cities by addressing social and economic problems. He wasn't supposed to get shot. He wasn't supposed to die. What the hell was I doing on the bathroom floor? I was not supposed to be there. I was supposed to be at my new job as a copyreader at the *Wall Street Journal*. The Dow-Jones publication had hired me after *Plain Dealer* assistant City Editor, Russ Kane, told the *Journal*'s Cleveland Bureau Chief, Clayton Sutton: "I think he's gotten politics out of his system." Sure I had, bullet by bullet.

The assassination of Robert Kennedy left me fed up with politics and the whole rotten system. I said so, to *Plain Dealer* political editor Jim Naughton, during a visit to the *Plain Dealer* City Room after Kennedy was murdered.

Naughton answered me with in his Sunday political column: "Lost Hope? He Had More Cause." The message was that Kennedy believed in change through the system and that he had endured all kinds of tragedy to pursue such change. There was no reason to lose hope, Naughton wrote, because as bad as the system was, Kennedy still believed it could be changed. I didn't like the system. It brought a world of poverty, racism, crime, war and death. But could I change the system by staying outside of it? I knew I had to find that place inside of me which had the courage to go on whatever disappointment, whatever the odds, if I really wanted to change the world. Maybe I hadn't gotten politics out of my system, but I certainly had something in my system that I wanted to get rid of before it got rid of me.

I struggled to set myself on the toilet seat. I bent over and waited. When I got up I looked into a bowl that was dark and red. I didn't want to call the doctor. That would mean time away from work, and I had just gotten the job. I didn't think the *Wall Street Journal* would carry a sick person on its payroll, and my studies were in trouble. I had just finished making up work I missed during the final weeks of the 1968 spring quarter. I didn't need more postponements in my college education. I was already twenty-two years old and barely into my senior year. Mind over matter. It will go away. I was on the floor again, rocking back and forth. I fell asleep. When I woke up a few hours later the pain was still there. I had nothing left to vomit. I had not eaten in a day. My neck and chest muscles were sore from the dry heaves that wracked my body. I was so weak, but still I did not want to call the doctor. I would wait one more day. Maybe by tomorrow it would pass.

I went back to the kitchen table to watch the steel mills form their wispy palette of grey, white and red smoke, to see white lights outline the Clark Avenue Bridge and the mills and the other heavy industries of the flats, to see automobile headlights extinguished in the parking lot of Clark Field, providing young lovers with the protective cover of darkness. I put my head down on the table. I could hear the hot steel crashing. I could hear Jan Krzmien's pigeons cooing in the backyard coop. I could hear my baritone bowels repercussing. I fell asleep. I woke to discover it was not my dreams that had been petrifying, but my waking hours. I was frozen in pain that locked everything that was inside of me and would not permit any food to enter in. My intestines felt knotted. Whatever it was it would not go away. I could not wish it away. I could not will it away. It was a twisted fact. I had to admit it as it screamed at me from inside. I changed my clothes. My pants were quite roomy around the waist. My shirt felt oversized. I had to go to the doctor's.

I boarded a Number 84. As it worked its way through the southside, I hoped that maybe there was still a small chance that something would change, that the assault would end. When the bus arrived downtown, I felt just as awful as I had when I got on it. I transferred to the Broadway bus, which would take me to Fleet Avenue.

I sat in the back of the hot, stuffy bus, feeling queasy as chills swept over me. I fell asleep but woke up at my stop. I rushed to grab the bell and rang it several times. The bus driver stared into the rear view mirror. Disgusted, he opened the doors once more. The temperature was at least 90 degrees. I plodded along Fleet Avenue—Warzawa, little Warsaw as it is called—a street of Polish bakeries, delicatessens, butcher shops, travel agencies, insurance companies, funeral homes and churches. This is a community of commerce and worship; of friends congregating and rowdiness from the dozen bars where liquor is poured in many European languages. Fleet Avenue is a street of grand parades, of Polish Veterans marching grandly, flourishing the Polish red and white alongside Old Glory's red, white and blue. It is the street a President must walk down to say he was truly in Cleveland.

This morning Fleet Avenue was a street of pain, a tarry street with heat waves flowing from the pavement, a forever street with a far-off mirage of a doctor's office. Little bubbles! Little bubbles? What, where are those little bubbles coming from, percolating in front of my burning eyes, dancing above the hot pavement, floating in the air? Where's the doctor's office!? Oh, there, across the street. I had to sit down and rest. I sat on the curb, nodding, my head between my legs. Two old women who passed by squinted at me and shook their heads. Obviously a young wino was regurgitating some cheap swill into the gutter, what's this neighborhood coming to? I vomited more mucus, raised myself up and stumbled across the street to the office of Dr. Javier Lopez, the Kucinich family physician. It was a long climb to the top of the stairs.

Dr. Lopez had just opened his office for the day. He was a stout man, balding prematurely. He looked somewhat older than his thirty years. His heavy brown-rimmed glasses framed knowing dark eyes that widened when he saw me appear in his waiting room.

"Dennis, what happened to you?" His brow was furrowed. Did I look like something had happened to me?

"I, uh, don't feel well. I feel awful."

"I'm sure you don't feel well. Here, let me help you on this scale. My goodness, you have lost a lot of weight. What happened?"

I weighed in at 110 pounds, twenty-five pounds off my normal weight. He helped me to a leather examining table.

"Lie back now." He felt my abdomen. It was very tight.

Everywhere he touched, it hurt, but I didn't want to make a big deal out of it.

"My, my," he shook his head. "This is very bad, Dennis. You will have to go to the hospital right now. I will call for a bed. Did anyone drive you here?"

"No. I came by bus."

"You came all the way here, like this, by bus?" he shook his head again. "Dennis, Dennis, Dennis." He usually spoke in cool Colombian tones, but his voice expressed such concern that I knew it was bad. I had known Dr. Lopez for about ten years. I met him when he took over Dr. Hall's practice on Broadway and Harvard. We renewed our acquaintance when I was a technician at St. Alexis Hospital and he was a member of the surgical staff. He was my friend as well as my doctor.

"Wait one moment and I will drive you to the hospital."

On the way to the hospital I explained to him that I had been living alone, except for an occasional visit from my cousin Ray, who was home from the Air Force. I explained that I ate mostly TV dinners and fast foods, chili-dogs, hot dogs, hamburgers, and fried chicken. I drank about six twelve-ounce bottles of cola every day. I always had enough to eat. I told Dr. Lopez that whatever it was, I didn't want to stay in the hospital very long because I had things to do.

"Let's find out what is wrong first," he said. He asked me about my studies. He had been one of the people who encouraged me to go to college.

"My grades are good, but the last time I was in the hospital I lost a lot of time...."

"Dennis, you cannot worry about anything else right now. You must get well first and then you will have all the time in the world to think about what you will do next."

I was admitted to St. Alexis and sent directly to x-ray for a series of gastro-intestinal studies, including a barium swallow and a barium enema which made me want to resign from the human race. I felt like I was a roll of hard salami being paddled back and forth by expert hands. The hum of the Picker machine, the ghostly hues of the x-ray room, the muttering of technicians, the solemn tones of doctors consulting behind the window of the lead screen seemed unreal, like this was happening to someone else, except for the barium enema, which made it all too real.

"Dennis, your intestines are totally obstructed. Nothing is getting through. There are some ulcerations and perforations, too. How long have you been in pain?"

I just looked at him and winced.

"I am afraid we must operate on you. It will be very serious surgery, but you are not ready for it, yet. You are too weak right now." He sent me to a room and ordered intravenous feedings.

One week later he came into my room and explained that he would have to remove some of my intestines. He could not say how much until he got inside to take a look. I understood.

"You know I will do everything I can to help you, Dennis."

I was afraid, but I trusted him. The seriousness of surgery began to settle in. I remembered being an orderly on this same floor. I had walked into the room of a very young patient who had had a large section of his intestines and his colon removed. He spent about a month in the hospital. He had it very rough. I remembered his cries, his screams for something to relieve the pain. I had thought at that time how odd it was that someone so young would end up having so many physical problems and need to have so much of his intestines cut out; now here I was in a similar predicament. I knew the routine that would follow, and I dreaded it.

An orderly came into the room the evening before surgery with a pre-soaped sponge and razor kit to shave me from chest to thighs. It is a very vulnerable feeling, having someone work with a razor below one's navel. Then came the enema. I hated giving them or taking them. When that was over they told you to have a good night's sleep. Sure. A nurse brought an NPO (nothing permitted orally) sign and taped it to the front of the bed. This was easy enough, I hadn't taken anything by mouth for at least a week, except a few deep breaths as I sighed.

It was morning. I did not remember falling asleep. The nurse was at my bedside asking me to roll over. She administered an injection which was supposed to make me feel drowsy, but I fought it. I wanted to be aware of everything that was going on. I was transferred to a surgical cart and counted the rows of lights along the ceiling as we moved towards the electronic doors to the surgical division. My friends were there as I came to the operating room corridor. Ladies I folded clothes with, old men I scrubbed the floors with, nurses I scrubbed with on surgical cases, Miss Tercek, anesthesiologists, surgeons—hey, this was just like old home week. Let me get off this cart and shake everybody's hand. What the hell, can I scrub at my own surgery? I mean, I knew all the tools, I saw the way the instruments were arranged on the Mayo. Rows and rows of clamps, assorted retractors, saline irrigation basins, and, scalpels. This was all so familiar. Those lights shining down on me—I'd worked under them hundreds of times. The resident surgeons assisting Dr. Lopez began to paint my belly with an iodine-type compound. I knew the whole routine. Everything was going according to standard operating procedure. Very efficient.

"Dennis, can I have your arm?" the anesthesiologist said. "Make a fist, please." He found a vein and inserted a long needle attached to a plastic catheter hooked up to a bottle labeled "Sodium Pentathol."

"Now I am going to ask you to count backwards." Yes, that is exactly what he says to everyone; this is easy, Doc.

"Ten, nine, eight, seven, s...."

I gripped the metal rails.   I was awake on a recovery room cart as the first post-operative sensations penetrated deep inside my body. Needles pinched my arms and legs. A clear plastic nasogastric tube tightened in my throat; it carried a brownish-red substance into a bottle below my bed. A green catheter inserted in my other nostril brought oxygen. Body fluids moved out of tubes below my waist. I was immobile.

"Nurse," I rattled hoarsely to a recovery staff member.

I noticed it was daylight outside, then I fell asleep. Next thing I knew it was night. There were no other carts in the recovery room.

"We are going to take you back to your room, Dennis," a nurse said.

I fell asleep. I woke up in a dimly lit room. Aunt Betty, her eyes bloodshot, tears streaming down her face, wiped perspiration from my forehead.

"You're back in your room, Dennis. How do you feel?"

I had a terrible time trying to talk and I couldn't understand why I felt...I...felt...like I was going to die. I couldn't move. My chest was heavy. The pain was unimaginable. I held onto the railings of the bed and gritted my teeth. A single tear came from my right eye. I blinked at Aunt Betty and she turned away briefly. She was crying again, I knew it. Why the hell was she still crying? She could see I was awake. A special nurse entered the room.

"I'll pay you by the day," Aunt Betty said to her. "Here's my home phone number, please call me to tell me how he is doing. I've been here since early this morning. I have to go home and get some sleep.

"By the way, nurse, did you look at his chart? Is there any change in his condition?"

"No ma'am. His condition is still critical." The tall black special duty nurse leaned over the bedside and began to take my pulse.

"Don't you worry, Mrs. Gannon, I'm going to take good care of this young man. He'll make it all right. Now you go home and rest."

Critical condition? Jesus Christ! There must he some mistake. "Critical" is a polite way for doctors and nurses to say, "Hey, if he doesn't make it, don't say we didn't tell you so."

This can't be! The room was tranquil. The pale yellow light over the bed gave my arms a sallow cast. Critical condition? What the hell happened? I've got a birthday next month. I'm going to be 22! I'm too young to die. Let me out of here. I dozed. A shaft of light opened my eyes. The hospital chaplain, dressed in a black robe, put his hand on my shoulder. It was Father Roztas, I knew him from when I worked the late night "on-call" surgery shift.

He whispered in my ear: "Dennis, do you desire God's grace?"

"Yes...Father...uh...." Oh no. This is it! He took out his annointing oils and set them on the stand. He ran his hand through his reddish-brown hair, took off his glasses, wiped them and put them back on his gentle face. He brought out a purple stole, kissed it, placed it around his thick neck and drew near again.

"Son, do you wish to make a confession?" Hey, how can you go to confession with someone who knows you and look him in the face the next day?

"Dennis, can you hear me? Do you wish to make a confession?"

Let's see, what the hell have I done lately? Yeah, Father, not going to church on Sundays and holy days. I was tired of all the blather about money, money, money—and what did the Church have to say about the war in Vietnam? What else? Oh, honor thy father and thy mother. Well, I hadn't seen them much lately. I didn't want to go visit and then get yelled at for not visiting. What else? Oh, the usual, just the usual. *My confession?!* Hey, I wasn't really sure that there was a heaven and a hell, aside from what we experienced here on earth. Could I take that gamble right now? I was really big on reincarnation, although I had no idea where I came from or where I was going. Maybe I needed a few more Philosophy of Religion classes and a few more chapters of Augustine and Aquinas to balance out Cayce and Blavatsky before I came to any conclusions. Maybe I just better play it safe, make a good confession and not screw around and risk waking up in Hell tomorrow morning, which would be a real shame after all those years of serving mass.

Oh yes, Sister Estelle warned me about the effect certain kinds of reading could have on my faith, something about "Pride goeth before destruction, and a haughty spirit before a fall." I cleared my conscience, made my peace, and covered my bets.

"Oh my God, I am heartily sorry for having offended Thee. I detest my sins because I dread the loss of heaven and the pain of hell, but most of all because I have offended Thee, my God, Who art all good and deserving of all my love. I firmly resolve with the help of Thy Grace to confess my sins, to do penance and to amend my life. Amen."

This better work. Father Roztas then began to bless my forehead and my feet with the chrism. He was giving me the Last Rites. I didn't have to be convinced any longer that I was really sick. Oh Jesus, was I in a fix. Father gave me his blessing. "In nomine Patris, et Filius, et Spiritui Sanctus."

I was crying as he left the room. The nurse did not return immediately. I loosened the binder on my right arm, reached and nudged the phone receiver from the nearby nightstand onto the bed. I asked the operator for the information desk. I had to find out.

"The information desk is closed for the evening, I'm sorry."

"Then give me nursing service," I rasped.

"Nursing service, can I help you?"

"Yes," I was having trouble speaking. "I want to know the condition of a patient."

"Which patient?"

"Dennis Kucinich."

"I'm sorry I can't give that information out. Are you a member of the immediate family?"

"Yes," came back a gravelly voice. "We're real close."

"I'm sorry. His condition is critical."

I put down the phone receiver. It bounced off the floor just as the special nurse came back to my bed.

My last confession. The Last Rites. Well, this was it. This was the fight I had been waiting for. I fought to stay awake. I measured my breaths. I prayed to live. I wanted a chance to do something with my life. I thought of all those people I met in the 1967 campaign. I had found a home in the streets of Ward Seven. I believed that my life had some value. I was only twenty-one years old. I had so many plans. I was going to make a difference. There were so many people in the world I wanted to help. I fought with every ounce of strength to stay awake. I want to live. Jesus, can you hear me? I want to live. This was the fight of my life. I was determined to win it. This was a big wall I had to run into, and then through it, under it, up it and over it. I wasn't going to stop. I had only to stay awake.

"Nurse! Don't leave. Come here! Don't let me fall asleep."

Chapter Forty-Nine

OUTSIDE THE WINDOW of my room, the sun and smoke hovered over the somber mills. The smell of sulphur dioxide and autumn was in the air. The treetops were yellowing and red dust painted the neighborhood houses. Gritty particles came through the hospital windows, settling as a dark film on the inside window ledge.

I had been keeping time by counting my pain shots. I did not know how many days I had been in the bed.

"Nurse, what day is it?"

"It's the first day of October."

I raised my eyebrows and asked her, "How am I doing?"

"You've had a rough time, but you are going to be okay."

"Where's my Aunt Betty?"

"She has been here every night. She'll be here tonight, too."

"Is Dr. Lopez around the hospital?"

"He was in earlier to check on you. He is giving you bathroom privileges beginning this afternoon. You'll be getting up and around more and more. We don't want to keep you here much longer, you know. You've been here for four weeks already. So, are you ready for some visitors today?"

"Visitors? Sure! Who? Gee, that's real nice. When?" Fortunately, friends from surgery and student nurses kept me from being totally alone during the day.

"Well, some of your friends are outside right now. They wanted to surprise you. They're from your old high school class."

I looked forward to visitors. They must have been cleared by Aunt Betty. There were some people she would not let see me, like Mom and Dad. I didn't know why.

My former classmate, Terrie, had a puff of strawberry hair atop her head. She was frail, but she had looked that way ever since I met her at St. Colman's. Her blond boyfriend, Bob, had not changed much since the days he was a stocky halfback on the Cantius varsity.

"Hi!" I said, with all the exuberance I could muster. No time for torment. Lace up the boot—er, belly—and grin.

Something Terrie saw eclipsed her smile. There was a stunned look on her now ashen face. She turned, headed for the door and fainted. Bob knelt at her side as he called for a nurse. I pulled the cord to signal the nursing station.

"Can I help you?" asked the voice over the intercom.

"Uh...I'm alright, I think, but a girl who came to visit me isn't." Gee, I hoped it wasn't anything serious. What had she seen that caused her to swoon? There was no one else in the room but me; the older fellow in the next bed had passed away the week before. Hmmm. It sure was strange to see her take two steps into the room and then close her eyes and faint. I sat up in bed, leaning forward just enough to catch a glimpse of the mirror recessed into the center wall. I didn't see the confident, fierce look I saw when a younger football player looked into the mirror after a tough practice and said to himself: "I did my best."

My God! Who was that creature in the mirror, that thing with the cherry pustules and coffee blisters on what might have been a face? I knew why my visitor dropped. Maybe the nurses weren't telling me everything. Maybe I was so juiced up with pain shots I really didn't know what was going on. Maybe I was just sort of lingering, and they were simply trying to handle this whole thing in a humane way. They couldn't fool my visitor—no, she wasn't in on the game. I was shocked. I rang for the nurse.

"Please come in here, right away, PLEASE."

The head nurse hurried to my bedside. She looked at me with such concern, her eyes asking "What's the matter my poor dearest, is there anything I could ever do for you?"

My eyes strained to tell her: I blew it. I had the chance to go before anything else went wrong. First it showed up in my belly, now it had crawled outside to my skin. Okay, I quit! I'll just lie here, perfectly still. I'll close my eyes never again to see the blight. Just pull the sheets over me and forget it, quick, you won't have to tell me another gentle lie.

Somehow she understood. "No, Dennis, you aren't going to die, and you aren't going through puberty again. You have had a bad reaction to some of the large doses of antibiotics you have received. It will clear up in a few weeks, really."

"Nurse, I don't want any more visitors." I wished my eyes could focus to read, then the time would go faster. I wished I could have afforded to rent a television. I just couldn't ask Aunt Betty to pick up any more hospital bills.

The 1968 Presidential campaign was in its homestretch and here I was, flat on my back. I couldn't even watch TV to try to figure out whether Nixon or Humphrey would win. I felt so distant from events. All I wanted was to think about something other than myself.

The nurse who walked into my room told me I had a visitor waiting. She didn't know I wasn't interested in seeing anyone until I got out of the hospital.

"No. I'm sorry. I don't want any visitors."

"You will want to see this person. Besides he can't stay long. He's got to go back to work at the *Plain Dealer*."

The *Plain Dealer*? Hey, I quit the *Plain Dealer*. What did anyone there want with me? Oh sure, I had friends there. But I didn't think that they knew I was in the hospital. Dennis Rini came into the hospital room with a gift-wrapped box and a card.

"I can't stay. The guys around the office signed this card and took up a collection to get you something to help you pass the time here. We all want you to get well quick."

I was speechless. "Look," he continued. "I have to stay here until you open this." I opened the card; there were about sixty signatures on the get-well message. Dennis helped me to unwrap the box. He unpacked some styrofoam shipping material, reached in and brought up a battery-powered television with an eight-inch screen.

"The guys chipped in. They thought you might like this," he said with a wide grin.

"You tell them I'll be back. I'll be coming up to the City Room myself to thank them for this. You don't know how much this means."

"Yes, I do," he said. Then he shook my hand and left. Gosh, sometimes people are so nice that it makes you want to cry. I was so happy. I could concentrate on the outside world instead of the clock. I began to devour current events again, particularly those reports relating to politics. The more I thought about politics, the more I wanted to get out of the hospital and get involved again.

I placed a phone call to a woman who had helped in my first campaign. Florence Gioitta was a southside housewife who always had her ear to the ground. She knew everything that was going on in our neighborhood, and in many other neighborhoods as well. Her husband was an Italian produce salesman who sold fruit and vegetables from his small panel truck. Florence was an O'Rourke, straight Irish, with flaming red hair, pale blue eyes and the inside track on everything going on.

"Hi, Florence. What do you hear?"

"I hear you are going to die," she said. "Are you?"

"No, that's old news. Who told you?"

"Someone who works in the hospital is the daughter of a woman in the Bilinski organization. The word is that there is no way you could survive that surgery and no one will have to worry about you running for anything anymore."

"Who's worried anyway?" I asked. "I got beat in the last election."

"Are you kidding?" A tone of disbelief registered in her soft voice. "You caught them off guard last time. They are obsessed with you. They don't think your vote was a fluke. They would be happy if you just died. They would probably all come to your funeral."

"Oh they would, huh? Well I'm going to disappoint them again. I just may be around to run again."

"Are you sure?"

"Sure I'm sure. Hey, I'll be out of here in no time and back to business as usual." I looked at the intravenous feeding line. It was time to inform the nurse that the dextrose had run out. I pulled the cord.

"Look, Florence, if you get a chance, visit me, huh?"

Doctor Lopez entered the room.

"I see you are feeling better, spending time talking on the phone. You should not be on the phone too much. I want you to rest.

"When can I go home, Doctor?"

"You will be here for a few more weeks, and then maybe you can go home. Is there anyone at your house who can take care of you?"

"No."

"You will need to stay with someone, to make sure there are no complications. How about your Aunt Betty? Can you stay with her?"

"I'm sure, if I asked her."

"That would be best. I don't want you living alone right now. It will be a long time before you are totally healed. You must be careful not to open or strain the incisional area." I lifted up my hospital gown to examine the long packing across my abdomen. He loosened the bandages, quickly inspected the wound and reset the packing.

"Doctor, how long before I can go back to work at the *Wall Street Journal*?"

"Dennis, why are you in such a hurry? Are you going to lose your job?"

"No. The bureau chief sent me a letter telling me that I will have a job there when I return."

"Then what are you worried about? You should not go back to work too soon. You should think only about getting well."

"I don't understand. Why should it take so long? I feel fine."

"Dennis, I removed five-and-a-half feet of your small bowel and two-and-a-half feet of your colon."

"You did?" I knew my *Grey's Anatomy*.

Dr. Lopez took out a pencil and on the back of a lunch menu began to diagram the surgery, the resection and the anastomoses. It all looked like a new plumbing job.

"We can only hope that surgery will end the problem, but I cannot promise you that it will. You have what is called Crohn's Disease, or regional ileitus. You had many obstructions and fistulas. Your intestines were inflamed and blocked. The disease was causing a progressive deterioration of the walls of your intestines. It must have been developing for years and years."

Years and years? I thought of a kid on the ground of the Holy Name churchyard, rolling around, looking up under the fire escape while yellow gas fermented deep inside of him. That was normal for me for a long time. I felt heavily weighted.

"If you do not have a recurrence of the inflamation within the next five years, there is a good chance that you will recover. Of course, there will be other problems you will have as your body adjusts to the changes which surgery will bring, but we will talk about that later," he said.

"Doctor, what if it comes back?"

"Then I will have to remove more of your intestines, but that would be very difficult and dangerous surgically. You would have a permanent colostomy then. That is why you must be very careful. Your insides are delicate. There is only so much left, so you are going to have to get plenty of rest and you must avoid stress of any kind."

"Stress?"

"Yes. You should not be exposed to any great amounts of stress. It could cause the Crohn's to flare up."

"Doctor, I was thinking of running again for City Council."

"I do not think that would be advisable, Dennis. No, that would not be a very wise thing for you to do. I do not think your body could stand up to the physical stress of a political career. You are too sensitive a person."

I studied his face as he talked. He was very serious. His was not a political judgment but a medical one. My thoughts became as straws blowing in a storm.

As my life was being scrambled, I was nearly incoherent.

"But Doctor, are you saying, I shouldn't be, shouldn't run, politics?!"

He put his hand on my shoulder and said in a kind, fatherly way, "Dennis, there are many other things you can do in life. I just hope you are not thinking of running again for political office."

What else did he think I was dreaming about all these days in bed? Of course I was planning to run for City Council again. I was now 22 years old. I was making a lifetime of plans, plotting out the next ten, fifteen years. I knew exactly where I wanted to go and what I wanted to be. When you are in a hospital bed fighting for your life, what else do you do with your time besides plan for the future? That's when you can see the future better than at any other time.

"Does this mean I may not have long to live?"

"No," he smiled. "You should live a long life, if you are careful. Some people with Crohn's can live to be eighty-five or even older; but others, if they are not careful...."

"But Doctor, what if I do decide to run again? What can happen?" He patted my arm.

"You will make that decision, Dennis. Now get some rest."

I lay back in bed, feeling very sorry for myself. Sure, there were other things I could do with my life. Yeah, the Occupational Inventory Test I took in my sophomore year at St. John Cantius said I was best suited to be a banker. I think I was sick the day I took the test, or maybe the paper rags man hawking his cart around the Tremont Triangle distracted me and I marked the wrong boxes. Besides, those tests never measured what's in a person's heart. After

I left the *Plain Dealer*, I even tried for a job as a public relations man at the Cleveland Electric Illuminating Company. They wanted someone with more experience. They were a little put off when I wrote on my job application that I was planning a political career.

"We frown on politics around here," said the man who had interviewed me in a small cubicle at 55 Public Square. Instead I was hired as a copy reader at the *Wall Street Journal*. I could caddy. I could work as a surgical technician, a hospital orderly or I could write sports. There were a lot of things I could do in life, as the Doctor had pointed out.

But quit politics? Nothing seemed as important as being involved in trying to help shape a better future for people by standing up for them inside the government. I turned my face toward the window. The flames of autumn licking across the valley began to flicker as pools of liquid melted the scarlet, marigold and steel harvest. I buried my face in my pillow. I was not to be consoled.

Aunt Betty attended my recovery at her suburban Spanish villa home overlooking the Seven Hills south of the Cleveland metropolitan area. From her front window I saw autumn slip into the icy tendrils of a premature Cleveland winter, moving like a frosted shadow across the hillside. A few crisp orange leaves weathered the siege, waving in defiance at the approaching greyness. Against this enthralling canvas I had time to meditate with Emerson, Tennyson, Shelley, Keats, Whitman, Frost, Browning, Fromm and many others; time to let my thoughts expand with the frozen sky. I could begin to see for miles and miles.

In the evenings Uncle Lenny played on the electric organ and performed sleight-of-hand with coins and cards as I applauded enthusiastically. My spirits began to lift. I could feel my strength returning under my Aunt's faithful nursing. I was ready to go home to Brayton Avenue.

"Don't you think it's too soon, Dennis?" Aunt Betty asked.

"Really, I'll be fine. I just have to get back there and try to pick up where I left off. The doctor says I can go back to work in a few weeks. Gee, the year is slipping by, isn't it? It's almost Thanksgiving and Christmas is just a month away."

"You'll be here for Thanksgiving Dinner, won't you?"

"Aunt Betty, what I have to give thanks for is *you*. Of course I'll be here."

"You'll check with me every day?"

"Yes. I'll call you every evening to give you a report."

I turned the key to the Brayton Avenue apartment. The front room had a strange quiet. The small office I had set up was ready for business. Papers and files were neatly arranged atop a large mahogany desk. Hundreds of books were stacked against the walls. Aunt Betty walked to the kitchen.

"Dennis! What on earth?! These dishes! They haven't been done in months."

"I was planning on throwing them out," I said sheepishly.

"Look, you better not live like this from now on or you'll catch it from me."

She threw out the green and white dishes piled in the sink, tidied around the apartment and then left. I walked to the kitchen window and looked out over the industrial valley. I knew I had a lot of work to do before I was back in good health. Dr. Lopez, the nurses and Aunt Betty all did their part. Now it was up to me.

I purchased a set of springs to exercise my hands and arms and to rebuild my chest muscles. I carried a rubber ball with me at all times to get back my grip. I began simple calisthenics the next morning. I worked up to an hour of exercise at the beginning of each day. I put on my old football pants and a hooded sweatshirt and walked to Tremont Field so that I could begin short sprints.

The sprints soon stretched into longer distances. I traced the rutted acres of Tremont, running stiffly into the wind. My cheeks stinging, my eyes tearing, each chilled stride in unison with each frozen breath; my leg, chest and back muscles straining. My body was propelled not so much by my weak and wobbly legs as by determination. I didn't give a damn what anyone said about my frailty. I wasn't going to let anything beat me, not even this Crohn's Disease. I could beat this thing. I knew I could. I ran and ran. At the end of each morning's session I walked slowly up St. Tikhon Hill, a steep incline under the shadow of the great cupolas of St. Theodosius. The day soon came, as I knew it would, when I completed my chase around the field and I faced the bottom of St. Tikhon determined to run straight up the hill. It would be like running up the side of a mountain. But the mountain was not simply the 50-degree incline that stretched 200 yards to Brayton Avenue at its summit.

The mountain I had to climb was inside me. It was the physical barrier of self I had to surmount because it was there. So I began to run home, running harder than ever. I ran straight up the hill. The shoulder of my spirit was set against the rock of my body. I pushed it up the hill. My life depended on it. Occasionally I stumbled along the pitted macadam and fell backwards. The worst part was getting up. My body said I could not get up. My legs were burning. My lungs were screaming: "Quit!" but I got up again. My spirit steeled against the rock of my body. I started to run—driving, digging, daring my shaking legs to carry me to the top of the hill. I arrived as I knew I could.

A light snow dusted the street. Small flurries were swirling as if someone had just shaken a glass bowl containing Brayton Avenue and the hill. I turned for a brief moment to look out at the power and the beauty of the industrial valley. It was at that moment, right then and there, that I decided I could accomplish anything.